The Search for Meaning

The Search for Meaning

A Short History

Dennis Ford

UNIVERSITY OF CALIFORNIA PRESS

Berkeley   Los Angeles   London

University of California Press, one of the most distinguished
university presses in the United States, enriches lives around
the world by advancing scholarship in the humanities, social
sciences, and natural sciences. Its activities are supported by
the UC Press Foundation and by philanthropic contributions
from individuals and institutions. For more information, visit
www.ucpress.edu.

University of California Press
Berkeley and Los Angeles, California

University of California Press, Ltd.
London, England

Library of Congress Cataloging-in-Publication Data

Ford, Dennis, 1947–.
  The search for meaning : a short history / Dennis Ford.
    p.   cm.
  Includes bibliographical references and index.
  ISBN-13: 978-0-520-25300-1 (cloth : alk. paper)
    1. Meaning (Philosophy).   I. Title.

B105.M4F67   2007
140—dc22   2006032566

Manufactured in the United States of America

16 15 14 13 12 11 10 09 08 07
10 9 8 7 6 5 4 3 2 1

This book is printed on New Leaf EcoBook 50, a 100%
recycled fiber of which 50% is de-inked post-consumer
waste, processed chlorine-free. EcoBook 50 is acid-free and
meets the minimum requirements of ANSI/ASTM D 5634-01
(*Permanence of Paper*).

To Dana, Justin, and Ann

Every intellectual effort sets us apart from the commonplace, and leads us by hidden and difficult paths to secluded spots where we find ourselves amid unaccustomed thoughts.

José Ortega y Gasset

CONTENTS

PREFACE: WHEN MEANING
BECOMES A QUESTION

Does life have meaning? Before the question is asked, we live in a state of innocence. But once the question becomes a question, once we ask whether life is meaningful, there is no turning back. The possibility that our lives may be pointless leaves us naked and vulnerable. All of us seek a life of meaning and purpose, but finding such a life is difficult.

Thoreau was wrong when he observed that most of us lead lives of quiet desperation. Most of us, I think, lead lives of denial. Like children passing a graveyard, we hold our breath as we pass the shadow of meaninglessness that darkens our lives. The image evoked by the nineteenth-century preacher Jonathan Edwards in his sermon "Sinners in the Hands of an Angry God"—being held precariously by a string over the vapors and fires of hell—becomes for us the feeling that that we are dangling over an abyss of meaninglessness. Denial is better than the alternative: if the heights are frightening, don't look down. How could we go on living if we were to admit that life is utterly meaningless?

For those who have experienced meaninglessness, words of explanation are unnecessary. For those who have not, words of explanation are insufficient.

"Why?" is a simple, childlike question. Someone dies, a friend has a baby with a birth defect, or we read about a devastating flood in Indonesia, and we ask "Why?" Harold Kushner's 1981 best seller *When Bad Things Happen to Good People*, written after his three-year-old son was diagnosed with a deadly degenerative disease, was a heartfelt response to the question. In such cases, we are not so much seeking a scientific explanation or cause as asking for a reason or justification. Without an ability to answer "Why?" such catastrophes remain unassimilated and without meaning.

If the *why* question emerges in response to specific losses or tragedies, it also arises when we look at our lives as a whole. Does my life, with its joys and sorrows, loves and betrayals, add up to something meaningful? If called upon to justify my life, how would I answer? What would I say if I were to write my obituary? Was my life meaningful because I lived in conformity with God's law, because I made a billion dollars in the stock market, or because I found a cure for cancer? When the urban commuter on her daily drive to her cubicle confesses that her life seems meaningless, she is not responding to a specific event or tragedy; she is saying something about her entire life experience. Questions about the existence of God and life after death are, at root, questions about meaning, the presumption being that if they exist, our lives are somehow meaningful.

How do people go about answering the question of whether their lives have meaning? How do they find meaning in their lives? These are the questions I pursue.

Many popular books attempting to answer the meaning question adopt a single, authoritative approach. Thus, for example, people identify the elements of a purpose-driven life in scripture and Christianity. In contrast, *The Search for Meaning* studies the range of options people have used to invest their lives with meaning. As we shall see, the question of meaning does not have just one answer. How people discover purpose, how they define a "meaningful life," and how they go about attaining it differ from one person to the next and, indeed, for the same person depending on age and circumstances. The way meaning enters the life of a Native American may be radically different from the way it arose in the life of a scientist working on the Manhattan Project. The question "What is the meaning of life?"—implying as it does a single answer—conceals the many ways meaning reveals itself. Because people invest their lives with meaning differently, my study does not offer or advocate a single answer. Rather, it takes a step back to examine the *various* ways people have gone about answering the question, whether mythical, philosophical, scientific, or other.

In so doing, *The Search for Meaning* addresses two audiences. First, it speaks to those who are engaged in a personal quest for meaning. We all want to answer the *why* question, just as we all want to forge a life with purpose and meaning. For some of us, the answers provided by traditional religions no longer work or, worse, seem to work only for the most extreme and fanatical believers in our midst. As a result, many are looking for new ways both to understand and to answer the question of meaning. The history of meaning discloses both old and new examples of and tools for finding meaning in our lives. Second, the book addresses students who want an introduction to the study of meaning. Meaning is a central and defining question in both religion and philosophy. More than that, it is a key to understanding major currents in Western thought. By examining how people have invested their lives with meaning, we come to see how they answer other questions in their lives as well. "Why?" is asked of events and lives, but it is also, for example, the foundational question in ethics: Why do this rather than that? Why be good? Meaning is thus a vehicle for introducing students to the fundamental epistemological, ontological, and axiological dimensions of religion, philosophy, and ethics.

Addressing students may seem incompatible with addressing those engaged in a more personal, existential search. The student's interest in knowledge appears at odds with the pilgrim's desire for enlightenment. But, as will become clear in this study, pragmatism and postmodernism have undermined this conventional division between objective and subjective knowledge. They have shown us how even the most objective study is infused with personal interests and biases. As an introductory text, *The Search for Meaning* offers accurate and authoritative descriptions of the various approaches people have used to find meaning. But as a postmodern work, it also openly acknowledges that the impetus for the study is a personal quest. Setting aside the pretense of uncontaminated objectivity, the book readily admits references to *I* and *me* and *us* and the more personal, engaged commitment those words suggest. I hope this approach will enable both of my audiences— students and seekers alike—to see the intimate relationship between scholarship and personal interests more clearly.

VIOLATING A LAST TABOO

To admit that a text in religion or philosophy also expresses personal interests violates both academic and cultural boundaries.

Talking openly about meaning and meaninglessness is one of the last taboos. The question of meaning makes us uncomfortable.

I discovered this several years ago. Over lunch with a group of software and electrical engineers, someone asked me what I was currently reading. I hesitantly mumbled in reply that I was reading about meaning, as in the question, "What is the meaning of life?" An embarrassed, awkward silence followed. Interspersed between casual conversations about politics, morning traffic, and housing prices, my words had suddenly, unintentionally conjured up a ghostlike presence, which everyone felt but no one was comfortable talking about. Once the question was asked, we couldn't pretend it hadn't been uttered.

Like talk about other taboo subjects, talking about meaning both repels and attracts. Conversations about meaning and meaninglessness sound grandiose and audacious. If my companions had been less polite, I can imagine their saying, "You're going to tell us the meaning of life. Yes? Is that it? And while you're at it, how about a cure for cancer and a unified theory of the universe as well!" Our era is distrustful of and uncomfortable with high-sounding abstractions that tend to begin with capital letters, such as Truth, Reality, and Meaning. Speaking of these things elicits the same awkwardness many of us feel when we attend a funeral. We may follow the solemn rituals and evoke the timeless prayers for a better life beyond death while secretly wondering to what or to whom we are praying and doubtful that anything exists on the other side of the grave. We are nominalists despite ourselves: *meaning* is a name or category, but we can't help wondering whether it really denotes anything substantial, as the word *horse* denotes the animals that run in the Kentucky Derby.

Evoking the question of meaning also repels us because those who possess a sense of meaning too often seem fanatical. It would appear that, as W. B. Yeats observed, "The best lack all conviction, while the worst/Are full of passionate intensity." The terrorists who flew into the World Trade Center uttering the words "Allah is Great" were filled, I am sure, with a sense of meaning and purpose. They did not question whether life was meaningful; indeed, an intensely meaningful life led them to murder and death. If living a meaningful life means fanaticism, then who can blame us for falling silent when someone broaches the subject of whether life has meaning? The meaningful life, no less than a life without meaning, has its dangers.

For the engineers with whom I was talking, there were also philosophical reasons for the taboo. The question of meaning is not immediately practical in the same way as a question about relieving traffic congestion, increasing sales, or accessing our e-mail remotely. These are the sort of pragmatic *how* questions with which our age is most comfortable. In contrast, we are uneasy with the more contentious *why* questions evoked by the challenge of meaning. Tactical questions are easier than strategic questions: determining the means of getting from Topeka to Seattle is easier than explaining why getting from Topeka to Seattle is important. What's more, efforts to resolve the *why* questions seem interminable and subjective, because there is no agreed-upon or measurable basis by which to validate an answer. Without verifiable facts and measurable data, our answers are based on arbitrary feelings or opinions. I say life is meaningful, someone else says it's meaningless, while many others—including my silent companions perhaps—would say that the question itself is altogether useless, because inherently unresolvable. Our vocabulary for speaking about and resolving the question of meaning is limited and halting.

Finally, if talk about meaning is useless, it's also embarrassing and subversive. To ask "Does life have meaning?"—and, even more so, to offer an opinion on the subject—is enormously self-revealing. To say "I wonder if my life means anything in the end" is to invite concerned friends to ask whether you are depressed or unhappy. "Is everything all right?" they will ask. The language of doubt itself assumes that life should be meaningful; meaningless-ness, after all, is the absence of a more normative meaning. Similarly, to ask whether life has meaning is subversive because it implies that the meaning we are *supposed* to find in life—as defined by parents, Church, career, culture, and politics—is found wanting. To ask whether life has meaning is to challenge and subvert the legitimacy of the answers others provide.

Alternatively, to say "Yes, I think life has enormous meaning and purpose" is to risk being labeled a Pollyanna or a member of a privileged minority unacquainted with poverty and injustice. Asking a question about a historical fact or what Plato said about art or virtue does not suggest the same level of intimacy and per-sonal engagement as the question of meaningfulness. We are reluctant to talk about meaninglessness and meaning because of what it may reveal about us. Like comments about sex and money, I can't say much about whether life has meaning without saying something about my own experience. And so, fearful of exposing ourselves to others, especially in connection with such an intimate yet critical subject, we remain silent.

If we are thus repelled by speech about meaning and meaning-lessness, on the one hand, we are nevertheless drawn to it, on the other, almost like a biological urge. "Is life meaningful?" is an essential and inescapable human question. We are less human when we fail to ask it. What if the universe is meaningless? Wouldn't that change everything? Isn't the concept of meaninglessness an abyss beyond which we cannot imagine? On a popular level, the persistence and tenacity exhibited by opponents of evolution express an unwillingness to accept the meaninglessness implied by the proposition that we are here for no better reason or higher purpose than random selection. If the greatest fear of liberals is fanaticism, the greatest fear of conservatives is meaninglessness. Once asked, the question of meaning is inescapable, and the answer—however we may answer it—never seems settled. We go along merrily from day to day until someone close to us dies unexpectedly in an accident. One's efforts to create a happy family end in betrayal and divorce. One is young and vigorous, and then old and infirm. Experience would seem to compel us to be utterly without hope, but then someone says, "I love you," or holds your hand. Martin Luther King Jr. emerges to confront injustice. The Boston Red Sox win the World Series against the Yankees in the seventh and deciding game. Miracle of miracles! Suddenly, the world seems whole again, full of grace, full of meaning and purpose.

The question of meaning—or, more accurately, the search or nostalgia for meaning—preoccupies much of nineteenth- and twentieth-century philosophy, literature, and theology. One thinks of the lineage stretching from Nietzsche to Hemingway, Sartre, and beyond; indeed, it is difficult to think of a prominent twentieth-century writer for whom meaning has not been a defining question. The very prominence of these authors and the fact that so many gave them a hearing testify to the longing of the age to which they spoke. What's more, questions of right and wrong, the existence of evil, and the need for redemption are secondary to the question of meaning. What do these questions signify if the universe itself is meaningless? Even if we are reluctant to talk openly about meaning, we are nevertheless drawn to read and note the talk of others—from a safe distance—just as people who avoided speaking about the taboo subject of sex in the 1960s were secretly thinking about it and reading Masters and Johnson's *Human Sexual Response*. People both want and don't want to talk about the presence or absence of meaning.

WE ARE AMPHIBIOUS CREATURES, BETWIXT AND BETWEEN

The Search for Meaning is predicated on two assumptions. First, the meaning otherwise available in our culture—including that offered by historical and institutionalized religions—is no longer persuasive, and, second, living without meaning is unacceptable. This book thus looks at the landscape in between, a place where we are comfortable neither with what seem the false or hypocritical answers provided by culture nor with a life lived existentially in an otherwise meaningless here and now. In both cases, we yearn for something more.

By confessing to the first assumption, we simultaneously confess an experience of deculturation and join the ranks of those whom Colin Wilson called "outsiders" in a book that was an overnight sensation when it was published in 1956.[1] For whatever reason, we are in league with those exiles for whom the itch for meaning and purpose is not soothed by sports, a career in the ascendancy, or the achievements of our children. Even if all our wishes came true, we'd soon become bored, satiated, and discontented with our lot. Adam and Eve, after all, were malcontents even in Eden. No entertainment, no degree of affluence, no relationship can silence the small, insistent voice saying, "What's the point?" We and everyone we know will die and fade from memory. The earth is only a futile and insignificant dot in the expanse of time and space that is the universe. Like Tolstoy, I wonder how people can live knowing the futility of life and the indifference of the universe. Can we live happily only so long as we deny the question?

Of course, like many others, I looked to religion for answers to such questions in my youth. Sin, salvation, accepting Jesus as my "personal savior," and earning "eternal rewards" all had something to do with the answer, although I was never quite sure how. Christianity provided great solace and comfort for others; it just didn't work especially well for me. Attending a seminary served only to provoke more questions. Eventually, I became an outsider to Christianity, as well as to American culture, and increasingly I could take nothing for granted about my beliefs. "Question authority" was the mantra of my generation. My beliefs about the world and about what was real and false thus became an impediment to faith. And, too, I must confess, I didn't feel particularly sinful and in need of salvation, or at least not the type of salvation one gained by believing in Christ. If I didn't do "bad" things, it was not because I thought I was going to burn in hell if I did. All of this is to say that I did not find in Christianity an immediate or simple answer to the question of meaning.

While finding conventional Christianity inadequate, I did not—like many others—abandon the search for meaning along with my juvenile understanding of religion. I began looking elsewhere for examples of how people invest their lives with meaning—or, perhaps more accurately, I began to acknowledge that meaning might have sources other than Christianity and the historical religions. As a consequence, I often, though not exclusively, define religion functionally as any set of symbols and rituals that provide a sense of life meaning and orientation, regardless of whether they are drawn from traditional religions, philosophy, psychology, or aspects of an otherwise secular culture, such as sports or popular entertainment. The question of meaning signifies a religious search, but it is also a philosophical, psychological, and mythical search, to the extent that each of those disciplines asks similar questions about what constitutes the good and meaningful life, even if they answer those questions in fundamentally different ways. I have chosen to discuss the question of meaning outside traditional religious categories—at least initially—simply because for some people the conventional religious symbols and categories no longer have currency. (I define religion ontologically and thus more conventionally—and see what difference that makes—in chapter 8.) However legitimate or even true it may otherwise be, the conventional theological language of sin and salvation, predestination and grace, may fall on deaf ears. In a secular, technological culture, people may stumble toward a sense of life meaning without necessarily seeking it in conventional religion. Many seek to be "spiritual" without being "religious." The question of God and the question of meaning are thus distinguishable: people can find meaning without looking to a conventional deity. This book is accordingly about a search for meaning rather than a search for God.

In *Moby-Dick*, Ishmael begins his adventure by describing how, in the drizzly November of his soul, he finds himself "involuntarily pausing before coffin warehouses and bringing up the rear of

every funeral I meet." In a similar fashion, I have found myself pausing involuntarily over passages in my reading and conversations
about meaning and purpose. The book that follows is the result.
Others may be drawn to the business pages of the newspaper or to
the calculations of quantum physics, but if, like me, you are
drawn to questions of meaning, then this book is for you. Because
we can't take the world for granted, because we find ourselves
wondering why there is something rather than nothing, we insist
on an answer to the question "How do people—and, in particular,
how do I—invest life with meaning?"

Paths and journeys are familiar images in accounts of spiritual
searches, including the search for how people invest their lives
with meaning. Meaning is not only something we once had but
have now lost; meaning is also something toward which we are
always moving. In that movement, we can always benefit from a
good guide. Accordingly, I acknowledge the good guides on
whom I have relied, and who are referenced in my notes and bibliography.[2] In their company, we are no longer solitary, isolated
exiles; on the contrary, we are more like apprentices at the beginning of a great adventure, novitiates of a great mystery. What the
French mountaineer Gaston Rébuffat (1921–85) said about
becoming a climber applies equally well to a study of meaning:

> I often think of [the master guide] Moulin and how he initi-
> ated me. I have now made rather more than a thousand
> ascents in all seasons. I sometimes have the feeling that the
> mountains are my domain, and yet, each time I break through
> the invisible barrier, although I "feel" very good, I am always
> aware of a slight trembling inside. As Moulin "knew" all those
> years ago, I "know" now. But even if I had climbed every
> mountain by every route, I should never know everything
> about this world I love. I shall be always on my way.[3]

CHAPTER ONE

Introduction

The greatest mystery is not that we have been flung at random
among the profusion of the earth and the galaxy of the stars,
but that in this prison we can fashion images of ourselves sufficiently powerful to deny our nothingness.

> Maurice Friedman, *To Deny Our Nothingness:*
> *Contemporary Images of Man*

ASKING WHY?

The question "Why?" is the fulcrum on which the question of
meaning hinges. Before asking why, we take the world for
granted. We go to work, have children, eat meat, attend church
on Sunday mornings perhaps, but we do all of these things
unself-consciously and without deliberation. We simply accept
the norms of our culture and community without awareness or
questioning; in a sense, we are living and acting on automatic.

In contrast, asking "Why?" signals the point at which we self-
consciously step back from what we are doing to look for a reason
or justification. With this simple, childlike question, the taken-
for-granted quality of our life suddenly loses its foundations, and
we are left exposed to the threat of meaninglessness. Why do

good people suffer? Why do I choose to go to work in the morning rather than walking barefoot on the beach? Why am I a Christian rather than a Buddhist or a Muslim? Why do I merrily go about my daily activities despite the prospect of my own death and the deaths of all those I love? Meaninglessness represents the inability to persuasively answer the *why* questions about either our beliefs or our actions. Without an answer to the *why* questions we may continue to exist, but we will fail to thrive.

PERPLEXITY AND ARREST

With the skill of a great novelist, Leo Tolstoy described the debilitating effects he experienced once he began to ask "Why?" and "What for?" Nearing the age of fifty, prosperous and in good health, Tolstoy reported experiencing occasional moments of "bewilderment" and "arrest" when these questions brought his life to a halt and he knew neither what to do nor how to live. Life, which had been intoxicating to him, was suddenly sober, flat, and meaningless. The novelist's own words speak more powerfully than any paraphrase:

> At first I thought these were pointless and irrelevant questions. . . .
>
> It happened with me as it happens with everyone who contracts a fatal internal disease. At first there were the insignificant symptoms of an ailment, which the patient ignores; then these symptoms recur more and more frequently, until they merge into one continuous suffering. . . .
>
> . . . The questions seemed to be such foolish, simple, childish questions. But as soon as I laid my hands on them and tried to resolve them, I was immediately convinced, first of all, that they were not childish and foolish questions but

the most vital and profound questions in life, and secondly, that no matter how much I pondered them there was no way I could resolve them. . . .

If a fairy had come and offered to fulfill my every wish, I would not have known what to wish for. If in moments of intoxication, I should have not desires but the habits of old desires, in moments of sobriety I knew that it was all a delusion, that I really desired nothing. I did not even want to discover the truth anymore because I had to guess what it was. The truth was that life is meaningless. . . .

. . . And there I was a fortunate man, carrying a rope from my room, where I was alone at night as I undressed, so that I would not hang myself from the beam between the closets. And I quit going hunting with a gun, so that I would not be too easily tempted to rid myself of life. . . .

. . . If not today, then tomorrow sickness and death will come (indeed, they were already approaching) to everyone, to me, and nothing will remain except the stench and the worms. My deeds, whatever they may be, will be forgotten sooner or later, and I myself will be no more. Why, then, do anything? How can anyone fail to see this and live? That's what's amazing! It is possible to live only as long as life intoxicates us; once we are sober we cannot help seeing that it is all a delusion, a stupid delusion! Nor is there anything funny or witty about it; it is only cruel and stupid. . . .

The former delusion of the happiness of life that had concealed from me the horror of the dragon no longer deceives me. No matter how much I tell myself that I cannot understand the meaning of life, that I should live without thinking about it, I cannot do this because I have done it for too long already. . . .

"My family . . . ," I said to myself. But my family, my wife and children, are people too. They are subject to the same conditions as I: they must either live the lie or face the terrible truth. Why should they live? Why should I love them? Why care for them, bring them up, and watch over them? So that they can sink into the despair that eats away at me, or to turn them over to stupidity? If I love them, then I cannot hide the truth from them. . . .

. . . Had I simply understood that life has no meaning, I might have been able to calmly accept it; I might have recognized that such was my lot. But I could not rest content at this. Had I been like a man who lives in a forest from which he knows there is no way out, I might have been able to go on living; but I was like a man lost in the forest who was terrified by the fact that he was lost, like a man who was rushing about, longing to find his way and knowing that every step was leading him into deeper confusion, and yet who could not help rushing about.[1]

I have often thought that the cover of Tolstoy's *Confession*, from which these passages are excerpted, should carry a parental warning: Keep this book out of the reach of children. Pornography and obscenity are trivial compared to Tolstoy's narrative of disillusionment; reading his account is an antidote to the happiest of moods. Who can read Tolstoy's sobering account with immunity, even when reduced to brief excerpts?

Five observations about Tolstoy's narrative frame our subsequent discussion. First, Tolstoy clearly makes a distinction between appearances, including the habits of his former, intoxicated life, and reality or the truth. The happiness of life, before the questioning began, was a delusion, a concealment and lie perpetrated by the conventional answers of success and fame and material comfort that the culture provided. In contrast to this intoxication, there is the sober perception that life is meaningless, cruel, and stupid. This perception becomes the compelling force, which he describes as a fatal disease, in Tolstoy's life.

Second, the question of meaning arose for Tolstoy when he was in otherwise happy circumstances. He was a respected, successful writer, a landowner, and enjoyed good health and the affection of his family. Why or when does the question "Why?" arise? Typically, it does so when people suffer events or experiences that they do not choose or wish for or are forced to participate in activities that they do not value. A man works because he has to earn a living, rather than because he is engaged in what he considers a meaningful activity. Illness, old age, or loss descends on a woman in a way that precludes deliberate choice and a future. Social upheavals—the loss of a job, war, the transition from a rural to an urban society—call into question the world and values on which one has relied. In contrast to all these triggers, nothing in Tolstoy's life at the time explains why these questions were provoked. Indeed, the absence of these triggers suggests that the impulse to ask "Why?" may be innate. We ask the question because we are human, and we fail to be fully human whenever we fail to ask it.

Third, once sobriety happens, one cannot return unselfconsciously to either innocence or intoxication. The symptoms, as Tolstoy describes them, become both more severe and more frequent. He cannot go back to *not* thinking about the truth because, as he says, he had done that too long already. The door only swings one way; after the fall, Humpty Dumpty cannot be put together again. Apparently, one cannot deliberately live a life that is perceived to be a lie or delusion. In the excerpts quoted above, Tolstoy rejects the option of turning his family over to "stupidity"—meaning to the conventional customs of his community—even if that were possible. Seeing the truth marks one as irreversibly an "outsider,"[2] alienated and at a step removed from social conventions.

Fourth, the experience of sobriety and truth is, emotionally at least, negative. Cultural symbols and rituals protect us from being exposed to the truth, including the truth that we and everyone we love will die one day. Ernest Becker makes this argument in his classic, Pulitzer Prize–winning book *The Denial of Death*. Whenever cultural symbols fail, and we are exposed to the truth, our condition is close to madness. Tolstoy hides the rope, quits hunting, and speaks of "the horror of the dragon." It is possible to live, he says, only when intoxicated. The sense that life is meaningless undermines all desire and the choices based on those desires. If a fairy granted him a wish, he would not know what to wish for. Tolstoy thus demonstrates the cynical adage "Those who seek the truth deserve the penalty of finding it."

Fifth, Tolstoy could not rest content with the idea that life was meaningless. He intuited that there was, so to speak, a Truth behind the truth. Beyond the truth of meaninglessness that is revealed when culture fails, there is a deeper Truth. As he says, he was not a resident of the forest but a person lost in the forest with a longing to find a way out. Tolstoy does not explain the source of that longing—although in his case Augustine's "My heart is restless until it finds its rest in Thee" comes to mind—but he is clearly comfortable with neither the despair that eats away at him nor the stupidity of his former life. He simply "longs," like a person lost in the forest, for a way out. Unlike those who have not asked the questions, at least he knows that he is lost. Tolstoy is caught in between the question "Why?" on the one hand, and, on the other hand, a longing for another level of Truth beyond that first level of disillusionment.

BEFORE THE QUESTION IS ASKED

The existentialists had one thing right: life is full of choices. However, most of these choices are made unconsciously or instinctively. Our family cat Gypsy, for example, is not faced with the bewildering questions of what to believe or how to act; she is already perfect in her catness. Guided by instincts, she knows what to do without thought, doubt, or emotion and acts without hesitation to fulfill her identity as a cat. Gypsy never doubts or asks whether she should eat the mouse, nor does she feel remorse or guilt when she does. Gypsy never asks "Why?" because instincts preclude her from having to ask the questions.

In contrast to Gypsy's, only a portion of my own beliefs and actions are instinctive. Eating when I am hungry is instinctive, but whether I eat meat or am a vegetarian is not; trying to swim once I'm submerged in water is instinctive, but jumping into a pool on a hot day in July is not. Many, perhaps the majority, of my beliefs and actions are neither instinctive nor biologically determined, unlike Gypsy's. Beyond the limits of the animal instincts I share with Gypsy, there are an immense number of questions about how I should act and what I should believe, from the most mundane (what should I have for dinner?) to the most momentous (do I believe in God?). In normal times, and for most people, these questions are answered by the norms and directives embodied in the symbols, ideologies, and rituals of culture, which constitute the everyday world I take for granted. On a typical day, I don't stop to think self-consciously whether to choose to have a cup of coffee or read the morning newspaper or drive to work. Within our twenty-first-century American culture, all those things are a part of the taken-for-granted landscape.

At any point, I could step back and question whether by drinking coffee I'm contributing to the destruction of tropical rain forests and, as a consequence, decide to drink water instead. Similarly, I could step back and question the belief that newspapers accurately reflect the events of the previous day and decide that they are useless, distorting instruments of economic or political bias and self-interest. But most mornings I don't raise such questions; most mornings I let the culture decide for me. I simply have a cup of coffee while reading the morning newspaper. Similarly, most of the time, I don't ask myself whether I believe in God or an afterlife. I let the culture decide for me, because if I had to make a conscious decision about every aspect of my life—from what I eat, to what I wear, to what I believe—I'd become immobile. Cultures function as peculiarly human forms of instincts. At the point where animal instincts fail, what's awkwardly been called the "surreality of culture"[3] takes over to guide our actions and beliefs.

CHOICE AND MEANING

When cultural symbols and rituals are compelling, and the social group that supports them is coherent, culture works with the efficiency of Gypsy's instincts. People living in what are mistakenly described as primitive cultures act unreflectively and unerringly in a way that is almost instinctual. One consequence is that the question of meaning, along with a host of other questions, does not arise. Our beliefs and actions require no justification or explanation, because we take the world for granted. As long as we are immersed in culture, we are not challenged to step back from or step outside of day-to-day living to ask: "Why?"

However, whenever cultural symbols and rituals become weak, answers to questions about what to do and what to believe become muted or inconsistent. Personal or social tragedies—the birth of a deformed child, the Holocaust, or when one culture clashes with another—can challenge the answers that my culture provides. When this happens, cultural instincts begin to fail and Tolstoy's *why* and *what for* questions become more insistent, and the answers become less and less certain. Culture leaves large areas of choice and belief open where preferences are arbitrary and need no justification or reason: I like vanilla ice cream; you like chocolate. But in other, culturally defining areas, such as whether one eats meat or has an abortion or engages in adultery, to violate a culturally instinctive norm is taboo. To ask the questions "Why?" or "Why not?" cheat on income taxes or permit physician-assisted suicides is already to stand outside the unquestioned norms of the dominant culture.

Should same-sex marriages be sanctified by the Church or sanctioned by a civil ceremony? A century ago, I suspect, that question never became a question. The culturally based instinctual reaction to homosexuality was revulsion and disgust. Now, however, those instinctual reactions are less sure. We may have friends or co-workers who are gay or lesbian and whom we like and respect. The mainline Episcopal Church elected a gay bishop, while, concurrently, the pope warned American lawmakers that it would be "gravely immoral" to legalize same-sex marriages. What should we think about homosexuality? Should I support the ordination of gay priests or should I oppose it? Why? The culture is clearly no longer providing an unambiguous, instinctual response. As a consequence, our own actions and beliefs are less certain, and we tend to look for answers either by being attentive to only one portion of the largely, pluralistic culture or by examining our own Protestant consciences.[4]

We shall discuss later the factors that weaken the strength of culturally based instincts. For now, it is sufficient to say that whenever a culture fails to supply unambiguous answers to the questions of what to believe and what to do, no action or belief seems justifiable. The question "Why?" does not elicit a convincing answer. As a result, all actions and beliefs seem arbitrary or subjective. "Everything is relative," as some people like to say. Pluralism and diversity reign. Choice is a matter of personal (i.e., nonpublic) preference or whim. There is no better or worse; there's just difference. The landscape is flat because there are no high and low points. There is no error because there is no one truth, or, as a character in Steven Soderbergh's movie *Solaris* (2002) expressed it: "There are no answers, only choices." Choices are instrumental acts to achieve meaningful ends, but when those ends lack justification, choice is arbitrary and meaningless. In a world without meaning, choice is a futile gesture. Meaninglessness occurs when the *why* questions—*once they are raised*—remain unanswered.

Of this world, in which every action and belief is equally meaningful and equally meaningless, we can say two things. First, this is the free, but empty, world in which many of us now live and about which much has been written. This is the world we inherited from Nietzsche, the existentialists, and their progeny. I shall describe the features of this world in more detail a bit later. Second, the experience of living in an entirely flat world has proven to be, for most of us, as emotionally devastating as it was for Tolstoy, the equivalent of catching the flu, rather than of falling in love. What the theologian Michael Novak describes as the "experience of nothingness"[5] is not neutral; on the contrary it tends to make us positively unhappy and brings us to the edge of insanity. The experience of nothingness is terrifying, Novak observes, because it makes all attempts at speaking of purpose, goals, and meaning spurious. If the flat landscape of our postmodern culture made us happier, if saying that one choice was as good as another demonstrably contributed to a better world, and if we were content with that world, then the human, symbolic needs provided by the secondary instincts of culture would be satisfied and our actions would be sure and unerring. But that's not the way it is. Tolstoy hid the rope and stopped hunting with a gun.

TOLSTOY WRIT LARGE: THE CULTURAL TRIUMPH OF UNCERTAINTY

That people fail to see what he sees—that life is trivial when seen against an infinite, indifferent universe or futile in the face of death—that's the "amazing" thing according to Tolstoy. One wonders how widespread Tolstoy's experience was during his day or for that matter during different historical periods. There is no way of knowing for certain the answer to that question. However, it is clear that the experience is, in our own day, neither peripheral nor extraordinary; on the contrary, it is both central and widespread.

Stringing together scholarly endorsements of this assertion is easy to do: philosophers, psychologists, sociologists, theologians, and writers attest to the fact that the issue of meaning has become the central question of our time:

Bruno Bettelheim: "[O]ur greatest need and most difficult achievement is to find meaning in our lives."[6]

Michael Novak: "The experience of nothingness is now the point from which nearly every reflective man begins his adult life."[7]

Robert C. Solomon: "The world is no longer ours. The old habits keep us moving, robot-like through the paces of life, but we are not wholly there. The 'why' has no answer and that is the singular fact that now defines our existence. . . . I believe that it [the absurd] is still the dominant philosophical conception of our time. It is not a philosopher's invention. It follows with merciless logic from our most everyday thinking."[8]

James E. Edwards: "Thus nihilism—the self-devaluation of our highest values—seems the secret logic of Western culture: the worm was in the bud all along."[9]

Wilfred Cantwell Smith: "The intellectual problem of the modern world is how to be a relativist without being a nihilist."[10]

Viktor Frankl: "We have heard that man is a being in search of meaning. We have seen that today his search is unsatisfied and thus constitutes the pathology of our age."[11]

Richard Tarnas: "Our psychological and spiritual predispositions are absurdly at variance with the world revealed by our scientific method. We seem to receive two messages from our existential situation: on the one hand, strive, give oneself to the quest for meaning and spiritual fulfillment; but, on the other hand, know that the universe, of whose substance we are derived, is entirely indifferent to that quest, soulless in character, and nullifying in its effects. We are at once aroused and crushed. For inexplicably,

absurdly, the cosmos is inhuman, yet we are not. The
situation is profoundly unintelligible."[12]

Erich Fromm: "Once skepticism and rationalism were progressive forces for the development of thought; now
they have become rationalizations for relativism and
uncertainty."[13] "Doubt is the starting point of modern
philosophy."[14]

Whereas many scholars identify the problem or question of
meaning as cultural—as either the failure of culture altogether
or as conflict between our deepest desires and a scientific culture
that proclaims that the universe is indifferent—the theologian
Paul Tillich argues that the question of meaning, and the anxiety
of living it provokes, is an inescapable aspect of the human condition. It is not the result of an individual's personal or cultural
history but, Tillich says, "belongs to existence itself." Tolstoy's
life was good; he was successful and in excellent health. But no
matter how good life may be otherwise, there is what Tillich
called the "ontological anxiety" occasioned by the inescapable
awareness and threat of nonbeing, including death. Anxiety in its
nakedness is always the anxiety of ultimate nonbeing, the remedy
for which, Tillich argues, is what he calls "the courage to be."[15]
The experience of nothingness may thus be at the heart of the
human experience, as well as the underlying impetus for culture.

WHERE DO WE GO FROM HERE?

If the questions "Why?" and "What to do?" find an answer neither
in our biological instincts nor in the secondary instincts of our
postmodern culture, then what to do? Where do we go from here?

What do we do when the truth is exposed and the truth is that life is meaningless?

Shorn of the secondary instincts provided by culture, it is not surprising that many people fall into depression. The prevalence of depression is well documented; by some estimates it will affect 7.9–8.6 percent of adults during their lifetime. While the biological and psychological reasons for depression are complex, at least some forms of depression are associated with a sense that life is without meaning or purpose. Whether depression leads to these feeling or whether, alternatively, a sense of meaninglessness leads to depression is a classic "chicken and egg" problem. Regardless of which comes first, the close association between depression and meaninglessness is nevertheless strong.

Several, ultimately futile possibilities exist on both the individual and social levels for at least temporarily denying meaninglessness and its associated depression. One strategy is to return to our primary instincts. The pioneering sociologist Émile Durkheim described the failure of culture as *deculturation*, a state, he said, that reduces its victims to the animal level of chronic fighting or fornication. If I find direction or meaning neither in culture nor in more self-conscious attempts to answer the *why* questions, then I may find solace in my body, emotions, and pure, unmediated experience. From the perspective of these strategies, meaninglessness is not the problem; thinking self-consciously is the problem. Avoid or deny the questions, concede that you are nothing more than an instinctual animal in an indifferent universe, and you've solved the problem. Alcoholism, drug addiction, sexual obsessions, and adventurousness—in which meaning remains, but only while engaged in extreme and risky activities, including violence—have all been attributed to misguided and finally self-destructive attempts to suppress the question of meaning by drowning in instinctual behavior. The climber Mark Jenkins articulates perfectly the experience and joy of losing oneself entirely in the body this way: "At this moment, all I know is movement. I'm not even thinking; I'm just climbing. I shut down the brain and let the body be what it is: an animal. Unbeknownst even to myself, somewhere high on the Sheila Face, I unlatch the cage. . . . The cage door swings open and out steps the beast."[16]

On a social level, as early as 1941, Erich Fromm was writing about our collective *Escape from Freedom.* Why the need to escape? From what are we escaping? Fromm argues that a long history of liberation—from first nature, race and family, the authority of the Church and then the state (the Reformation and the rise of democracies, for example)—terminated in the achievement of individual freedom. But having attained that cherished goal, the question became "freedom not from what but for what?" Having progressively rejected the guidance and authority of revelation, community, tradition, and reason, freedom becomes a burden, and we have the absurd situation of being free to choose anything we wish but having no choices worth making.

Knowing neither what we must do nor what we should do, nor even what we wish to do, Fromm argues, we typically look for clues by watching what others do, or willingly abdicate the burden of freedom by reverting to the authority of others, whether the latest guru, pop celebrity, or political leader. Conformity and authoritarianism are thus collective strategies for relieving the anxiety that absolute freedom elicits. We willingly exchange our anxiety and freedom for compulsive activity and the answers provided by others. Conformity to the cultural norms modeled by members of our family, friends, and associates or obedient loyalty to the goals of our leaders and nation protects us from the debilitating experience of nothingness resting at the heart of modernity.[17]

Philosophically, the modern, debilitating ideology that humankind is nothing but a complex mechanism of chemical reactions or social forces and its attendant experience of nothingness is, itself, the culmination of a long skeptical tradition. The notion of the Absurd arose when humankind's desire for meaning and purpose confronted the indifferent universe that the skeptical tradition projected. On the one hand, modernity was a necessary prerequisite for the emergence of the existential vacuum, and thus a source of the problem. On the other hand, modernity is also a solution. If one believes that the universe is indeed indifferent and without purpose, then the absurd is merely nostalgia for a world that never existed. The modern idea that the universe, and in turn humankind, is meaningless, without intrinsic value or purpose, is both a cause of and a solution to the problem posed by the experience of nothingness. Living in the modern universe of indifferent and mechanical causation may require honesty and courage, but it is finally not absurd, whenever the nostalgia for purpose and meaning is abandoned. All one has is this world as it is, and many would claim that that is sufficient. Firmly within a modern perspective, there is no answer or resolution to Tolstoy's question "Why?" Our best course of action, as a consequence, is to enjoy and make the best we can of this world as it is. Or as the literary critic Lionel Trilling expressed it poetically: "If we are in a balloon over an abyss, let us at least value the balloon. If night is all around, then what light we have is precious. If there is no life to be seen in the great emptiness, our companions are to be cherished; so are we ourselves."[18]

A BEGINNING POINT

To go somewhere, we must know from whence we start. My starting point is delineated by four assumptions, which together explain why how we go about answering the *why* question is important.

First, the childish questions that Tolstoy asked are both fundamental and inescapable. They are fundamental because we are paradoxical or liminal creatures, half-animal and half-symbolic, beyond nature and her instinctually driven behaviors, on the one hand, and yet embodied creatures who are subject to sickness and death, on the other. Because humans are more than animals, because we are half-symbolic, if you will, questions of meaning are inescapable. They must be and are answered, either by our culture or our own self-conscious efforts. Failure to adequately answer these questions, or an absence of answers altogether, results in individual and social pathologies. We cannot for long deny our amphibious natures. Individuals and societies cannot thrive in the absence of meaning and purpose. Fromm highlights the difference between animals and humans this way: "The animal is content if its physiological needs—its hunger, its thirst and its sexual needs—are satisfied. Inasmuch as man is also animal, these needs are likewise imperative and must be satisfied. But inasmuch as man is human, the satisfaction of these instinctual needs is not sufficient to make him happy; they are not even sufficient to make him sane."[19]

Unlike our organic or natural needs, our uniquely human or symbolic needs have no inherent limits. Symbolic needs cannot be satiated in the same way that our hunger is satisfied after a Thanksgiving dinner. Robert Solomon asks whether "philosophy, which brought us to the Absurd, [can] carry us through it as well?"[20] Perhaps not, perhaps not philosophy, but some sort of "thinking" resolution is required if we are to satisfy our uniquely human—that is, symbolic—natures.

Second, the fact that both the question and the answer to meaning is symbolic explains why I seek guidance and the solace of fellow travelers in the thoughts and reflections of others, rather than through activities such as building a Habitat for Humanity house or volunteering to work with Meals-on-Wheels. I do this because, as a human being, the meaningfulness of my acts is not inherent in the acts themselves, but in how I understand those acts, and the motivations I have for performing them. Strategy—the *why* or ends questions—trumps the tactical *how* and *by what means* questions.

The fable of three men carrying stones to build a cathedral is often used to illustrate how what people think affects how they invest their work with meaning. The first man is a slave, and for him the work is meaningless, no more than drudgery to avoid the overseer's lash. The second man is a laborer. The meaning of his work is the pay he will receive at the end of the day, which will feed and shelter his family. Finally, the third man working on the cathedral is a religious pilgrim. The meaning of his work is glorifying God with acts of devotion and obedience. The physical activity of these three is the same, but the meaning is entirely different in each case. As human beings, meaning is "in our heads," in a way that makes activity necessary but insufficient.

The lesson of idealism, the philosopher and novelist Iris Murdoch, reminds us "is that what is material can only find its truth by passing into thought."[21]

The meaning lodged in our heads can either be unself-conscious and cultural or deliberate and self-conscious. Although the strength of and commitment to self-consciously held beliefs are arguable, the secondary instincts of culture are clearly more powerful than our biological instincts. Mind informs the body. Witness the suicide bombings in the Middle East, crash diets, celibacy, mountaineers struggling on high and dangerous peaks, or a thousand other examples of how the mind overcomes instinctual boundaries that no animal, acting on instinct alone, would cross. The culture in which we live, as well as how we think more deliberately, informs how we feel and act. Reductionism says that we are driven by economic or class interests, organic chemistry, or unconscious residues from our past. In contrast, I join those who assert that culture and self-conscious thought are independent variables and thus not reducible to biological or social factors.

Third, the creation and employment of symbols—what we think *about* nature, our fellow travelers, and ourselves—dramatically affect our emotions and actions. However abstract it may other-wise seem, thinking has practical consequences. Thought and feeling, the head and the heart, are not diametrically opposed. Thus I subscribe to what is sometimes referred to as a "cogni-tive" or "constructionist" theory of emotions. For example, I am angry with Jim, and, because I am angry, I treat him in a differ-ent way; I am less friendly, less forgiving, and less likely to respond positively to him if he should ask me for a favor. Criti-cally, my anger is dependent on a matrix of social practices, cultural beliefs, and judgments. My anger that he has treated me unfairly is based on how "fairness" is understood in my culture; similarly, if I were angry because he was having an affair with my wife, that anger is sustained by a symbolic and cultural understanding of marital fidelity. If I were in a culture in which marital fidelity was not a value, or if I discovered that—contrary to my earlier beliefs—Jim had not in fact had an affair with my wife, my anger would dissipate. In short, my changing thoughts would be preliminary to my once again treating Jim as a friend. My cat acts instinctively, but without anger. In contrast, "thinking" about anger—when it is justified, whether being angry calls for certain actions rather than others, how it relates to other emotions I may have toward Jim, such as friendship or kinship—has consequences for how I feel about myself, about Jim and about the tonal quality of the universe. The person who "thinks" that the universe is neutral and without purpose lives in a different universe—not only cognitively but emotionally—from one who thinks that the universe is sustained by God's continuing grace. Or as the popular writer Wayne Dyer says, "When you change the way you look at things the things you look at change."[22]

Lastly, the search for how people invest their lives with meaning is prompted by the intuition that, at least for those of us who live in relative security and affluence, meaninglessness is a greater threat than fanaticism, and faith and commitment are a greater challenge than doubt and skepticism. Skepticism and doubt, an ingrained habit of questioning authority and asking "Why" at every turn, is our Protestant/Enlightenment birthright, as Reinhold Niebuhr explains in his *Nature and Destiny of Man*. Whereas this was once an instrument of liberation from oppressive beliefs, many of us now need liberation from the inability to believe. Skepticism is itself an expression of more fundamental beliefs, not dissimilar to the faith traditions of the great religions. A study of meaning exhibits skepticism and doubt about skepticism and doubt. It looks beyond a habitual skepticism about answering the *why* question to see what we can learn from people who have invested their lives with meaning through myth, philosophy, and the other ways I explore in this book. Skepticism and doubt undermine fanaticism, but fanaticism flourishes in the soil of meaninglessness when the fanatic is the only one who has found a meaning worth dying for. Fear of fanaticism prevents us from identifying and confronting evil. Martin Luther King Jr. often spoke about how the greatest impediment to the civil rights movement was not the racists but the indifference of otherwise good people. Evils persist whenever otherwise good people fail to answer the *why* question in a way that fortifies them for action.

PROSPECTS

Regardless of the cause—whether personal experience (Tolstoy), the human awareness of death and doubt (Tillich), or because we live at the terminus of a long and inherently flawed philosophical tradition (Solomon et al.)—we find ourselves in a dark wood, in an age in which questions about why and for what purpose do not find ready answers. Much of twentieth-century literature, philosophy, and theology represents attempts to create a pathway out of the wood. The variety of these attempts is confusing; there are too many possible directions, too many pathways that cross and intersect. To reduce that variety and confusion, in the following chapters, I develop a typology of basic and recurrent directions in which we can move. Part I of this book looks at the classical sources of meaning, aspects of which will be familiar. My purpose in revisiting them here is not primarily historical but philosophical; that is, I do not assume that the sources of meaning are progressive, where a later source invalidates an earlier one, but that each source is a genuine type or archetype. The classic and recurring ways of thinking about the question of meaning are the mythic (chapter 2), the philosophical (chapter 3), the scientific (chapter 4), and the postmodern (chapter 5). While it is convenient to discuss these types as they unfolded sequentially in history, each type is also found in any historical period, most especially our own. What's more, no type or way of thinking is pure. Most people, most of the time, exhibit more than one type of thinking, if not at the same time, then sequentially.

Analyzing how people invest their lives with meaning into four types provides a simplified structure for comparing how the questions of meaning and purpose can be addressed. Mine is finally a comparative approach, only instead of comparing Augustine with Albert Camus, existentialism with vitalism, or Buddhism with Christianity, I compare how meaning is addressed by myth versus philosophy or by science versus postmodernism. A comparative approach is important because the nature of the question, the direction of our search, and what we accept as a legitimate or satisfactory answer change according to which way of thinking we employ. Indeed, I hope the reader will come to appreciate how my own approach to the question of meaning is prejudicial and goes in one direction rather than another, as it must. To say that life does or does not have purpose and meaning is insufficient. To reach that point in our search is not the end.

Beyond that point, we need to ask, "Yes, life is meaningful—or not—but what do we mean by meaning? What would make life meaningful, and what does life lack when it seems meaningless?" What the philosopher accepts as constituting a meaningful life is not the same as what a postmodernist finds meaningful, nor does the pragmatist understand meaning in the same way as the naturalist. The development of a comparative typology, like all analytical thought, is not only a technique of simplification; it is also a technique for liberation from a myopic vision that says that meaning can be found in only one way.

Like the primary colors of cyan, magenta, yellow, and black, the four archetypal sources of meaning—myth, philosophy, science, and postmodernism—can and have been combined to create a more subtle and complex palette. In part II of the book, on contemporary sources of meaning, I extend the search initiated in part I to more contemporary expressions in pragmatism (chapter 6), archetypal psychology (chapter 7), metaphysics (chapter 8), and naturalism (chapter 9). Although each chapter of the book is largely independent, I recommend that the classic approaches in part I be read sequentially before reading the later chapters in part II, because these later chapters require the background provided in the former. Thus, for example, an understanding of Aristotelian Forms, as described in chapter 3, is germane to understanding the archetypal psychology described in chapter 7, just as elements of science and postmodernism (chapters 4 and 5) are expressed in pragmatism (chapter 6) and naturalism (chapter 9). If "history doesn't repeat itself, but it at least rhymes," as Mark Twain is reputed to have said, it does so in such a way that the classic options find new depth and complexity in more contemporary expressions.

Taken together, chapters 2 to 9 present eight strategies people have used to instill their lives with meaning. These strategies provide a resource for answering the questions "Why?" and "What for?" and provide tools for analyzing intractable cultural and moral conflicts. The nature of the questions and what people accept as legitimate answers vary. Accordingly, for clarity's sake and to assist comparison, each chapter has a summarizing section that asks four questions: What do we know? How do we know? What does the approach being examined emphasize or neglect in our experience? and, finally, What does the chapter have to say or contribute to the way we create or discern a meaningful life?

Lastly, in chapter 10, I conclude by briefly reflecting on themes and motivations both different and shared by the various ways people invest their lives with meaning, and suggest the archetype that the search for meaning exposes. The reasons and justifications we use in answering the question of meaning say much about who we are and help explain persistent social and moral conflicts. The religious extremists and citizens of modern, secular societies live in very different worlds because they invest their lives with meaning in fundamental different ways. *The Search for Meaning* seeks to make those differences clearer. If I have succeeded in my study, the typology I've described will provoke its application to the analysis of more complex ways to invest life with meaning and, in so doing, prove the usefulness of the perspective it affords.

PART I

Classical Sources of Meaning

CHAPTER TWO

Myth and Meaning

CHARACTERIZING MYTHS

To talk about myth is already to violate it.

Imagine yourself watching an action-packed movie or a romantic comedy in your local theater. It's a Friday evening after a hard week at work, and you willingly suspend any disbelief or critical faculty you may otherwise have in order to be entertained. Arresting images of exotic places and eccentric characters pass by in succession, and you are captivated by the sights, sounds, and feelings they evoke. Happily for one who is trying to relax, the seduction is sufficiently strong that the mind is able to go from one thing to the next, unimpeded by what is going on either at work or at home. What "should" happen is what "does" happen as the unfolding narrative pulls your attention and sympathies now this way, now that. What counts in viewing a movie is finally not what it means or whether it accurately corresponds to historical events but whether it, for a time at least, holds one's attention completely.

A "bent of mind that sees things exactly, each for itself" is the first characteristic of what the classical scholar John H. Finley calls "the heroic mind."[1] Although Finley developed the concept to explain the works of Homer, the heroic or mythic mind applies equally well to explaining the experience of watching movies. The use of the word "see" here is not accidental, for movies are visual and display physical actions that unfold as movements in time in a series of doings by persons or agents. The proper question to ask of myth is not "What does it mean?" but "What happens next and how does it end?" The mythic mind is a mind of becoming rather than of static being. Whatever grand ideas or intentions a movie director may have can be expressed only through sights, sounds, narrative, and the succession of our sympathies as they follow one character after another. If an idea or theme can't be seen and acted out, it can't be said; all we have with myth is the story itself and what Finley calls the "luminous surface of things."

By staying close to the surface of things, myth is not only sensual and unfolds in time; it is also encyclopedic and pluralistic. Finley says of the mythic mind that it was not "blunted" to fit into a conceptual scheme, but mimicked sights and actions as they were found, however random. In a world of bright particulars, experience takes precedence over concepts or ideas. My self-conscious ideas about violence, for example, ought to preclude me from watching the multiple murders I witness in television shows and movies. Similarly, if I were to ask what constitutes a worthwhile life, myth would answer, in fact, could only answer, with the stories such as those of Jesus or Gandhi, Mother Teresa or Martin Luther King Jr. To observe and categorize these lives as "worthwhile," however, is already a step removed from myth, because "worthwhile," as an abstract category, cannot be seen or narrated. The mythic mind simply talks about a life, in Eric Havelock's words, "without knowing anything about it . . . what he [the mythic story-teller] is doing is simply painting word-portraits of what . . . [in our example, lives] look like in a thousand different confusing situations."[2] The mythic mind is one in which direction is given by landmarks, rather than with a global positioning system and an abstract grid of longitude and latitude: "Go to the red house, take a left, go straight until you reach the McDonalds, turn left . . ." No thematic or conceptual summary of a myth is possible, because its essence is in the bright particulars.

Paradoxically, although thus embodied in the bright particulars, myth presupposes another, sacred plane that is ontologically different from and prior to our day-to-day profane world. Without denying the contingencies of this profane world, the mythic mind sees through and apprehends a sacred realm. To the mythic mind, every object in this world can be transparent to transcendence. The scholar of religion and myth Mircea Eliade proposed the word *hierophany* to describe those occasions— narrated by myths—when the sacred, a "reality that does not belong to our world," is manifested in the objects and events of our natural, taken-for-granted world. For the mythic mind, nature is at the same time both immediately in front of us and a manifestation of something else, is at once real and significant. By manifesting the sacred, any object can be transformed into something else, yet remain itself. "A sacred stone remains a *stone*," Eliade remarks. "[A]pparently [or, more precisely, from the profane point of view], nothing distinguishes it from all other stones. But for those to whom a stone reveals itself as sacred, its immediate reality is transmuted into a supernatural reality."[3] In the Christian tradition, to cite a common example, the bread and wine of the Eucharist remain bread and wine, yet paradoxically they are also the body and blood of Christ.

The sacred realm as articulated by myth is universal, impersonal, timeless, and transcendent. As such, it contrasts sharply with the everyday, profane world that is particular, personal, and time-bound. The bright particulars and surfaces of myths are unchanging and timeless because they also exist in a mythic time and place. Our lives are constantly in flux; we live with contingencies of place and time. Nothing is permanent; we come into and depart this world alone. In contrast, the world expressed by myth is unchanging and eternal; the myths do not change; the gods and actors always play out the narrative in the same way. There are no surprise endings; there is no progress. Oedipus always marries his mother; Ulysses always returns home; Rhett always tells Scarlett that he doesn't give a damn. The important thing about myth is not the new, creative, or novel but the old and the typical. The traditional hymn got it right: "Tell me the old, old story."

By identifying with the universal and unchanging narratives of myth, by seeing the stone as *also* a manifestation of the eternal, we achieve transcendence. We are lifted out of our normal lives. We see something fixed and enduring in the midst of universal flux. Contingency and change is seen through. As a consequence, the reality of the day-to-day becomes secondary to the enduring and eternal reality of the sacred. I shall describe later how philosophy fulfills our human need for order and stability with abstract—universal and timeless—categories and ideas. Here I wish to say that myths fulfill these same needs not conceptually, but by returning to and identifying with unchanging mythic stories. What is constant and unchanging are the myths, and the sacred realm that the myths articulate. The mythic story is not idiosyncratic to me or to my time and place; it is not "my" story. On the contrary, myths are impersonal and universal; they are there equally for all those who hear and identify with them. Contingent on neither a particular place nor a particular time, they exist in a mythic, that is, universal and eternal, time and place. The story of Christ or Buddha is the same regardless of who I am, where I am, or my historical circumstance.

The characteristics of myth can be illustrated with a contemporary example. Consider the civil rights movement in America. For many, this was at once both a social movement and a manifestation of the Exodus myth. The leaders of the civil rights movement—based as they were in African American churches—clearly identified their struggles with the biblical story of an oppressed people gaining freedom from Egypt. By making this connection, participants in the civil rights struggle became contemporary with that primordial place and time. In so doing, two things were accomplished. First, the participants were able to escape or transcend chronological time and achieve hope. Even though things may seem hopeless, there is hope if one can return to and live within the original, eternal story of liberation and the Promised Land. And second, the participants learned who they were and what they needed to do by living out—reenacting—the primordial history of the Exodus. Who are we? We are an oppressed people, like the people in Egypt. What are we to do? We are to resist oppression and move toward the Promised Land like the Israelites. How can we hope to become free in the face of overwhelming social and economic prejudice and oppression?

Our hope is not logical, pragmatic, or calculating but rests on our identification with those whom God set free in the past, a liberation that our reenactment makes present. This secular world of oppression, violence, and discrimination is "unreal" and fleeting in comparison to the permanent world of the Exodus myth. Whenever we find ourselves going back to and identifying with a paradigmatic story—whether it's the Eucharist, the Exodus, or the legends of the American War of Independence—we are in the presence of myth. Myths are able to structure and provide stability from one moment to the next, because any moment can be transcended and related to an exemplary, unchanging mythic time and event. For participants in the civil rights struggle, time and circumstances were annihilated through the auspices of the Exodus myth.

MYTH AS BELIEF; MYTH AS FAITH

> Man is excluded from the reality of whatever he may do if his heart be not engaged.
> William Cantwell Smith, *Faith and Belief*

However important knowing the characteristics of myths may be, we miss something essential if we do not distinguish between knowing *about* myth and *living mythically*.

The word *about* connotes a separation between the knower and the known that is alien to genuine myth. One can formulate propositions that are either true or false about an object. Persons outside a myth can characterize and describe myth, as I am doing here, but knowing about a myth is different from living from within it. I may know all the statistics of the Atlanta Braves baseball team—how many games they've won and lost, their team batting average and ERAs—but that is different from being a fan who identifies with the team and the mythology of baseball.

What separates a fan from someone who knows *about*—one who is inside a myth from one who is outside—is emotional identification, ritual, and imaginative reenactment. The fan identifies with the team and its heroes. The fan is happy when the team wins and is despondent when it loses. Similarly, the person living within a myth identifies wholly with the characters and events of the myth. Eric Havelock emphasizes that the ritual oral performance and retelling of Greek myth elicited an active, hypnotic identification of the audience with the myth. The audience was not merely watching a performance of a myth; it was ritually engaged in a reenactment and identification with it. In these circumstances, audience and performer become one. Within myth, I do not think *about* Achilles; rather, I wholly identify with Achilles; in a sense, I become him, as long as I submit myself to the incantation. This fanatical identification with the myth annihilates my autonomous, separate ego. I no longer live "as if" but in and within the myth.

The absolutely critical distinction between knowing *about* myth and *living within* myth is clarified by Wilfred Cantwell Smith's discussion of faith and belief. Belief is analogous to knowing *about*. It is both propositional and provisional. Belief is "the concept by which we convey the fact that a view is held, ideationally, without a final decision as to its validity."[4] Thus, it is reductionistic. Belief rests between complete skepticism, on the one hand, and certain knowledge, on the other. From the outside, we say of someone that they believe in, rather than know, the Resurrection, the four Noble Truths, and the superiority of the Red Sox to the Yankees. And, as we all know, beliefs can be true or false, whereas knowledge is unassailable. In contrast, faith elevates belief to a religious level. Faith is a total, engaged response to and identification with myth that annihilates the critical distance between it and me. It is through the eyes of faith that one sees whatever one sees, not as a proposition that can be true or false, but as the way things are. Faith engages heart and soul. It is not enough to know *about;* one must directly experience and respond through the auspices of faith.

Knowing mythically is not disinterested and objective but engaged and tacit, like the knowledge one has of riding a bike, hitting a tennis ball, or greeting a neighbor. As Smith observes, one does not believe a symbol. "Rather one responds to it, one is more or less successful in seeing what it means, in seeing and feeling and being moved by that."[5] Within myth, the faithful hardly believe in anything; they simply and unself-consciously respond to the world they perceive with the aid of the myth, a world, moreover, that they see as real. The beliefs we observe in others are, for the insiders, invisible and taken for granted. The fan does not believe the Red Sox are the best team; he knows it. The devout don't believe Jesus is the Christ; they encounter Jesus directly as the Christ. The myth implicitly presents the world as it is, not as it may possibly be.

I think Joseph Campbell is pointing to the priority of faith to belief when he writes: "People say that what we are all seeking is a meaning for life. I don't think that's what we're really seeking. I think that what we are seeking is an experience of being alive, so that our life experiences on the purely physical plane will have resonance with our innermost being and reality, so that we actually feel the rapture of being alive. That's what it's finally all about."[6]

William Cantwell Smith observes that the total, engaged response to experience that is faith can be expressed in any number of different ways: in dance, music, and law, as well as verbally.[7] Beliefs—explicitly *about* statements—are, he says, a particularly Western way of approaching questions of faith. Statements by the faithful about their beliefs are actually a way of "bearing witness." When the believer says, "There is no God but Allah and Muhammad is His Prophet," he is bearing witness, in Smith's words, to the facts as he sees them, "as realities in the universe not belief in his mind. . . . The witness formula affirms that he is relating himself in a certain way—of recognition, obedience, and service—to a situation that, already, and independently, and objectively exists. He is corroborating it, not postulating it."[8] Similarly, talk *about* myths—about the beliefs myths contain—are secondary and reductionistic in comparison to the primary experience of living mythically. We become concerned with beliefs and myth at the point where faith and living within myth fails. We begin to ask *why* and *what for* when faith and myth become self-conscious.

Most of the time, we are distrustful of faith and of those who live mythically, and for good reason. We are heirs of the Enlightenment, which sees faith as "blind," "naïve," or "fanatical," just as in common parlance, myth denotes a "false," "deceitful," or "fabricated" story. The Nazis identified with and lived within the myth of the Aryan race, just as contemporary Islamic terrorists are comforted by the myth that they will have a place of honor in heaven because of their martyrdom. Myth can thus convey meaning and purpose, but it does so with a price and a danger. That's what it looks like from the outside. But from the inside, it doesn't look that way. From inside of myth, we become more authentic, and life gains greater significance and meaning, the more we identify with the mythic tale. For the outsider, Westminster Cathedral is a tourist attraction; for the devout, it is a place of worship.

In the following section, I shall often talk *about* myth. The reader should keep in mind, however, that *about* emerges from *within*, and the movement from the one to the other is critical. Before I close, I shall have occasion to discuss contemporary examples of myths that are more invisible and thus closer to faith, even for those who would claim their liberation from those irrational, authoritarian, false stories. Before moving to those considerations, however, four comments.

FOUR COMMENTS

First, let us note that the timeless and universal character of myth finds expression in repetition. Myths are repetitive. The repetitive elements can be exact, as in archaic myths, or they can be adaptive and typological. When myths are typological, we do not ritually return to an original, timeless, unchanging story so much as repeat a variation of the "core" story, clothed in the specifics of our own time and place. A typically male hero of uncertain heritage and reputation emerges from an obscure town to save an otherwise hapless and doomed people though an act of often violent self-sacrifice. The Christ story, yes, but also the story of the cowboy, Captain America, and Luke Skywalker. Typology seeks order through allusion and suggestive semblances. In the biblical narrative, Eden is succeeded by the Promised Land, Jerusalem, the rebuilt Temple, the Kingdom of God, and Heaven, whereas, negatively, the Wilderness and Sea are succeeded by Egypt, the Philistines, Babylon, Antioch, Rome, and Hell.[9] With typology, we return to the same mythic core, albeit disguised, even when we encounter what we believe to be a new story.

A consideration of typologies suggests that we err if we think mythic thinking is limited to stories of the gods and goddesses of Greece or other archaic cultures. We are self-deceived if we think we have abandoned or outgrown childish myths by merely rejecting the ancient stories of Moses or the god of thunder. The gods are not so easily dismissed. "The latest incarnation of Oedipus, the continued romance of Beauty and the Beast," Joseph Campbell famously said, "stands this afternoon on the corner of 42nd street and Fifth Avenue, waiting for the traffic light to change."[10] *Star Wars* seems like a new story about the future but is actually a very old story from the past, as the movie's opening text tells us.

Second, many questions we might like to ask—such as, What constitutes a worthwhile life?—cannot be asked while we are living mythically. From inside myth, the question of meaning never arises. All myth can do is tell compelling stories. To ask critical or abstract questions of a myth—how the stories are related or what ideas they represent, for example—is already to violate the mythic mind. Plato asks such questions, but these are not the questions of myth but of myth's detractors, questions one asks from outside rather than inside. Myth is neither allegory nor philosophy but identification. The most important thing about myths is not the depth of ideas they contain—remember, I said they calm the mind precisely by staying on the surface of things—but whether they are compelling. To remind a companion who emerges in tears from a viewing of *The Last*

Picture Show or some similarly sad movie that "It's only a story; it's not real" is both to miss the point and to misunderstand the compelling nature of, and total identification with, myth.

Third, myth works because of our identification with the story and its characters. With myth, the criteria for successful and meaningful action are not pragmatic or calculating; they are imitative and representational. A popular career-planning book does not cite statistics about potential earning power or the demographics of demand; rather, it encourages those who are seeking their path to consider with which mythic character they identify. Are they a hero, a magician, a warrior, or a scholar? If you can identify the myth that "fits," the mythic story will provide direction as to what to do and become. Our central mission is not to be pragmatically "successful" but to be faithful to the mythic pattern.[11] Christians are admonished, "Go thou and do likewise"—that is, imitate Christ—not, "Analyze the situation and see what's best."

Fourth, and finally, we can never mount an abstract argument against a myth. We cannot ask of a myth whether it is true or false (truth and falsehood are, after all, abstract notions); we can only testify to whether the story is compelling. If you doubt this, try arguing with a biblical literalist or a Red Sox fan. The mythic mind is one in which, in the search for what is true and real, faith is more important than comparison, reflection, and doubt. When our sympathies are fully engaged by a story, we never ask whether we "believe" it or question its "point." As long as we are fully engaged, we are victims of its enchantments. The scholar of religion David L. Miller maintains simply: "Religion means being gripped by a story."[12] Myth eliminates critical distance. It works to the extent that we submit and are obedient to its spell.

I repeat this point because of its central importance: we do not "believe in" a myth the way we might believe in Santa Claus; rather, we directly encounter a compelling force whose power we can never question. "To acknowledge something as (one's) god," James C. Edwards observes, "is to surrender to that power: to let its immediately experienced willfulness have sway over one, to serve that power. A proper relationship of profane to sacred is maintained or restored when the compelling power at the heart of things is acknowledged and then allowed to rule."[13] The only way to challenge a myth is to confront it with another, more compelling myth. One moves, not from falsehood to truth, but from one god—or baseball team—to another.

A STORY-SHAPED WORLD

In the opening chapter of his classic study *Myth and Reality*, Mircea Eliade says that he is going to examine societies in which myths are—or were until very recently—"living," meaning that they are models for human behavior and, in so doing, supply meaning and value to life.[14] The difference between a "merely entertaining" story and a true or paradigmatic story, that is, a myth, is thus functional. Both the story and the myth are narratives, both embody their meanings through actions and characters, but the former can be dismissed as being only "fictional" or "merely" a story, whereas the latter has authority. Myth gives direction, because we identify with its compelling characters and actions. *Myth*, then, is an honorific title reserved for stories with a compelling force and authority.

Understood in this way, many studies have addressed the relationship between stories, myths, and behavior. Oscar Wilde's saying "Life imitates art" is a cliché because it acknowledges the commonsense notion that we learn how to act by watching others, including the others found in narratives and stories. Although at times dauntingly psychological, Bruno Bettelheim's *The Uses of Enchantment* examines how fairy tales function to raise and resolve the basic life problems of children and adolescents, especially problems involving the struggle to achieve maturity. Cinderella is a complex tale, with many themes, including sibling rivalry, the triumph of goodness and purity, the unimportance of humble beginnings, the necessity of establishing independence from one's parents, and the achievement of intimacy, among others. On the one hand, there is the positive conviction that deceit and mean-spiritedness are not rewarded; on the other, there is the negative Cinderella Complex, in which young girls wait as passive and submissive victims until they are rescued and fulfilled by a handsome prince. Whether these lessons are finally positive or negative is debatable and, for our purposes here, unimportant. What's important for us is that Bettelheim shows how stories function mythically by subconsciously informing children's thoughts and actions as they move toward maturity.

A more amusing and lighthearted example of how stories influence behavior is found in Susan J. Douglas's *Where the Girls Are: Growing Up Female with the Mass Media*. How do women learn how to act? Certainly from their parents, peers, and families but also, according to Douglas and many others, from the models provided in the mass media. The television sitcom *The Mary Tyler Moore Show*, for example, both articulated and encouraged the way "new" women were beginning to act during the early 1970s.

For those unfamiliar with it, *The Mary Tyler Moore Show* depicts the life of a single career woman living in Minneapolis.

That may sound like an unremarkable story line today, but, in its day, the show was pioneering in its depiction of the life of an unmarried working woman. In contrast to the conventional depictions of women that preceded it, the main character— Mary Richards—is shown making it on her own, outside the home and a stable marriage. She is no Cinderella waiting to meet her Prince Charming at a ball. Shockingly, she calls up men for dates, and she fends off men she doesn't like. Mary makes it clear that she prefers solitude to spending time with some oaf just because he is a man. Expressive of the ambiguity surrounding the increasingly ambiguous role of woman during the era, Mary is both assertive and submissive, at times—often at the same time—both feisty and meek. Her boldest and most righteous assertions are immediately tempered by smiles, an uncertain tone of voice, and the use of words and qualifying phrases such as *maybe, perhaps,* or *have you considered* to cushion the impact of her requests. Traditional role models for women—primarily those of wives and stay-at-home mothers— were being eroded during the 1970s, and the contemporary mass media obliged with new models, among them Mary Richards.

I feel sure that Bettelheim and Douglas would claim that the influence of stories on behavior is often, if not largely, unconscious or nondeliberate and thus mythical. I may deliberately and self-consciously try to imitate the way Tom Hanks dresses or jokes in *Sleepless in Seattle,* but more often I go about acting as I do without any conscious identification of why I act in this way rather than in that. Indeed, whenever I do interrupt my actions to reflect on *why,* the question of meaning and purpose will most likely occur. Because explicit stories can be questioned, at least in principle; because I can ask deliberately whether I wish to imitate this character or a particular aspect of a character, the spell, or, as Bettelheim says, the "enchant-ment," of the story is always vulnerable. As a result, the fairy tale of Cinderella and the contemporary sitcom of Mary Richards remain "mere" stories, and their authority for our thought and behavior can be denied whenever it becomes demanding or uncomfortable. However insightful and interest-ing Bettelheim and Douglas and their colleagues may be (and they are), they do not in the end go far enough because they remain centrally concerned with stories and not myth. At the level of myth, I am asked to sell all my worldly goods to follow Christ; at the level of story, Jesus is an inspirational example, an important and vital story—don't misunderstand me—but still only a story. Myth works at a far deeper level than story, in a way that is pre- or subconscious, making its suasion or spell all the more compelling. Or to say this in another way, genuine myth is invisible.

THE INVISIBILITY OF MYTH

What do I mean by saying that myth is invisible, and how are we to talk about a ghost?

Genuine myth is invisible in two ways.

First, as Eliade argues, the "majority of men 'without religion' still hold to pseudo religions and degenerate mythologies."[15] As an example of this, Eliade cites the mythological structure and eschatological content of Marxism. On the surface, Marxism explicitly rejects religious mythology—religion is, after all, the opium of the people—but on a deeper or latent level it is one of the world's great eschatological myths:

> [T]he Just (the "chosen," the "anointed," the "innocent," the "messenger"; in our day, the proletariat) . . . are destined to change the ontological status of the world. In fact, Marx's classless society and the consequent disappearance of historical tensions find their closest precedent in the myth of the Golden Age that many traditions put at the beginning and the end of history. Marx enriched this venerable myth by a whole Judaeo-Christian messianic ideology: on the one hand, the prophetic role and soteriological function that he attributes to the proletariat; on the other, the final battle between Good and Evil, which is easily comparable to the apocalyptic battle between Christ and the Antichrist, followed by the total victory of the former.[16]

Eliade finds what he calls "degenerate" forms of myth in war, individual combat, psychoanalysis, and, ironically, reading and scholarship. What's important about these latent myths is that they are genuine myths, first, in the sense that they provide paradigmatic solutions to how and why one should act and, second, in that the mythic element remains invisible and unacknowledged. For persons living within a myth, the rise of the proletariat or alternatively psychoanalysis is rational and objectively descriptive of what is the case. It's not myth; it's what's real. Within myth, the question of whether I should go to war when my country calls is never asked. I simply respond. Within myth, I do not see the myth itself, just as I do not see the lenses in my glasses; on the contrary, I see through the invisible or transparent myth in apprehending the world as—from my perspective—it simply is.

Another, perhaps more accessible, way to talk about the invisibility of myth is to consider the nature of historical writing. Conventionally, history is thought to describe and correspond to "real" events—to facts—in contrast to fictions that refer to imaginary events. History at its best approaches the objectivity and disinterest of science; the more one introduces a personal or ideological bias into an interpretation of history, the further one strays from the objective, true description of what happened. Understanding in history occurs when our descriptions mirror what actually happened.

In contrast to this conventional understanding of history, the historian of consciousness Hayden White persuasively argues that all history, no matter how seemingly objective, is a combination of fact and generic story form that encodes or configures data into the familiar story types of our culture. Understanding is a process of rendering the unfamiliar familiar by a process that White variously describes as emplotment, encoding, or configuring. In this process, otherwise random facts are apprehended through the familiar story types of our culture. Historiography thus "*constitutes the objects* which it pretends only to describe realistically and to analyze objectively."[17] We understand or find meaning in facts to the extent that they yield to and are identified with the myths available in our culture. In short, we learn by going back to and repeating the sacred stories. Indeed, to take this one step further, these stories—myths—not only configure existing facts, they determine which facts we seek out and notice. White summarizes his influential notion of historical understanding this way:

> The reader, in the process of following the historian's account of those events, gradually comes to realize that the story he is reading is of one kind rather than another: romance, tragedy,

comedy, satire, epic, or what have you. And when he has perceived the class or type to which the story that he is reading belongs, he experiences the effect of having the events of the story explained to him. He has at this point not only successfully *followed* the story; he has grasped the point of it, *understood* it, as well. The original strangeness, mystery, or exoticism of the events is dispelled, and they take on a familiar aspect, not in their details, but in their functions as elements of a familiar kind of configuration. They are rendered comprehensible by being subsumed under the categories of the plot structure in which they are encoded as a story of a particular kind. They are familiarized, not only because the reader now has more *information* about the events, but also because he has been shown how the data conform to an *icon* of a comprehensible finished process, a plot structure with which he is familiar as a part of his cultural endowment.[18]

For anyone who has been exposed to Kant's concept of the a priori imagination, White's discussion of how we see and comprehend facts in terms of "the categories of the plot structure in which they are encoded" will be familiar. Even our perceptions of the objective laws of nature, according to some scholars, are informed by nonrational myths.[19] We can never think entirely outside of myth; to say that we find meaning in the facts themselves is merely to suffer from a certain lack of self-consciousness.

FOUR QUESTIONS

As a way of summarizing our discussion of mythical thinking, let us consider four questions: (1) What do we know? (2) How do we know it? (3) How does thinking mythically influence what we notice and what we ignore in our experience? Or to put this in another way, what questions does mythical thinking permit us to ask and what questions does it ignore? And finally, (4) What does mythic thinking say about the question of meaning?

What Do We Know?

First, whether consciously or subconsciously, we know a body of stories and plot structures that function mythically by providing us with authoritative examples of who we are and how we should act. Because they are authoritative, we know that we can resolve the uncertainties and ambiguities of life by taking our bearings from the actions of mythic characters. As we have seen, White suggests that being a member of a culture means configuring the world according to the "genetic code" provided by our inherited myths. Thus, the meaning of being an American involves knowing and identifying with narratives of the American Revolution and the Civil War, just as children know and repeat the stories of Superman or Luke Skywalker. At a deeper level, myth subconsciously structures how we emplot or configure our experience— most persuasively, before we "step back" to consciously imitate the actions of a hero or God. There is no uninterpreted experience; on the contrary, experience takes shape and becomes visible because of the subconsciously held myths we employ. These subconsciously held myths tell us what to notice and what to ignore, what is meaningful and what is not.

Second, we know sights and sounds and narratives that unfold in time, not ideas or pragmatic ends. Myth presents us with a surface of "bright particulars" that, paradoxically, is also a transcendent world of timeless and universal actions. Mythical thinking testifies that image and example move us more than concept and argument. Advertisers know this well; attractive, affluent people seductively seem to invite us to be "just like them" as they drive the latest car. It may not make rational sense to go into debt to purchase a new car or a bigger house but, seduced by myth, we can't stop ourselves buying a bright red BMW. Product placements as a form of advertising inform our choices without calling attention to themselves. We know that our day-to-day, taken-for-granted world can be "seen through" and that our life gains authenticity and meaning to the extent that it imitates and corresponds to the transcendent world of myth. We know that our time-bound, particular lives can become universal and timeless through myth.

How Do We Know?

We know by identifying our experience with the narrative accounts found in stories that function mythically. That is to say, we know through imitation, identification, and repetitively or ritually following the concrete, sensual examples of heroes and the gods, rather than, for example, a causal sequence, abstract ideology, or list of explicit commandments. Children display the wisdom of the mythic mind by unself-consciously identifying with the heroes of popular culture and athletics. The reason or explanation for an event or action is in the imitation and identification with the mythic narrative itself, not in sociological or biological factors. We are liberated from the existential burden of knowing what to do and who we are by identifying our actions and desires with the characters of myth. We know, not by knowing *about* myth, but by *living mythically.*

What Does Mythical Thinking Emphasize and What Does It Neglect?

Ironically, mythical thinking—when we are fully seduced by its spell—does not permit us to formulate an abstract or conceptual question such as "What is the meaning of life? Or "Why do good people suffer?" Nor for that matter, does myth permit us to ask whether a hero's actions are consistent or true or pragmatically useful. Myth does not permit us to step outside of myth. It permits us only to tell more or less compelling stories, one after the other. We can ask of myths whether they are alive or dead, compelling or boring, but not whether they are true or false. Within myth, the dancer cannot be separated from the dance. Faith and commitment are more characteristic of mythical thinking than are doubt and skepticism. Myth highlights the reassuring experience provided by continuity, repetition, and the acceptance of authoritative examples. I am writing this passage during the Christmas season, and I am reminded that, within myth, novelty and creativity are less important than hearing the same *Lessons and Carols* and responding, "As it was in the beginning, is now, and ever shall be, world without end."

Myth and Meaning

Myth is our original condition. Myth is the world in which we live before we ask whether life has meaning. Myth is how we live when we are fully and unself-consciously engaged; when we identify and participate fully in our actions.

As we have seen, the proponents of mythical thinking argue that we are never outside of myth. From this perspective, what seems to us like a movement from myth and superstition to reason and causality (what's been called the Enlightenment myth) is actually a movement from one myth to another, albeit secular, myth. Meaninglessness is impossible because we are always within myth, even if that myth is saying that life is meaningless. Nihilists embody their own form of meaning in their denial of meaning, just as rebellious teenagers embody their own form of conventionality in their unconventional dress and behavior. What's more, to the extent that we cannot self-consciously create a compelling myth, we are captured and enchanted by forces beyond our direct control. We wait expectantly for a new god, a new love, a new enthusiasm to come to us as a revelation and gift. Theologically, we are saved through grace and not our own works or righteousness. A mythic strategy is the primary strategy for meaning, because it is inescapable; we are always living within myth, the more so when we do not recognize it.

Such thoughts challenge everything we believe in the modern era. We resist the notion that we are not free, autonomous persons who make deliberate, self-conscious judgments based on objective information. The thought that our actions and experience are not new and creative but old and repetitive seems ludicrous; we are tutored from an early age to be our own persons rather than to imitate others. We can grapple with myth and faith as outsiders, can reduce it to a set of beliefs that we can compare and accept as either true or false. But belief and living mythically are different. The myths of philosophy and modernity tutor us to distrust the older myths of gods and anthropomorphic forces. Because of that distrust, it is easier to understand a mythical strategy for meaning by seeing how or when myth fails.

First, loss of meaning occurs because we have "forgotten" the mythic stories. Simply stated, we cannot relate our current experience to the life-informing stories of myth *if we do not know the stories*. From this perspective, meaning has been lost because we have failed to learn the sacred stories and the social practices that support them. We have acquired the knowledge provided by philosophy and science but neglected the wisdom found in myth. An encyclopedia of mythic stories and cultural images constitutes a vocabulary of sorts through which our own experience can be uniquely articulated. Without that vocabulary, our experience remains humanly uninformed and meaningless. Conversely, a mythic strategy for meaning requires learning the vocabulary of myths and being attentive to the social practices and rituals that sustain them.

Second, the problem of meaninglessness may be attributed to the adoption of what can be called the "nihilistic myth." Nihilism, as classically expressed in the existential stories of Camus, Beckett, and Vonnegut, for example, is itself a culminating mythology of a long skeptical tradition that says that there is no meaning in an otherwise objective or neutral universe without purpose. Ironically, the myth of a meaningless universe is itself a way of infusing meaning into the experience of meaninglessness. Nihilists have their own emplotments of experience. According to this myth, we gain authenticity, dignity, and meaning by honestly and bravely accepting that the universe is without intrinsic meaning. The myth tells us that we are superior to those who live false, inauthentic lives by believing in one myth or the other, whether that myth be the American Dream or a socialist revolution. There's nobility and art in creating meaning in an otherwise meaningless universe. Paradoxically, a mythic strategy is effective for investing life with meaning even when the myth is telling us there is no meaning.

Thirdly, the compelling nature of mythic thinking breaks down whenever we become reflective or self-conscious. Meaning is the price we pay for self-consciousness. This implies that a strategy of living mythically is both vulnerable and fragile, fanatical and dangerous. Remember that mythic thinking is characteristically concrete and focused on the bright, luminous surface of things. If I can't see it or apprehend it with my senses, it cannot be articulated in myth. Myth contains no depth, ideas, or hidden meanings but reflects our response when we are fully engaged and unquestioning. Questions of meaning never arise when we are in love or, as we say, "lost" in sport or conversation, when we are living out the myth unself-consciously. For those who live mythically, there is no myth or distance between the knower and the known; the world in which we live simply is, and we respond. In response to tragedy, we can only say, "It's God's will." In contrast, whenever we "step back" to reflect—when we compare the directives of one myth against another or ask the question "why" a story or an act is either important or right—we already move outside of myth. We start to think *about* myth, rather than living mythically. Recall how Tolstoy was undone once he stepped back and began what proved to be an endless sequence of *why* and *what for* questions. Stepping back, reflecting on what one is doing and whether what one is doing is consistent, corresponds to an idea, or is pragmatically useful—rather than just unself-consciously doing—can be one's undoing. Robert C. Solomon describes the point at which the spell of mythic thinking is broken and we transcend ourselves, not by entering myth through identification, but by stepping back from myth to reflect:

> Yet we once were certain of an answer, that is, until we asked. Having only heard the question mentioned we knew: "Of course life has meaning—there is happiness and one's fellow men, love, and life's little pleasures . . ." But as we ask, we step back from living, as we might step back from love, and there is that quiet ominous sound like the ripping at the seams of a tight fitting fabric. We immediately recognize what we have done. Our step backward has severed that intimacy which once served to answer our question, before it had been asked. . . . That final "why" has undermined everything. . . . Everything remains as before but deadened, emptied of meaning. The world is no longer ours: We observe it. . . . The old habits keep us moving, robotlike, through the paces of life, but we are not wholly there. The "why" has no answer.[20]

"Stepping back" from living mythically announces the beginning of the philosophical mind. The origins and characteristics of this mode of thinking, and how it adds to a discussion of meaning, is the subject of the next chapter.

CHAPTER THREE

Philosophy and Meaning

In Plato's dialogue *Meno*, Socrates asks for a definition of virtue. Meno—speaking for the Sophists—confidently replies by saying first what virtue is for a man—he should know how to administer the state for the benefit of his friends and harm to his enemies— and then for a woman—she should order her house and obey her husband. And then, sounding very much like a contemporary relativist, he goes on to say that "every age, every condition of life, young and old, male or female, bond or free, has a different virtue; for virtue is relative to the actions and ages of each of us in all that we do." Socrates mocks Meno's answer. "How fortunate I am, Meno," Socrates responds sarcastically, "When I ask you for one virtue, you present me with a swarm of them."[1]

What follows is a dialogue that seeks to discover what the "common notion" is among the various virtues. What is it that permits one to apply the word *virtue* to both the actions of the master and the slave, to both an old man and a young girl? In what will become a familiar strategy, Socrates goes beyond appearances—the "bright particulars" of the heroic or mythic mind—to discover the defining concept or principle or finally the Platonic Form of Virtue per se, a category that can be universally applied to all acts of virtue, whenever and wherever they occur. A Homeric saga might contain a thousand narratives of how virtuous persons act in various circumstances, and we might, for example, admire Mother Teresa and Martin Luther King Jr. equally. But, behind the apparent differences between the woman from India and the American social revolutionary, what is it that they have in common that we admire?

In the *Republic*, Plato says that people delight in beautiful tones, colors, and shapes—of a woman, a sunset, or a building, perhaps—but that they do not have "the power of thought to behold and to take delight in the nature of Beauty itself." Plato contrasts the difference between the beautiful and Beauty, appearance and Reality, this way:

> Now if a man believes in the existence of beautiful things, but not of Beauty itself . . . is he not living in a dream? Consider: does not dreaming, whether one is awake or asleep, consist in mistaking a semblance for the reality it resembles? . . .
>
> Contrast with him the man who holds that there is such a thing as Beauty itself and can discern that essence as well as the things that partake of its character, without ever confusing the one with the other—is he a dreamer or living in a waking state?[2]

It's a rhetorical question, of course, because the immediate reply is: he is very much awake. The person who can behold Beauty itself and discern its essence behind the appearances is very much superior.

Like Socrates and his pupil Plato, the Greek historian Thucydides also looked beyond appearances. Whereas they found unity behind a plurality of virtuous exemplars, he discerned the universal forces and a guiding scheme beyond the apparent randomness of historical events. Through his eyes, the battles and conflicts of the Peloponnesian War became *illustrative* of forces that were inherent in political conflicts that would reoccur, human nature remaining the same, in other times and places. During the war, he writes, "People changed in usage the normal relationship of words to deeds: insane daring was judged loyal courage, cautious delay was called specious fear, temperance the mask of cowardice, and general intelligence general futility. . . . A violent man was always credible, his opponent suspect."[3] History is not, as someone has said, simply "one damn thing after another," nor is it subject to the whims of capricious gods. On the contrary, history exhibits a discernable pattern, an order that only the mind—as distinguished from the senses—can grasp. Grasping this intelligible order within the otherwise random events of history is a form of genuine, and useful, knowledge. To us, the idea that history contains lessons seems commonplace, hardly worth mentioning. But when seen against the mythical backdrop from which it emerged, Thucydides' act of looking beyond the appearances was revolutionary.

The classics scholar Eric Havelock contrasts the mythic mind with the emerging philosophic mind of Socrates, Plato, and Thucydides this way:

> Simply put, a narrativised experience says: "The storm-god launched the river against the wall and swept it away." An abstract version rearranges this to say "The river had a force of such and such . . . and the wall had a weight (or mass or inertia) of such and such; the weight and the force when

calculated and compared yield the result that the wall has to give way before the stress imposed on it." But this particular result now depends on concepts of force and weight which just "are" and which become the terms of equations which "are." These in Platonism would become the "Forms" of force and weight, and their participation in each other becomes a law governing the relation of pressure to inertia. . . .

Or again, Agamemnon challenged by Calchas to give up the priest's daughter is very angry; yet he adds: "For all that I will give her back if that is better. Rather would I see my people whole than perishing. Only make you ready a prize of honour forthwith lest I alone of all the Argives be disprized, which thing is not proper. For you all behold how my prize is departing from me." This series of acts and events sharply but separately imagised—"I will give her back—the people must not perish—but get me a substitute—I am King—I am the only one to lose my prize"—these can be rearranged as the expression or illustration of moral principle or social law: "The good of the army is paramount and this forces me to return the girl. Nevertheless my status is also paramount; justice therefore requires that I receive a substitute." Here the "good" of the army, the "'status" of Agamemnon, and the "justice" of his demand are cast in a language which presumes some general standard of good and of propriety and of justice, by which the particular good and the particular propriety of the present situation can be estimated. The standards have to be expressed in ideal laws which just "are."[4]

CHARACTERIZING THE PHILOSOPHIC MIND

These brief examples offer clues for characterizing the philosophic mind.

First, the heart of the philosophic mind is discontent.[5] It is hard to overemphasize this point. As Richard Tarnas observes in his popular survey of Western thought, the "Greeks were perhaps the first to see the world as a question to be answered."[6] In contrast to the mythic mind that preceded it, which uncritically follows one story after another, we see Socrates objecting to Meno's giving now this definition of virtue, now that, depending on the circumstance, gender, and status of the person. Socrates asks for a single definition of Virtue and is not content with the swarm of definitions he receives in reply. The philosophic mind is not content with the inconsistency and absolute contingency implied in the saying "When in Rome, do as the Romans do." Socrates was not an existentialist; his was a philosophy of Being rather than one of an ever-changing becoming. The philosophic mind is not content with disorder and changing appearances.

Furthermore, the philosophic mind is also not content with the capriciousness and lack of predictability exhibited by the mythic mind. It seeks a stable, universal order behind the kaleidoscope of appearances. A willful storm-god pushes our boat now this way, now that; the gods of war favor this side, now that. In response, the mythic mind is largely passive and obedient. Abraham does not question the God who asks him to sacrifice his son Isaac. If we arrive in port a day late because of God's will, then so be it. In contrast, the philosophic mind wants a stable order or structure that enables those who perceive it to act consistently and predictably. Knowing the principles of force and weather, we can actively and repeatedly maneuver our boat to port; knowing what justice demands challenges our self-interest and provides an abstract standard against which to judge the actions of ourselves and others, including the gods. Politically, this is the rule of law in contrast to the rule of capricious, willful men or gods. The mythic mind is obedient to divine commands;

the philosophic mind holds even the gods to an abstract standard of justice. If nothing else, it seeks an explanation based on something more than arbitrary, unpredictable power.

Discontent with the seeming randomness of life can be overcome through dialectic and a process of abstraction. A second characteristic of the philosophic mind, then, is that it is abstract. "Abstract" has several meanings in this context, and the first is literal. Socrates requires of Meno that he examine the virtues of a man and of a woman and "abstract" the essence of Virtue per se. In so doing, Virtue is separated from a particular gender, place, and time. This abstract conception of Virtue applies to all instances of virtue and, ironically, is not fully realized in any particular instance. Likewise, to discover Beauty, I need to discern the beauty common to the painting on my wall, the music to which I am listening, and the photographs of Ansel Adams. Philosophy abstracts from the particular shapes, colors, and locations in which either virtue or beauty is embodied to reveal the universal, permanent, and timeless Form that all things Virtuous and Beautiful share.

Abstract has another meaning. Abstractions, in radical contrast to the mythic mind, are nonsensual. Abstractions are grasped by the power of the mind rather than by the senses. I can listen to a beautiful song or see a beautiful sunset, but I cannot directly see or hear Beauty per se. I can follow the narratives of a war, and my senses can be assaulted by the sights and sounds of battle—whether it be the Peloponnesian War, the American Civil War, or the Vietnam War—but I cannot "see" the universal principle of war that "Truth is the first casualty" in the same way that I can literally see the flash of light and hear the percussion of an exploding shell. On the one hand, myth presents us with examples that *must be* acted out concretely in space and time in particular—if nevertheless concurrently representative—circumstances. Myths do not contain an answer or principle that can be separated, perceived, or communicated apart from the myth itself. Myths are both the question and the answer fully embodied. In the mythic phase of language, we are reminded that all words are concrete and there are no true verbal abstractions. The philosophic mind, in contrast, presents us with nonsensual concepts that can be grasped *only* by the intellect. You cannot point to and see Beauty in the same way that you can point to and see a yellow flower. Virtue or Beauty per se must be abstracted from their particular sensual embodiments. Philosophy reduces the sensuality of narratives to their thematic, allegorical, or essentialist meanings. In the contrast between the mythic and Platonic minds, Havelock discerns the difference between two "classes of human beings: those who like opinion (*philodoxoi*) and those who like what is intellectual (*philosophoi*)."[7] Or we have, in my manner of expression, two Minds: the mythic and the philosophic. Tarnas says it well: "The Platonic perspective thus asks the philosopher to go through the particular to the universal, and beyond the appearance to the essence. . . . Plato directs the philosopher's attention away from the external and the concrete, from taking things at face value, and points 'deeper' and 'inward,' so that one may 'awaken' to a more profound level of reality."[8]

It is important to note that the abstractions that are grasped by the intellect in this context are not, as we now tend to think of them, humanly created generalizations from classes of particulars. For Socrates, Plato, and their metaphysical heirs, Beauty is not a convenient, humanly created category that we arrive at

inductively by adding up and averaging the beautiful characteristics of flowers and symphonies and paintings. On the contrary,
Beauty—like all the Forms—possess a quality of being and a
degree of reality that is ontologically superior to the concrete
world. The eternal Platonic Forms transcend this transitory
world of changing appearances. What's more, the particular
thing is what it is by virtue of the Form or Idea literally informing it. Something is beautiful because it participates and
expresses the eternal and universal Form of Beauty.

Platonic Forms—that is, the unifying abstractions grasped by
the intellect—are timeless, universal, and changeless. As such,
they are unlike any experience we have of this material, sensual
world of appearances. In the material world of particulars, nothing is permanent or timeless or universal. In contrast, the essence
of Virtue is the same regardless of circumstance; Beauty exists
whether it is found in a sunset or a building, whether it occurred
in ancient Greece or yesterday. What's more, the Forms exist
whether or not they have specific embodiments. The beautiful
flower may pass away, but the Form of Beauty remains. We live
in evil times, but Virtue remains, even if we cannot find it or
have never experienced it in our own lives.

The autonomous, universal status of the Forms means that the
yellow daffodil with the radiant green stem on my desk "veils"—
and is secondary both ontologically and epistemologically to—
the essence of Beauty it embodies or incarnates. The flower that
is red or yellow, that grows and then fades, is only the incomplete
imitation of the Form of Beauty per se, "only" as James Edwards
observes, "its dim reflection, distorted by the recalcitrant materi-
ality of the medium within which the reflection occurs."[9] For the
philosophic mind, the "is" (what exists in this world) cannot be

confused with the "ought" (what exists in the Ideal, abstract world of Forms.) Here we have expression of the familiar dualism in Platonism between pluralistic appearances and a single Reality; the often contradictory sensory perceptions and rational Truth; the material and the spiritual; becoming and Being.

The philosophic mind has another characteristic. The Forms to which it is attracted are impersonal. Like mathematics, the Forms constitute an a priori cosmos hidden within appearances that is both changeless (because perfect) and "the same," or universal for all who are capable of grasping it. The abstraction $2 + 2 = 4$ is true whether it refers to cats or balls or coins, whether I am male or female, rich or poor, angry or elated, in Paris or Atlanta. What's more, if someone says that $2 + 2 = 5$, we say that that person lacks knowledge. The mathematical Form, like the Form of Virtue, provides an impersonal, objective standard by which we can judge the truth or falsity of a statement. The mythic mind does not ask whether a statement or action is true or false. It asks: "To what gods or stories are you faithful?" To answer the question "What am I to do?" I must first answer the question "Of what story or stories do I find myself a part?" In contrast, the philosophic mind asks: "What do you know? Have you properly grasped the essence or principle of human action and purpose that is veiled in the countless lives of humankind or your own apparently conflicting actions? Are your actions in conformity with the universal law or with human nature?" The mythic mind sacrifices the will in order to be obedient to the gods or the mythic stories. The philosophic mind sacrifices illusion and the seduction of appearances, the flashing bright particulars, to know and conform to an abstract, nonsensual Truth.

Finally, the distinction between appearances and the unifying essences or Forms provides a basis for distinguishing *opinion* from *knowledge*. Because all mythic or poetic knowledge is concrete, particular, and temporally conditioned, knowledge understood as a principle or essence that can be abstracted, articulated propositionally, and applied to different situations does not exist. Opinion is acquaintance and engagement with the realm of changing appearances; it is the willing suspension of disbelief we practice in following the dramatic sights and sounds of a movie. Knowledge, on the other hand, is grasping the movie's "theme," "meaning," or "essence" beneath the surface of bright particulars. It's what we say when someone asks us what the movie was "about." To know is to know that to which something refers, like grasping the meaning of an allegory. Once we grasp the abstract theme or the Form, of course, the bright particulars become less important. This "grasping" is of necessity accomplished by the intellect, because the abstract Forms cannot be grasped or perceived by the animal senses. Whereas opinion signifies acquaintance with the realm of appearances, knowledge signifies perceiving and intellectually grasping the realm of the Forms. Animals can perceive and respond to the imperatives of the senses, but only humans can perceive and respond to the imperatives of the Forms.

In summary, then, the philosophic mind seeks to grasp through abstraction and dialectic the eternal, universal, impersonal, nonsensual essences or Forms that are otherwise veiled or hidden in appearances. Philosophy is black-and-white photography in contrast to the sensual Technicolor of myth. For metaphysicians, these essences constitute a higher level of reality and are neither arbitrary nor humanly created. The philosophic mind seeks knowledge of these essences in contrast to opinion about the changing realm of concrete particulars.

Pundits and scholars continually remind us that we are living in a postmodern age, to which I would add that we also live in a post-mythic and post-philosophical age. What living in a "post"-era means in practice is that we remain conflicted between one age or mind and another. Ironically, notwithstanding his criticism of the poet's mythic mind, Plato uses the poetic myth of the cave to express the movement from opinion to knowledge. Similarly, we—as citizens of a post-Platonic era—are conflicted about the seductions of the philosophic mind.

Ours is not an era in which much store is placed in the realm of ideals or abstract truths. And this is for two reasons, I think. First, we are skeptical as to whether truth or courage or meaningful sacrifice exists, especially when they are invoked by self-serving politicians or corporate leaders. The whole realm of Platonic Forms seems, literally, unsubstantial. At best, grandiose ideals are expedient, nominalistic categories that we create and then discard when they cease to be useful. We are trained to trust only what we can see or hear or feel and, as we have learned, we cannot grasp the Forms with our senses. At best, the Forms seem like convenient conventions or arbitrary names we invent. Second, as heirs to a romantic legacy, something in us wants to rebel against the impersonality of the Forms. Something can be both factually true and totally meaningless. We would like to think that our truth, which is inseparable from our specific place and time and gender, is more important than a universal Truth. Freedom and individuality, ironically themselves abstract concepts, are more important than conformity to an impersonal, non-democratic standard of objective Truth. Living in a post-Platonic age as we do, abstractions fail to inspire or compel assent because they seem literally "out of touch" with reality, or, worse, the manipulative lies of an oppressive class.

But having said all of that, a counterexample of how abstract truth has inspired and functioned in recent history reveals both our conflict and the continuing seduction of the philosophic mind. "We hold these truths to be self-evident, that all men are created equal, that they are endowed by their Creator with certain inalienable rights, that among these are Life, Liberty and the pursuit of Happiness." Where would we be without the "Platonic" Form of human rights expressed in the Declaration of Independence? If we look around, humans appear enormously varied. They differ in race, language, gender, custom, intelligence, beliefs, and economic status—the list could go on and on. What do I, a twenty-first-century American sitting at a computer terminal in Atlanta, Georgia, have in common with a farmer subsisting on the high plains of Bolivia, say? Despite these apparent differences, the philosophic mind asserts that all humans are, *in essence*, the same and are endowed by their creator with certain inalienable rights. All our differences veil something we have in common. The Bolivian farmer has as much right to life, liberty, and the pursuit of happiness as I do. Equality is an abstract Form that goes against all that we know; we have never seen equality or justice in this world. We can see Equality and Justice only with our mind's eye. Nevertheless, the abstract concepts of Equality and Justice continue to seduce and inspire our actions and ignite social movements. Once grasped by the intellect, Equality and Justice are not arbitrary terms that we have made up and that can be abandoned if they become inconvenient. On the contrary, they signify Forms inherent in the ways things are and whose truth is undeniably self-evident and compelling. "We hold these truths to be self-evident, that all men are created equal. . . ."

The compelling force of concepts such as Equality and Justice is but one example of how the philosophic mind remains, perhaps unexpectedly, a forceful influence. Indeed, abstract philosophical thinking, what others would call "metaphysical" thinking, is currently undergoing a popular resurgence.[10] We are post-Platonic and thus conflicted: on the one hand, idealism is dead; on the other hand, the seduction of Forms still inspires us.

KNOWLEDGE BECOMES AN OBJECT

Beyond abstraction, and its manifold characteristics, the philosophic mind is critical because it was the first mind to make knowledge an *object*. What do I mean by this? What do I mean by saying that knowledge is an object, and why is this important?

Recall that in describing the mythic mind, I answered the epistemological question "How do we know?" by saying that we know by identifying uncritically with a set concrete, sensual exemplars or, less self-consciously, informing narrative structures. In this context, for example, I suggested that young women coming of age during the sexual revolution of the 1970s learned how to act by imitating *The Mary Tyler Moore Show*'s Mary Richards. Similarly, I argued that we unself-consciously adopt what I call invisible myths when we structure our experience through the lens of progress or Marxism. Heroes and stories are celebrated and become functionally mythic in a culture precisely because they serve as exemplars to be imitated.

The trouble with imitation and identification, however, is that a hero may act badly at some point in a narrative and well at some other point. Do I simply imitate and identify with a succession of actions and moods as they come and go, in the same way that someone who is polytheistic relies now on this god, now on that? What part of the narrative do I imitate and what part do I ignore? Jesus did not marry, hold down a conventional job, or contribute to a 401(k) plan. Are we to go and do likewise? And what of gender? How does a woman identify fully with the man Jesus, and whom does she imitate when she becomes a mother? Furthermore, what happens when heroes exemplify different actions? Do we imitate the political activism of Martin Luther King Jr. or the direct, largely apolitical compassion of Mother Teresa?

We know with the mythic mind by imitation and identification, but whenever we ask whether our acts are consistent, good, bad, or useful, we separate ourselves from our actions. We step back, as it were, from our actions and sever the unself-conscious, "instinctual" directives of our culture. We're no longer enjoying the party; we're watching the party. Instead of imitating Jesus and placing our faith in him, we begin to think *about* Jesus, and he becomes an object of belief, an object whose characteristics and actions we can examine and compare with others. We can enjoy the appearance and bright particulars of a beautiful yellow rose or we can think *about* a rose and how it is grown and how it compares with other flowers, or, more abstractly, what makes this rose beautiful and how this beauty participates in and reflects the Beautiful. I can act instinctively to give a homeless person a dollar in response to a plea on a street corner or I can think *about* the homeless person and whether he or she will spend the dollar on drugs, or *about* how homelessness exposes the failure of our social safety net. The philosophic mind, through dialectic, disrupts the fully engaged identification of the mythic mind, the culturally instinctive mind, by revealing the contradictions of appearances. In the process, it separates the knower from the known, the subject from the object, unreflective imitation and action from contemplation and reflection. We no longer ritually *become* our hero through identification; we think *about* our hero.

Again, Havelock provides a critical text for summarizing what happens when the unself-conscious identification characteristic of the mythic mind is interrupted:

> The Greek ego in order to achieve that kind of cultural experience which after Plato became possible and then normal must stop identifying itself successively with a whole series of polymorphic vivid narrative situations; must stop re-enacting the whole scale of the emotions, of challenge, and of love, and hate and fear and despair and joy, in which the characters of epic become involved. It must stop splitting itself up into an endless series of moods. It must separate itself out and by an effort of sheer will must rally itself to the point where it can say "I am I . . ."[11]

ACQUIRING A SOUL

When knowledge becomes an object, when we stop living instinctively and begin to think *about* our actions, or *about* what constitutes the essence of virtue, beauty, or justice, the question becomes, "What or who is the subject? Who or what is it that suddenly stands apart looking at the 'object' of knowledge?" Subject and object are a polarity; when the object emerged, so too did the subject, a "me" who is thinking *about* the object. In the quotation from Havelock that concludes the preceding section, notice how the stable, consistent "I am I" emerges from the "endless series of moods" more characteristic of the mythic mind.

The "I" that emerges with the objectification of knowledge can be looked at from another perspective, and not simply as a logical necessity to its polar opposite the object. I am a father and a son and a husband; I play tennis and go to work and take walks; I once rode a bicycle and delivered newspapers and lived without knowing how to drive a car or read a newspaper or operate a computer. But who am I? What has remained the same throughout my lifetime and the various roles I play? What, the philosophic mind asks, is the "essence" of my life and identity? These are questions the mythic mind cannot ask. Whenever we are advised to go and discover who we are, reminded that persons have dignity despite crushing poverty, or counseled to find our true calling or profession, we hear the necessarily silent but insistent voice of the philosophic mind.

That which remains constant throughout my changing life and circumstances is often associated with the soul. The soul emerges in the philosophic mind when the questions that were asked of Virtue and Beauty are asked about me, when "I" too become an object of self-conscious reflection. Beyond the red and yellow and purple flowers, there is the Form of the flower. Beyond the apparent differences between the virtue of a woman and the virtue of a man, there is the Form of Virtue per se. Beyond the apparent differences and conflicts between my various roles and actions, there is the unifying Form of my soul. The soul emerges when an "I" is separated—abstracted—from my actions, when "I" transcend my full engagement and identification with what I am doing at the moment and from moment to moment to ask how one action or role is related to, and normatively consistent with, another. When focused on myself, the Platonic mind seeks an essence, a Soul, beneath the passing appearances of day-to-day living. In the parlance of the day, the Platonic mind insists that I "get my act together" into a consistent whole.

Not surprisingly, as an abstraction that can be grasped only by the intellect, the soul shares the attributes of the other Forms examined earlier. Most important, the soul is nonmaterial. It is thus not surprising, though it is mistaken, to associate the soul with ghosts. As with the other Forms, I cannot see or touch or feel my soul, just as I cannot see or touch or feel Beauty. I can only apprehend the soul with my intellect. A uniquely human achievement, the perception of soul—like the perception of other Forms—is not unfairly associated with mystical experience. Like Beauty, my soul can be reflected or imperfectly expressed in material things, just as Beauty is reflected in the daffodil on my desk. The daffodil may wither, but Beauty remains. When I pass away, my soul (or more properly, my participation in Soul) will likewise remain eternal. My individual transient "ego" is secondary to the eternal, universal Soul, of which I am a pale and imperfect expression. The beauty of a flower becomes more real the more closely it approximates and participates in the Form of Beauty, which is prior to and more real than the beautiful. Likewise, I become more real to the extent that I more fully approximate and participate in Soul. Soul is prior to and more real than my individuality or ego. In transcending my particular history and setting, I acknowledge my membership in a universal community of souls. Chapter 7, on archetypal psychology, and chapter 8, on metaphysics, develop these themes further.

FOUR QUESTIONS

If the philosophic mind's grasp of the soul begins to sound like aspects of Christianity here, recall Nietzsche's observation that Christianity became "Platonism for the people." The Platonic mind's dominance was a long one, extending into the seventeenth century.[12] Before turning to the scientific mind, which succeeded it, let us again ask our four guiding questions: What do we know? How do we know it? What questions or aspects of experience does the Platonic mind highlight and ignore? and, finally, What does the Platonic mind say about the question of meaning?

What Do We Know?

We know, first of all, that we are dissatisfied with inconsistency, contradictions, and pluralism, with becoming and transitory appearances rather than timeless and unchanging Being. The philosophic mind knows that life pulls us in different directions; that obligations to job and family are often in conflict, that we grow old, and that moral imperatives to refrain from killing and to go to war drive us in different directions. Somewhere within us there is a need for unity, for an unchanging and permanent essence, orientation, or standard that finds expression in the discontent of Platonism. Existentialism and expediency have their limits.

The solution to the discontent that Platonism fosters is to grasp or know the Truth, as distinguished from mere opinion. Truth is unchanging, perfect, and transcontextual, whereas opinion can be identified by its propensity to change, whether that change occurs in time or from culture to culture. Truth is objective, rather than either individually or culturally subjective. In contrast to the volatile emotions that pull us now this way, now that, Truth is rational and intellectual. Truth is the law that everyone, everywhere must follow, regardless of their personal feelings or circumstances. Whereas the mythic mind knows and is guided by authoritative stories, the philosophic mind knows the authoritative Forms or Ideals. When we speak about idealism, meaning that people are motivated by their ideal conception of social justice, for example, we acknowledge that idealism can function mythically. That is to say, what we know can motivate us to transcend our self-interest or unself-conscious engagement with our nation, race, or time to work for a higher good. Driven to do what's right or what's fair, we can abstract ourselves from self-interest to join the universal community of idealists. No just society has ever existed, but people from the United States, the United Kingdom, India, and South Africa can come together to work for its realization. Abstractions, conceptions of an ideal or just society, provide hope of a world that is beyond anything we or anyone else has actually seen.

How Do We Know?

The philosophic mind knows through dialectic and conceptual thinking. Whereas the mythic mind knows by identification with the characters and actions of stories—that is, by submitting to their examples—the philosophic mind deliberately disengages from and objectifies knowledge. It knows by a process of "stepping back" to ask whether the virtue of a man is the same as the virtue of a woman, or how the beauty of a symphony is like the beauty of a flower. The Platonic mind abstracts the Mormon polygamist from his unquestioning cultural instinct that he should have more than one wife to ask how that assumption compares with the assumptions of his monogamous neighbors, and vice versa. In both instances, Platonism asserts that skepticism and contemplation are more reliable avenues to knowledge than faith, identification, and engagement. The 1960s catchphrase "Question authority!" has ancient Platonic roots.

The distinction between mythic and philosophic thinking is nicely captured by the changing meaning of the word "to know." In the mythic mind, knowledge carries the biblical connotation of carnal, fully engaged knowing, as when it is said that Lot "knew" his wife. In contrast, the philosophic mind defines knowledge as the correspondence between our mental images and distinct "objects." We can ask whether philosophic knowledge is true or false in a way that we cannot ask whether Lot's knowledge of his wife is true or false. Self-consciousness is both the reward and the price we pay for abandoning the mythic mind.

It is important to keep in mind that the philosophic mind knows by a process that begins in common experience. Unlike the mythic mind, it does not begin in a verbal or ritual artifact, or a canon of sacred stories or actions. The mythic mind knows by identifying with the stories; if the stories don't exist or are forgotten, knowledge cannot exist. In contrast, the philosophic mind asks not for stories but for reflection on what people actually do and say in a way that both reveals the differences and inconsistencies in how people act and suggests the common Form beneath appearances. In Plato's *Dialogues*, Socrates investigates the nature of Virtue by variously comparing virtue with mathematical figures, colors, health, and strength. Beginning with common experience, the philosophic mind proceeds—through a process of abstraction—to move from a plurality of appearances to a single "common nature" that applies to all instances of virtue. This common nature, it will be recalled, is perceived by the intellect rather than through the animal senses. More than a body of knowledge, philosophy is a technique that begins in discontent, skepticism, and the inconsistencies of common experience to achieve an intellectual grasp of a single Truth. We know philosophically by seeing with the mind's eye, rather than with the eye of the senses.

What Does the Philosophical Mind Emphasize and What Does It Neglect?

First, philosophic thinking emphasizes that the world is not as it appears. As such, it is a doctrine for those who are discontent with or alienated from this world. Not all are. Many, perhaps most, people are content with the appearances and find no cause to disengage from the instincts that their culture provides. But for those who are discontent, philosophy says that the world is not finally real. Hidden behind or beneath this world, there is another. Tolstoy articulates the feeling of many when he distinguishes his life as it appeared to others—that of a successful writer and parent—with his "real" life beyond or beneath the appearances. The philosophic mind is thus world-denying, ascetic, and dualistic; apart from the appearances and transitory nature of this world, there is the realm of eternal and changeless Forms. Socrates (like all martyrs) could calmly accept death because philosophy had taught him that this world of appearances, including the appearance of death, is not ultimately real. At least in its metaphysical expression, philosophy highlights the supremacy of the hidden world over the world of bright surfaces.

In addition to highlighting the unseen, hidden world beyond appearances, the philosophic mind highlights abstractions over the concrete and specific. This emphasis reflects the defining debate in the *Republic* between the poets and the philosophers. A philosopher will speak in abstractions about happiness and the happy life, whereas the poet will speak concretely by showing the happiness of someone who is newly in love, who watches his or her child succeed in riding a bicycle for the first time, or who achieves a sales goal for the year. Myths are territorial and localized, whereas philosophical abstractions are not. Again, the philosopher wants to know what happiness "is" per se—the abstract notion that unifies and describes what's common to all instances of happiness—whereas the poet wants to depict happiness in all its varying shades and circumstances. For the poet—that is, the mythic mind—happiness as an abstraction, apart from engagement, does not exist. There is only this specific happiness, on this specific occasion, for this specific person, even if that concrete universal has and will always mythically reoccur. In contrast, for the philosopher the many instances of happiness are secondary to the Form of Happiness that all the specific instances of happiness share in common. It's what they share in common that's important to the Platonic mind, not their differences. Without a rudimentary notion or abstract category of "happiness," we would not be able to self-consciously distinguish "happy" from "sad."

The Philosophic Mind and Meaning

Meaning is preeminently a question of the philosophic mind. It is an abstract question we ask *about* our life experiences.

We have seen how the philosophic mind attempts to unify and bring consistency to a plurality of appearances, whether those appearances depict virtue or beauty or justice. It goes beyond the bright surfaces characteristic of the mythic mind. The philosophic soul came about when this mind was self-consciously turned toward a person's own life; that is, when a person became an object to a disengaged, observing subject or "I." Thus, hidden beyond the many roles I may play in life as a child, a son, a brother, a father, a husband and an old man, a tennis player and an employee, ad infinitum, there persists an "I" that all those roles share. The philosophic mind is the mind that asks: What do these different appearances have in common? How do they all hang together? What is the constant identity beneath the changing appearances?

Similarly, the philosophic mind, unlike the mythic, is not satisfied that now this moment or experience appears meaningful and now that. On the contrary, the philosophic mind wants to know how all the experiences of meaning or meaninglessness hang together. "What does life, as a whole, mean, apart from a plurality of meaningful and meaningless moments" is a philosophic question. Just as Socrates wanted Meno not to give him a beehive of meanings for Virtue, so we want to know if life as a whole is meaningful. Does it all add up; does my life have a meaning that persists throughout and beyond it? Humankind seems to have a restless hunger to connect with something—a realm, spirit, or community—that is more universal and timeless than the lives we experience, filled as they are with birth, death, and sectarian conflicts.

It is a commonplace that many primitive cultures frequently do not have a word for religion. Ancient peoples may possess stories that function mythically in informing their actions and world-view; they may reenact seasonal rituals and offer sacrifices in places they consider sacred; and they may create images of their gods.

But fully engaged in their practices, they are unable to ask the abstract, philosophical question about how these various acts are connected. What ties all of these acts together? What we mean by the abstract concept of "religion," is a question they cannot ask. Similarly, no one asks *about* love when they are fully engaged in love, just as no one asks *about* the purpose or meaning of a basketball game when our favorite team makes the winning score on the final shot. Meaning is not a problem until the question is raised by a philosophic mind that attempts to discern what is universal and timeless in all our meaningful or meaningless moments. Before we ask the question, we go from one moment to the next, innocently guided and engaged by our biological and cultural instincts. Disengagement and rendering our life moments as "objects"—in response to discontent and frustrated expectations—create the question of meaning. Without philosophy, the question of meaning cannot be asked. Meaning is a concept that can be grasped only by the intellect. It has no feel, smell, or color.

I said earlier that the philosophic mind asserts that skepticism and doubt are more reliable avenues to truth than faith and engagement. But having said that, the consequences of questioning are monumental. By stepping back to raise the question of meaning, the philosophic mind—not surprisingly—will not find the answer in this transitory world of appearances. The philosopher is neither a poet nor an existentialist. Rather, the answer, if there is to be an answer, will be found in the realm of concepts and the Forms. Meaning means "reference beyond itself," or, in Camus's terms, requires an external "appeal." The phrase *ocean liner* means by virtue of its reference to a floating vehicle such as the *Queen Elizabeth* 2. Similarly, our life has meaning to the extent that it corresponds, points to, and participates in a higher or more real realm.

A soldier's death is judged meaningful because it is an expression of patriotism; my taking out the garbage and driving my children to soccer matches are meaningful because they point to a particular concept of being a good father and husband. Meaning is thus allegorical rather than symbolic. The philosophic mind, as a post–mythic mind, shares with the mythic mind the characteristic of looking beyond the here and now to something outside our experience. The mythic mind finds meaning by identifying with sacred stories and characters (one is a follower of Jesus or Buddha, for example), whereas the Platonic mind locates meaning by finding connections to timeless, abstract concepts, Forms and Ideals. In each instance, meaning is impossible without appeal, a "leap of faith" or a "mystical insight" that connects my life with something external to and more Real than the appearances of my day-to-day living. As we shall see, myth and philosophy are separated from science and postmodernism by their rejection of appeals to transcendent, ontologically higher realms. But I anticipate.

WHEN MEANING FAILS

Another way to see how the philosophic mind understands meaning is to look at what happens when meaning fails. To talk about when meaning fails within the philosophic mind anticipates the scientific mind that will follow it. Typically, meaning "fails" for the philosophic mind for three reasons, two of which have already been mentioned in passing. Meaninglessness occurs when (1) the realm of Forms or Ideals seems unreal and literally unsubstantial; (2) the realm of Forms becomes too intellectual, abstract, impersonal, and body-denying to satisfy our needs for sensuality and personal identity; or (3) the questions the philosophic mind was invented to ask and answer are bypassed for other questions that other minds are better equipped to handle.

First, the failure of meaning—that is, meaninglessness— occurs when we no longer believe in the object of our knowledge; that is, when the realm of Forms no longer seems real. Often a consequence of radical pluralism, nominalism is the doctrine that concepts are convenient, humanly created categories that do not have a separate, higher reality or ontological status than the realm of appearances. Indeed, for the nominalist, all our concepts are arrived at inductively through a process that moves from particulars to abstract generalities. Thus, a chair does not exist as a universal self-existent Form but is a concept that we develop inductively from seeing the very different chairs at my kitchen table, in my living room, at my desk, and on my porch. Similarly, virtue is a convenient concept that highlights the commonalities between many specific acts of virtue but, again, it does not exist apart from those many instances. Fatherhood or patriotism are not ideals to which I can appeal to make my life "meaningful"; they are simply ways of identifying patterns of specific acts. What does Virtue mean, and how can its objective, universal Form be sustained, when one culture eats beef, while another is vegetarian, one condones polygamy and another is strictly monogamous? Recall that meaninglessness occurs with the mythic mind when the myths no longer seem real; similarly, meaninglessness occurs with the philosophic mind when the concepts and ideals to which we appeal seem merely names and not members of a self-sustaining realm of Forms. Theologically, of course, the death of the Forms anticipated the death of God.

Secondly, meaninglessness occurs with the philosophic mind when we rebel against its severe intellectualism, asceticism, and impersonality. The abstract concepts and ideals to which the philosophic mind aspires cannot be grasped by our bodily senses. On the contrary, they can be grasped only by the intellect. The philosophic mind is an ascetic mind because it denies the sensual world of appearances in favor of the hidden realm of Forms. Regardless of how compelling concepts and ideals may sometimes be, they may nevertheless leave our need for sight, sound, and tactile impressions unfulfilled. We are philosophers, but we are also poets with animal bodies that need to be satisfied. Similarly, the philosophic mind also fails when we rebel against its impersonality. No matter how "objectively" true a notion of virtue or justice or even a chair may be, it lacks a compelling attraction until it is made relevant to me, my desires, and what I am doing. The world contains any number of indisputable truths—the height of Mount Everest is 29,035 feet—for example, but they do not "mean" anything until they find a context within my own interests. Because my context is always transitory and specific, whereas Forms are not, our connection to the philosophic mind is always tenuous and susceptible to being broken. A rebellion against the impersonality, asceticism, and severe intellectualism of the philosophic mind characterized the romantic movement that arose in response to the post-Platonic mind of modernity.

Third, and finally, the Platonic mind fails when questions arise that it is ill suited to answer. This is not so much a failure of meaning as it is a failure of the question of meaning. Typically, the philosophic mind, not unlike the mythic mind, addresses questions of purpose ("Why?"), identity ("Who am I?"; "What is virtue?"), or direction ("What am I to do?"). These are the paradigmatic meaning questions. Someone dies in an accident and we ask, "Why?" I play many roles in my life as husband and son and father, but who am I? Faced with a decision to contribute to the Republican party or join an intentional community in Montana, I ask what I should do and seek guidance in the example of Jesus or the abstract laws of the Ten Commandments. These are important questions that the mythic and philosophic minds are equipped in their different ways to answer, normally by reference to an external story or ideal to which it appeals. It is important to note that the meaning questions tend to be about events and entities we cannot change. We search for the meaning of virtue, say, but we do not work to change the nature of virtue. Similarly, we may explain the meaning of an event by seeing how it corresponds with a mythic story or ideal, but we do not work to change the event or prevent its reoccurrence. We can understand and find meaning in death, but we cannot change it. In contrast, the modern mind to which we are about to turn is characterized by a radically different set of questions. Even with a fundamental question such as the meaning of death, it does not ask "Why?" or "What for?" but simply "How?" In so doing, it replaces an appeal to an external, transcendent myth or Form with causality, metaphysics with physics. The *how* question overcomes the question of meaning or meaninglessness by abandoning the question altogether. But to say this is to tell only half the story. While the modern mind seemingly abandons the search for meaning characteristic of the mythic and philosophic minds, it nevertheless provides its own set of answers to the question of meaning. How the question of meaning and meaningless evolved and found new expression in the modern or scientific mind is the subject of the next chapter.

CHAPTER FOUR

Science and Meaning

THE ROAD THROUGH ARISTOTLE

The road from the philosophic mind to the scientific mind passes through Aristotle. Aristotle brought Plato "down to earth" and, in so doing, established the basis on which Kepler, Galileo, and Descartes, among others, would build the edifice of the modern mind. The scientific mind that Aristotle helped to create—as well as the postmodern mind following it—represents a radical departure from the myths and philosophy that preceded it, primarily because it rejected the metaphysical foundations on which myth and philosophy rested. Whereas myth sees daily life as a reenactment of sacred stories, and philosophy transcends daily life by appealing to the realm of Forms, science remains firmly and inescapably in this world. By remaining exclusively in this world, the scientific mind fundamentally changes our expectations about what constitutes a meaningful life and how it can be attained.

Aristotle's contributions to the scientific mind are immense, but for our purposes they can be reduced to four.

First, Aristotle distinguished primary from secondary qualities. The category of substance is primary and independent, whereas the other, secondary category is derivative. For example, the primary, substantive category of a horse is its "horseness" whereas the secondary categories of quality (white), quantity (tall), and relation (faster) are derivative. A horse can be white or brown, tall or short, fast or slow, without ceasing to be a horse, but "horseness" is primary and cannot change without changing the identity of the animal. The fundamental distinction between primary and secondary qualities would in time become the basis for the familiar modern distinction between objective and subjective, the former being the primary and thus the more substantive.

Second, Aristotle perceived that every substance consists of matter and Form. Matter is the possibility, the indeterminate "substrate of being" that is molded or shaped by the Form. The Form, which is inherent in nature and does not exist apart from its physical embodiment, provides intelligible structure to the otherwise amorphous matter. Thus, to use a contemporary example, the "matter" of carbon atoms can become either graphite or a diamond according to the form it assumes, just as DNA structures the growth of cells, determining that this cell will become a finger, while another will become a foot.

The distinction between matter and Form provides the basis for Aristotle's important distinction between potential and actuality. Matter moves from indeterminate potentiality to determinant actuality as it is literally informed by its indwelling Form. Form orders and motivates the development of a substance's potential so that it actualizes what it already is. Thus, to cite the classic example, the Form of the oak is implicit in the acorn. The "matter" and potential of the acorn becomes an oak rather than a dogwood because it possesses and is drawn forward by the Form of the oak. Similarly, Aristotle would argue that the Form and purpose of a child is to become an adult, just as the Form and purpose of an embryo is to become a child. Traditionally, opposition to contraception is based on the belief that we should not frustrate or impede the end, purpose, and Form of sexual intercourse, which is procreation. Form, for Aristotle, thus supplied not only an intrinsic pattern and intelligible structure to matter but also an informing hierarchical dynamic, end, and purpose.

For Aristotle, the Forms are *in* nature. Recall that for Plato, the Forms existed in a separate nonsensual realm. A chair was a "chair" because it imitated, however imperfectly, the ideal "chair." The Form of the chair existed independently of any particular chair and, what's more, was ontologically more real than any particular instance. All chairs are alike, because all chairs participate in the Form of chairness. In contrast, Aristotle argued that individual substances share common characteristics, which the mind can grasp, but that these common or universal characteristics are not independent entities apart from their particular embodiments. The universal or common characteristics of chairs, that they have four legs, for example, are conceptually distinguishable from any particular chair, but they are not ontologically independent of or superior to particular chairs. Beauty is not a transcendent ideal, in which the beautiful building and the beautiful painting participate, but a common trait and generalization that the beautiful building and painting share. By locating universal categories such as chair and beauty in the common characteristics that we find inductively in a host of specific instances, Aristotle turned Plato on his head. Plato's transcendent Forms became an inherent or imminent structure *in this* world. Because the Forms were now located in this, rather than in a transcendent world, this world became more important. The historian of philosophy Richard Tarnas succinctly summarizes the relationship between particulars and universals like this: "By replacing Plato's Ideals with universals, common qualities that the mind could grasp in the empirical world but that did not exist independently of that world, Aristotle turned Plato's ontology upside down. For Plato, the particular was less real, a derivative of the universal; for Aristotle, the universal was less real, a derivative of the particular. Universals were necessary for knowledge, but they did not exist as self-subsistent entities in a transcendent realm."[1]

APPEARANCE AND REALITY

The tendencies initiated with Aristotle—distinguishing primary from secondary qualities, substance from Form, the movement from potential to actuality, and replacing transcendent Forms with Forms inherent *in* nature—were revived and refined with the development of classical science from the sixteenth to the nineteenth centuries.

Early scientists adopted Aristotle's distinctions by defining the primary categories or qualities as those that are abstract, measurable, objective, and mathematical (size, shape, number, weight, motion), which inhere in the object "out there," whereas the secondary qualities are those that the senses perceive or the mind assembles, which reside in the human subject (such as

color, shape, taste, touch, smell, and ideologies). Galileo and
Kepler, the historian of science E. A. Burtt observes, make a "clear
distinction between that in the world which is absolute, object,
immutable, and mathematical; and that which is relative, fluctu-
ating, and sensible. The Former is the realm of knowledge, divine
and human; the latter is the realm of opinion and illusion."[2]
The measurable, quantitative qualities of a horse's weight, speed,
and dimensions are primary; the horse's color and smell are secondary and reflect only a subjective preference. If I am betting
on the winner of the Kentucky Derby, I want to know how measurably fast the horse runs, not its color. The speed of the horse is
a measurable "fact," not a matter of opinion.

The trouble with secondary qualities and the unaided senses,
as Copernicus would classically demonstrate, is that they are
unreliable. To our senses, the earth does seem immovable while
the sun rises and sets. To our senses, the moon on the horizon is
larger than when it is shinning directly overhead. To our senses,
the desk on which I am typing seems solid, but science tells me
that, if I could shrink to the size of an atom, I would see mostly
empty space, the ratio of matter to space being equal to a baseball versus a ballpark. If we come into a room from the cold, it
feels hot; if we enter that same room from a much warmer place,
the room feels cold. The movement of the heavens appears to
our senses entirely unrelated to the falling of an apple. The
"knowledge" that comes to us through the senses is thus demonstrably particular, contradictory, and untrustworthy.

How do we obtain more certain knowledge? Through a
process of abstracting, that is, separating, the primary from the
secondary qualities. Only the measurable, "objective" qualities
are to be considered primary, whereas the perceptible qualities

are to be ignored for being subjective and ephemeral. Or to say this in another way, the primary and more fundamental qualities are material and exhibit extension, whereas the secondary qualities are nonmaterial and immeasurable. What's more, as their designations imply, the secondary qualities are dependent on and do not exist apart from the primary ones. In short, for the scientific mind, "all that mattered was matter."[3] Physical matter contains an inherent structure or harmony that can be described by the alphabet of mathematical and mechanical principles or laws; we obtain knowledge to the extent that we progressively discover and more closely match our thoughts to this underlying, if invisible and abstract, order. Reminiscent of the philosophic mind, this order is grasped by the intellect, not through the deceptive senses. The distinction between appearance and reality is not new. What is new is the definition (reduction?) of "reality" to the primary qualities that are describable in largely mathematical and mechanical terms. Indeed, Kepler would go further and argue that, not only is there a mathematical structure or harmony inherent in nature, but that such order is the "cause" of observed facts, in the same way that an indwelling Form causes the acorn to become an oak.

In addition to distinguishing primary from secondary qualities, scientific explanations contain another crucial element: atomism, or the belief that matter consists of infinitely small indivisible atoms. Atomism assumes that what is small and molecular (including simple ideas) is more fundamental than what is large and molar. The atoms or the basic building blocks of the universe consist of the same material substances, whether they occur on earth or in the heavens, in nature or in mankind. Abstracted from their original context, H_2O is the "same" whether it occurs in the ocean, on Mars, or in a tear on someone's cheek. In adopting the perspective that phenomena could be analyzed and explained in terms of the combination and collisions of a limited number of more fundamental atoms or elements, Galileo and his successors revived aspects of ancient Greek philosophy and provided the foundations for what would become common sense.

CAUSALITY AND UNDERSTANDING

Atomism and the preeminence of the material, objective aspects of nature contributed to a new, modern understanding of causality and meaning. The final element contributing to that new understanding was a refinement of the distinction between potentiality and actuality.

Recall that for the mythic mind, understanding and knowledge mean the ability to see, identify, and participate in a correspondence between events and mythic narratives. Similarly, for the philosophic mind, they mean seeing and establishing a correspondence between events and Platonic ideas, or transcendent Forms. In contrast, for Aristotle to "know" is to understand the *causes of how something comes about.* Understanding translates or is reduced to causes. Understanding does not mean establishing a correspondence with either static narratives, ideologies, or Forms but explaining the *movement* from potentiality to actuality.

According to Aristotle, there are four categories of cause: (1) Formal; (2) material; (3) efficient; and (4) final, which respectively answer the questions (1) What is it? (2) What is it made of? (3) Who or what made it? and (4) Why does it exist, or what is it for? Thus, in the case of a statue, for example, the formal cause is the Form, or what we might call the "idea" of the statue, or that which it was intended to be. The material cause is the marble; the efficient cause is the sculptor; and the final cause is decoration, a memorial, or the glory of God. Similarly, the formal cause of a house is the design conceived by the architect, the material causes are the bricks and mortar, the efficient causes are the bricklayers and carpenters, and the final cause is the provision of housing.[4] Although this fourfold typology is easiest to understand when applied to humanly created objects, Aristotle also applied it to objects in nature, such as flowers and trees. Thus, the formal cause of a growing tree is the Form of the apple tree it is destined to become, the material causes are wood, leaves, and roots, the efficient cause is nature or God, and the final cause is to provide fruit for humankind or perhaps to symbolize the tree in the Garden of Eden.

Although all substances thus have four causes, substances move from potentiality to actuality because of their final cause, end, or *telos*. The question of final causality can only be answered in terms of purpose or use. Without the *telos* of providing shelter, the house would not be built; without the desire to glorify God or decorate a public square, the statue would not be created. Huston Smith remarks how "pleasing this sense of causation is, this notion that things move by being drawn toward what exceeds them, and will fulfill them to the degree that they refashion themselves to its likeness. For Aristotle, the entire universe was thus animated. Everything reaches toward its better in the effort to acquire for itself its virtues."[5] The traditional conception of nature was thus animalistic. It "projected a universe in which mind or spirit was ceaselessly at work, drawing and prodding creatures to their initially appointed ends . . . *thus the real explanation of all phenomena was metaphysical.*"[6] The highest knowledge, *sophia* (wisdom), as distinguished from either *empeiria* (experience) or *tekhnē* (art, skill), is to know why or for what purpose things come to be. To know something is not to know what it *is* but what it is *for*, or *the end toward which it is moving.* In the West, the focus on the end was reinforced by Christian notions of an eschatological end to history. The purpose of history was found in the end of history, just as the purpose of the individual life was found in the Day of Judgment. As heirs of both Aristotle and Christianity, we thus easily fall into saying that a life is "meaningless" if it has no purpose or meaningful end. Meaning always looks forward to, and is dependent on, a valued end.

Life is meaningless, then, if we cannot answer the question: What is it for?

In starkest contrast to Aristotle, the scientific mind denies final causes and thus purpose in the universe. Rather than finding the cause or explanation for something in the *telos* or end for which it is made or done, the scientific mind understands causality in terms of a sequence of events that precedes an effect. The scientific mind thus stands Aristotle on his head. Instead of looking forward to the final cause or formal end, science looks backward to the origins of a sequence of cause-and-effect events. The task of understanding and explanation thus becomes a process of analyzing events into a sequence of simpler, atomistic events whose cause-and-effect relationships are governed by unchanging, universal natural laws. Thus the cause of a flower is not the end of glorifying God or bringing beauty to humankind but a sequence of biological and chemical events that terminates in the flowering plant. God, no longer a final cause, is relegated to being the deistic first cause, the great, if now absent, watchmaker who created the self-sustaining mechanism of nature. Classical science looks at the sequence of material events *from which something has come, rather than that toward which it is going.* In so doing, it concurrently moves from metaphysics to physics, from philosophy to natural philosophy, from ends to origins. The scientific mind is concerned with *how* things work or happen rather than *why* or toward what end or purpose they do so.

In discerning a causal sequence of events, the scientific mind looks exclusively at the primary qualities of a substance, including the material, atomistic qualities of weight, size, and motion, which can be measured and described mathematically. These are the objective, universal qualities, in contrast to the subjective, secondary qualities. We may disagree about which car is better, the green Volkswagen or the blue Corvette, but we cannot disagree about which is measurably faster. The causal sequence progresses by analysis from the simple to the complex and from the earlier to the later. The sequence is a genuine and not an arbitrary sequence, meaning that one thing follows another according to natural laws that are inviolable, one-directional, deterministic, universal, and unchanging. Neither nonmaterial causes nor events without extension are permitted, nor can the sequence be violated or superseded by interventions, divine or otherwise. Not surprisingly, whereas Aristotle used biological metaphors to articulate his notions about growth and movement toward purposeful ends, the scientific mind saw the world in terms of clocks and machines. Indeed, according to the social critic Bryan Appleyard, the clock is a particularly apt symbol of the scientific outlook, because its placement in public places "emphasized that time now had an impersonal authority, an existence beyond ourselves and yet one which we could now control through our knowledge. Subjective time—our own private sensation of duration—was implicitly humbled and our modern obedience to objective, measured time was born."[7]

FROM EXPLANATION TO TECHNOLOGY

If the scientific mind had stopped at substituting its notions about causality for those of Aristotle or Plato, it would have succeeded only in reviving more ancient philosophies such as atomism and the distinction between primary and secondary qualities. The theological doctrine of transubstantiation, after all, distinguishes between the real spiritual body of Christ and the material bread and wine of the Eucharist. The critical innovation of the scientific mind was that it asserted that we could not simply deductively reason our way to truth, but that truth also required an inductive process of careful observation, experimentation, and public demonstration.

Science displays a movement from objectivity to taxonomy, and from prediction to control. Science is, first of all, based on intersubjective agreement. Emerging as it did during an era of interminable religious wars, that was one of its appeals. Secondly, however, science is predictive. Taxonomy, the classification of rocks and biological species, for example, is in some sense a science, or, perhaps more accurately, a pre-science, but it does not command the respect we accord to the predictive sciences. The great accomplishment of Galileo and Newton was that they could accurately and demonstratively predict the movement of the planets and the course of a projectile and could do so in a way that everyone could see. Scientific theory, no matter how intellectually appealing, is incomplete as science until it contains an experiment to prove whether it is true or false. If a theory cannot be tested for its falsity, it is not a scientific theory. The results of the test, and the ability to repeat the test, compel assent. More than prediction, however, is the science that can also control a sequence of events through experimentation and technology. It is one thing to observe and predict tomorrow's weather; it is something entirely different to make it rain by seeding clouds with iodine crystals. It is one thing to observe and predict the course of a disease but something entirely different to administer a polio vaccine or inoculate someone against smallpox. "This unarguable and spectacular effectiveness is the ace up science's sleeve," Appleyard concludes. "Whatever else we may think of it, we have to accept that science works. Penicillin cures disease, aircraft fly, crops grow more intensively because of fertilizers, and so on."[8]

Two comments on the scientific mind before we go further. First, the scientific mind is monotheistic. Its effectiveness and energy humble and marginalize alternative philosophies and local or cultural differences, which are dismissed as secondary and subjective. No matter what we may think or believe, we all want penicillin when our children are sick. Second, it's easy to make a "leap of faith" from science's effectiveness to its truth. Science becomes scientism whenever this occurs. Not surprisingly, the effectiveness of science led to a profound belief in the principles with which science succeeds: objectivity, material causality, measurement, analysis, and the dismissal of secondary qualities. "There is only one science and, in time, all cultures bow to its omnipotence and to its refusal to coexist," Appleyard observes. "The only reasonable conclusion appears to be that for some reason, science is the one Form of human knowledge that genuinely does give us access to a 'real' world."[9]

THE SCIENTIFIC MIND EXPANDED
AND ITS CONSEQUENCES

First applied to explaining the movements of the planets, the guiding principle of the scientific mind—that causality can be reduced to neutral, lifeless atoms and the physical forces that move them—was applied to more and more fields of study during the next three centuries. As the historian Carl Becker famously concluded, this new philosophy "ravished" the eighteenth century. Explaining phenomena from below, that is, as the result of a causal sequence of events rather than in terms of a teleological end, was successively applied to the motion of objects, the origins of rocks and minerals, biology, and finally to humankind. The seventeenth-century philosopher Benedict de Spinoza, precursor to many who would follow, declared that even the actions of men could be reduced to a sequence of physical causes, rather than teleological ends or reasons. "Most writers on the emotions and on human conducts," he declared, "seem to be treating rather of matters outside of nature than of natural phenomena following nature's general laws. They appear to conceive man to be situated in nature as a kingdom within a kingdom; *for they believe he disturbs rather than follows nature's order.* [Not so Spinoza:] I shall consider human actions and desires in exactly the same manner as though I were concerned with lines, planes, and solids."[10]

The great figures of the modern era share the common characteristic of explaining phenomena by tracing them to their simpler physical antecedents. Or, to say this in another way, each of them saw and explained the universe as a great machine. Huston Smith succinctly summarizes this history: "For Newton, stars become machines. For Descartes, animals are machines. For Hobbes, society is a machine. For LaMettrie, the human body is a machine. For Pavlov and Skinner, human behavior is mechanical."[11] Darwin and his successors traced the evolution of humankind to simpler and early forms of life and eventually to their chemical components. In so doing, human life lost its uniqueness. Marx reduced human history and idealism (including religion) to impersonal economic forces. We think we act independently and rationally, but founding sociologists such as Ludwig Gumplowicz (1838–1909) tell us that the assumption that men think is a great error, because it is not men who think but their social communities. Religious faith and sacred tests were demythologized, that is, "explained away" by tracing their origins to more fundamental historical, psychological, or sociological elements. Freud would go further and say that beneath the conscious mind we are driven by nonrational forces. Eventually, mind itself was reduced to chemical reactions and the neutralizing solvent of a wholly materialistic physics. Along with mind, of course, the scientific mind also dissolved free will, moral values, motivations, ideologies, politics, the soul, and meaningful ends, as each was, in turn, reduced to indifferent, mechanistic causes. From this perspective, the human spirit and its capacity for beauty and love is an evolutionary accomplishment. No *whys*; just *hows*; no ends, just origins and means; no reasons, just causes.

And the result of this great reductionism? A great irony and an old truth, expressed in a new way.

The great irony is that the more humankind gained the ability to predict and control nature, to understand its causes and to separate from its necessities, the more it was submerged into nature and became a determinant product of its meaningless mechanistic forces. Humankind achieved the power to cure disease and travel to the moon, but, at the same time, it was reduced to an "object" that was itself subject to the forces (physical, chemical, and electro-mechanical) it sought to control. At the moment of its triumph, humankind, and all the ideals it cherished, dissolved into a secondary quality. "We seem," Richard Tarnas observes, "to receive two messages from our existential situation; on the one hand, strive, give oneself to the quest for meaning and spiritual fulfillment, but on the other hand, know that the universe, of whose substance we are derived, is entirely indifferent to that quest, soulless in character, and nullifying in its effects. We are at once aroused and crushed. For inexplicably, absurdly, the cosmos is inhuman, yet we are not."[12]

And the great truth? The truth is that things are not as they seem. The scientific mind expressed Plato's intuition that appearances and reality are distinguishable in a radically different way. The historian of science E. A. Burtt says it well:

> The world that people had thought themselves living in—a
> world rich with colour and sound, redolent with fragrance,
> filled with gladness, love and beauty, speaking everywhere of
> purposive harmony and creative ideals—was crowded now
> into minute corners in the brains of scattered organic beings.
> The really important world outside was a world hard, cold,
> colourless, silent, and dead; a world of quantity, a world of
> mathematically computable motions in mechanical regular-
> ity. The world of qualities as immediately perceived by man
> became just a curious and minor effect of that infinite
> machine beyond. In Newton, the Cartesian metaphysics . . .
> finally overthrew Aristotelianism and became the predomi-
> nant world-view of modern times.[13]

PROGRESS

The scientific mind assumes that there is a real, non-mind-dependent objective world "out there," and that it can be understood. Science is a methodology that liberates us from secondary qualities and subjective distortions such as emotions, religion, political ideologies, and local custom. Coming as it did during a period of continual religious and political wars, the neutral, impartial framework of science and its appeal to a concrete reality that people could touch and weigh for themselves was welcomed for its ability to peacefully cut across all political, ideological, cultural, and religious boundaries. "Fact" became the ultimate honorific title designating genuine and substantiated knowledge, as distinct from either belief or opinion. In a courtroom, witnesses may say now one thing, now another about a case or the character or psychological profile of the defendant, but the question of guilt or innocence is settled if a fingerprint or DNA links the perpetrator with the victim. The scientific "fact" ends debate.

How do we know that science is true? As we have seen, we know because it works! Truth is defined not in terms of correspondence with myth or Forms, or, alternatively, in terms of internal consistency within a specific context or "game," but solely in terms of its results. The methods of science—experimental results that demonstrate prediction and control—have changed the world, eliminating some diseases, making agriculture more productive, and giving us the ability to communicate instantly around the globe. Debates about whether one should follow Christ or Buddha, the merits of Shakespeare or Picasso, and the degrees of justice possible in capitalist or socialist states are endless and inconclusive.

In contrast, the eradication of smallpox and the ability to fly coast-to-coast in an airplane are undeniable. Little wonder then that it seems to many that science is the only system of thought capable of producing genuine and permanent truth. "The history of science," the physicist Gerald Holton argues, "is the only history which can illustrate the progress of mankind. In fact, progress has no definitive and unquestionable meaning in other fields than the field of science."[14]

The ability of science not only to understand but to demonstrably change conditions for the better provides a basis for the notion of progress. The idea of progress projects a narrative in which humankind has advanced from its primitive origins, is now advancing largely through science and political enlightenment, and will continue to advance in the foreseeable future. We used to live in caves; we now live in air-conditioned houses. We once ate berries and roots; we now eat fresh vegetables and fruit imported from around the world. We used to communicate by means of hand-delivered parchments; we now communicate by e-mail, instant messaging, and cell phones.

The thesis that humankind progresses has several corollaries. First, progress is correlated with the slow, cumulative acquisition of knowledge that continually builds on itself. What's more, the acquisition of knowledge and the resultant progress is linear and one-directional. Once something is known, once humankind has discovered the "facts" inherent in the structure of nature, that knowledge is permanent and irreversible. The genie cannot be put back into the bottle. Third, and critically, the acquisition of knowledge is attributable entirely to human insight and ingenuity. Through the instrument of science, humankind no longer has to wait passively on divine intervention or inspiration.

Whereas the priest persuades people to endure their hard lot, or to understand it in a different way, the scientist follows a method that aims to do away with the hard lot altogether. Faith in divine agency is replaced by faith in the capacity of humankind to change things for the better. Prayer is replaced by vaccines, organ transplants, and pesticides. Placed in a fallen and imperfect world, our lives are progressively redeemed and fulfilled through the expansion of human knowledge.[15] If science tells us we live in a neutral, indifferent world, the ideology of progress reinserts purpose by saying we are on a journey of discovery and improvement toward a better end. Scientists feel as though they are making discoveries, not merely changing their perspectives or opinions. The smallest action of the scientist, tucked away in an obscure laboratory, is meaningful, because it contributes to and participates in the story of humankind's progress. It's little wonder that progress, with its humanly created "miracles" of science, has been described by the social critic Christopher Lasch as the "working faith of our civilization."[16]

Faith in the redemptive power of science and the demonstrable progress of humankind has two interrelated consequences. First, the energy, power, and effectiveness of science succeeded in shifting interests and the focus of commitments from either the mythic or philosophic world to *this* world. Increasingly, human fulfillment was defined exclusively in secular, that is, material, terms. In response to questions about God, immortality, meaning, purpose, or other metaphysical matters, science initially said that these questions were beyond physics and human reason. As a consequence, nature and religion constituted two separate universes, metaphorically, a book of nature and a book of God, approachable by science and faith respectively. It was not that science didn't yet know about matters of faith; it couldn't know. Science only deals with those problems that are amenable to its methods. Physics cannot speak authoritatively about metaphysics and vice versa.

The dualistic compromise between science and religion proved unstable and short-lived. Because the metaphysical sources of philosophy's answers were no longer believed, neither were the answers themselves. This was the second, if delayed, consequence of believing in science. Gradually, an initial tolerance for earlier forms of knowledge, including mythic and philosophic wisdom, became indifference, which in turn gave way to the perception that they were irrelevant. This is the second consequence of placing one's faith in science. As Appleyard aptly says, "Science begins by saying it can answer only *this* kind of question and ends by claiming that *these* [what we have described as the *how* questions] are the only questions than can be asked."[17] How could it be otherwise? As we have seen, by definition, science deals with primary qualities and systematically replaces purpose and the distortions of subjective, secondary qualities with causality, understood as a sequence of material events. What's more, as we have also seen, scientific questions can be resolved and publicly verified in a way that metaphysical questions cannot. Among other things, empiricism means offering evidence that others can see and agree with. The evidence in this case means that all phenomena, including ideas and beliefs, are explainable in terms of matter and a causal sequence. As a result, questions such as "Why do the good suffer?" or "Does God exist?" are marginalized, reserved for private solace or negatively seen as consoling lies. In the end, science—or more accurately scientism—is a monotheistic faith, incapable of coexistence, claiming as it does that it is not only a path to truth, but the *only* path. When our children are sick, we all want penicillin more than a theological explanation. What we want is a cause, not a reason.

HOW ARE WE TO LIVE?

Finally, how are we to live in the world that science reveals? That is, how are we to live in an indifferent, purposeless universe of material causes that operate according to the machine-like laws of nature, and that is alien to human values and aspirations? How do we make meaningful choices when choice is reduced to biological (Darwin), socioeconomic (Marx), or psychological (Freud) causes? One way is to believe in and work toward human, material progress, as we have already noted. The Final Cause or divine Form and intention banished by the purposeless universe revealed by science is reintroduced as human intention. Human intention becomes the Form to which a lifeless, neutral matter must conform. Matter moves from potential to actuality according to the Form of human intention, just as traditionally an acorn becomes a tree because of the Form of the oak. No one can deny that a noble cause like curing cancer instills purpose into the life of the working scientist. Beyond progress, however, science suggests that we live most truly when we live in conformity with what is, to the facts and natural laws as science has revealed them. Freedom in such a world is the recognition of necessity.

Two brief examples of how we are to be reconciled to what is. Freud is justifiably famous for explaining neurosis as sexual repression. That is, humans have sexual impulses that when repressed—in his day, by Victorian moral standards—cause mental disease. The solution to neurosis is to conform to what is, that is, to freely express the material sexual drives we share with all biological creatures. What's right and healthy is defined in terms of objective human behavior rather than subjective, debatable moral or religious standards and prohibitions. Norms are material and statistical rather than metaphysical. Traditional prohibitions against homosexuality or infidelity or even questionable accounting practices dissolve in light of statistics documenting the number of how many homosexuals or extramarital affairs there are. If they exist in sufficient number, then they are the norm. Similarly, analogies taken from nature, such as the Darwinian survival of the fittest, become the basis of social and economic policy. In short, the *is* defines the *ought*. Academic ethicists—notably David Hume—may argue otherwise, but teenagers have been expressing a scientific bias for years when they justify their actions by saying, "Everybody else is doing it."

The environmental movement, which Appleyard describes as a "quasi-religion," is the second example of reconciling ourselves to what is. For environmentalists and proponents of deep ecology, we live in a closed ecosystem, a Spaceship Earth that was most dramatically revealed to us by pictures of the earth from the moon. Because it is a closed system, interventions in one part of the system have consequences in other parts. As a result, the apparent achievements of science and technology are perceived as illusory and unsustainable. We conquer space by inventing the internal combustion engine and light our houses by burning coal, and in the process create greenhouse gases that raise the earth's temperature. We dramatically increase agricultural yields through the use of pesticides and fertilizers only to discover these same chemicals are carcinogenic. Nature is an autonomous, complex, and delicately balanced system. Human attempts to control or subjugate it constitute a rebellion against Mother Nature and inevitably end in fouling our only nest. It is within this closed system that reconciling ourselves to what is becomes an essential, "religious," imperative. Appleyard describes the relationship between environmentalism and a sense of religious meaning this way:

> To the environmentalist a day can be as full of religious observance as a monk's. He can choose his food to avoid chemicals, factory farming, and blighted origin. He can reject over-elaborate packaging, conscientiously reuse plastic bags and walk or cycle rather than drive. He can proselytize, campaign and demonstrate. . . .
> . . . For to the environmentalist, the world is suffused with baleful portents; it is enriched with meaning as in the vision of a saint. It is, above all, a world, a unity as opposed to the fragmentary, incomprehensible mass of facts provided by the scientist, or the modernist artist.[18]

For the environmentalist, the choice between paper or plastic is a moral issue, fraught with meaning. The attractiveness of the environmental movement is that, in a neutral universe without inherent value or purpose, it provides universal values and meaning. The teleological end is human survival. That is a goal about which we can all agree. Along with faith in progress, environmentalism is perhaps the faith most expressive of a scientific mind. Regardless of our cultural, social, or economic backgrounds, we all have a stake in the survival of the single planet that sustains us all. And like the older faiths, our task is to humble our assertive egos and conform to the authority of the true and the good, in this case to the objective, universal reality of nature and its imperatives as they are increasingly revealed to us by science. We achieve truth to the extent that our ideas more closely correspond, not with the stories of myth or the Forms of philosophy, but with what is the case. Ironically and ambiguously, with science, we seek control in order to conform. What is defines what we ought to do. Facts triumph over our subjective, private desires, provide an authoritative guide to our actions, and inform our connection with a universal human community.

The scientific mind is increasingly under attack. Postmodernism, as the name implies, is an attempt to move beyond modernism and its scientific assumptions. That said, however, postmodernism is largely confined to a small group of scientists, historians, and philosophers. Most scientists and engineers, as well as most people generally, hold to the foundational modern belief that an objective world exists "out there," and that the best way to discover that world is with the methodologies of science. Of the four minds we are examining—mythic, philosophical, scientific, and postmodern—the scientific is the one most educated people living today identify with and employ. Additional features of that mind will be exposed in the discussion of the still emerging postmodern mind in the next chapter. Before proceeding further, however, we need to ask of the scientific mind the questions we asked previously of the mythic and philosophic minds: (1) What do we know? (2) How do we know it? (3) What does the scientific mind neglect and emphasize? and (4) What does the scientific mind have to say about the central question of meaning?

FOUR QUESTIONS
What Do We Know?

The most fundamental thing we know with the scientific mind is that we can change our material circumstances. Responding to material discontent and desire, the scientific mind seeks, not just understanding, but control, or, more accurately perhaps, it seeks understanding as an instrument of control. Knowledge for the mythic mind means to see the present in light of mythic stories and rituals; for the philosophic mind, it means seeing a situation in terms of more universal and abstract ideals or Forms. For Aristotle, the highest knowledge meant grasping the teleological end or purpose. In contrast, knowledge for the scientific mind means discovering the simpler and temporally prior material entities and sequence of steps that cause an event to occur. Or to say this in another way, the scientific mind asks *how* not *why*. To know something for science is to know its causes, not its purpose, reason, or end. Like myth and Platonic Forms, the laws of nature discovered by science may be universal and timeless, but unlike for the mythic and philosophical minds, for the scientific mind, their value is not intrinsic but instrumental. Knowledge is always at the service of change and control. Or to paraphrase Karl Marx, the purpose of knowledge is not to understand the world but to change it.

In seeking its pragmatic truth, the scientific mind knows that the universe is composed of primary and secondary qualities. On the one hand, the abstract, primary qualities of size, shape, number, weight, and motion are objective, impersonal, material, and universal. These are the qualities that exhibit an inherent machinelike order and causality that is best expressed with the unambiguous and descriptive language of mathematics. On the other hand, there are the derivative secondary qualities of color, taste, touch, and smell, and the epiphenomena of human emotion, values, and ideas. The scientific mind knows that the realm of secondary qualities is subjective and "less real," because they are caused and explained by the more fundamental material and "factual" realm of primary qualities. The complex human Forms of the philosophic mind—love, virtue, justice, beauty, God et al.—are "explained away," as is the mythic mind, by tracing their causes to more basic political, social, psychological, and ultimately material facts. If the contingencies of life can be transcended with the help of more universal and timeless myths and ideas, science seeks a similar transcendence by discovering the universal and timeless natural laws hidden in the changing events and emotions of everyday life.

How Do We Know?

We know by a process of abstraction and by distinguishing the primary from the derivative and thus secondary qualities. Music is abstracted and reduced to mathematical harmonics; the subjective intensity of my morning run is translated into the objective digital numbers displayed on my heart monitor. We know, moreover, because our knowledge can be experimentally verified, and ultimately because it works. Whereas truth is broadly a form of correspondence for the mythic and philosophical minds, for the modern mind, it is insistently pragmatic and instrumental. The abstract knowledge of science and mathematics is verified in our day-to-day sensual world. We know because, through careful observation, measurement, and creative theories, we can demonstrate with controlled, repeatable experiments that we can predict and control our material circumstances. We know because the authority of our knowledge rests on intrasubjective agreement of undeniable facts and pragmatic results. Debate about the merits of Shakespeare or the right to an abortion may be interminable, but no one can deny the truth, the fact, that planes fly and that vaccine has eliminated smallpox.

What Does the Modern Mind Emphasize and What Does It Neglect?

Of course, from the perspective of the modern mind, it neglects nothing. Science describes the world as it is, in its entirety, and denies that other approaches to knowledge are valid. For those tutored on either the mythic and/or philosophic mind, however, science neglects and is unable to answer the interrelated questions of value, purpose, life meaning, and quality. Science neglects the *why* question for the *how* question, and replaces an emphasis on purpose with an emphasis on causality. How could it be otherwise in a universe that simply "is"? But having said that, can the *why* question be dismissed or ignored without pathological consequences?

Scientific values are exclusively instrumental. That is to say, knowledge, which was once an end in itself, becomes only a means to power. But power for what purpose? Science's inability to adjudicate between purposes or ends is exposed in contemporary conflicts. If the preservation of life per se is the end, science can place an elderly or terminal patient on a respirator and use heroic means to maintain life. On the other hand, if the end is the preservation specifically of a worthwhile life, science will provide the means for a patient to die with dignity. Similarly, science can tell us how to build a rocket to the moon or a rapid transit system, but it cannot tell us on which project we should expend our national resources. Science can take a survey to tell us descriptively that people place greater value on going to the moon than rapid transit, but it cannot prescribe what people ought to value most. Or to say this in another way, science is unable to answer the insistent, childlike questions that Tolstoy asked: *why?* and *what for?*

Of course, the ultimate *why* question is "Why are we here?" Does life, my life and life on this earth, have a purpose or meaning? Does the great disparity between rich and poor, the beautiful and the ugly, mean anything? Is there a purpose behind it all? We can blame Aristotle and Christianity for associating meaning with purpose and a final end; or we can blame science for making life seem "meaningless" by dismissing those ends as being merely subjective and metaphysical.

Finally, science is unable to make qualitative distinctions. Its emphasis on the primary qualities results in a corresponding neglect of the secondary, subjective qualities that add color and emotion to life. With science, the world is denuded of all human qualities: there is no better or worse, love or hate, beauty or ugliness, salvation or damnation. The universe simply is: neutral, indifferent, and without intrinsic value or purpose or soul. As a result, nothing is sacred, inviolable, or prohibited. Better and worse is replaced by more and less. In a wholly secular world, we are permitted to do whatever we can do and have absolute dominion. To the question, "Which is better, a beautiful old-growth forest or the jobs created by cutting it down?" science has nothing to say. Should marriage be defined as exclusively between a male and female? Science can descriptively tell us that many persons are homosexual, but it cannot say that heterosexual unions are better than those of gays or lesbians. Don't like your body? Science can give you larger breasts or a smaller stomach, but it cannot tell you whether it is better to be all "natural." Better and worse, good and bad are outside the descriptive vocabulary of mathematics. Normal is a statistical summary, not a prescriptive injunction.

Science and Meaning

First, the scientific mind says that "meaninglessness" is descriptively neutral. The universe has no intrinsic meaning, direction, end, or purpose. So what? That's just the facts; that's just the way things are. Deal with it. To use meaninglessness with negative connotations, to experience meaninglessness with a sense of loss or remorse is to be nostalgic for the ultimately subjective (a.k.a. delusional worlds) created by the mythic and philosophic minds, including Aristotle's final causes as teleological ends. The imperative of the scientific mind is to be reconciled to what is. In the world come of age, we need to abandon our childlike fantasies and live without appeal or justification by transcendent, nonmaterial gods, ideologies, values, and purpose. Alienation and the Absurd signify a failure to be reconciled to what is.

If we are to find meaning, it will emerge exclusively in *this* world, and in one of three ways. The first way it can emerge is through commitment to, and in conformity with, material pursuits and what *is*, there being nothing else. In this context, recall the scientific mind's commitment to progress and the ecological movement. By identifying and participating in progress or the environmental movement, we become part of something more universal and larger than our selves in a way that is reminiscent of our participation in a religion. On a more personal level, progress and commitment to this world may translate into a larger house or a sportier car. Keeping up with the Joneses, advancing a career, and getting one's children into good schools provide their own Forms of orientation and meaning.

The scientific mind—and the industrialized modern life it spawned—also prompted an opposing reaction. The romantic impulse and movement accepted the world bequeathed to us by science by becoming reconciled to what is, only, in this case, the world to which it sought reconciliation was a romanticized conception of nature. Nature became a place of refuge and meaning in reaction to the dehumanized, indifferent landscape represented by industrialization. This movement is nicely encapsulated in the title of M. H. Abrams's book *Natural Supernaturalism.*[19] In that classic work of literary and intellectual history, Abrams argued that the romantics found solace in the Other, as that Other was expressed in the "naturally sacred" world found in nature. If the scientific mind had thoroughly debunked the localized and personified God of Abraham, Moses, and Jesus, a universal divine spirit could nevertheless be perceived in nature.

A second way the scientific mind finds meaning in this world is through solving puzzles. As we have seen, by eliminating purposeful ends and the possibility of metaphysical transcendence, the scientific mind emphasizes the pleasures to be found in *this* world. *As long as, and only as long as, the question of meaning is muted or ignored,* the scientific mind finds intrinsic pleasure in solving the puzzles of nature in much the same way that intrinsic pleasure can be found in solving a Sudoku puzzle or in playing chess. On those occasions, the scientific mind does not look forward to achieving pragmatic ends; it looks only at the challenge of solving the puzzle immediately at hand. The *how* question can be sufficiently compelling that the *why* question becomes an afterthought or superfluous, at least temporarily. From this perspective, the scientific mind exemplifies an engaging form of play that points to other intrinsic pleasures available in this world, such as sports, aesthetic experience, intimate I-thou relationships, and games. The purpose and meaning of play is play, just as the purpose and meaning of joy is joy.[20] Life is meaningful so long as we are fully engaged in intrinsically satisfying experiences.

Third, and finally, meaning emerges with the scientific mind in association with Nietzsche and his existential heirs. If the universe is cold, lifeless, and without intrinsic meaning, then any meaning that exists is the meaning we create. Meaning is not discovered or perceived, nor is it objective, nor does it reside in a transcendental realm, whether mythical or philosophical. Whatever meaning there is is subjective, local, and without justification. Because the universe is meaningless, we are absolutely free to become who we are and who we wish to be through the choices we make. Science replaces final causality with human intention. There is no essential nature, human or otherwise; there are no universal values or divine purposes. Existence trumps essence; nothing is prohibited. The necessity of creating meaning without appeal or assurances is both a great liberation and an enormous existential burden. With the scientific mind, the will to believe that is evident with the mythic and philosophic minds becomes first a will to truth, beyond consoling illusions, and then the will to power first articulated by Nietzsche. The ability to live without illusions and to create purpose in an otherwise indifferent universe is a source of both pride and meaning.

But, with Nietzsche and the Existentialists, I anticipate. As we shall see, the themes they first articulated will become prominent as we move to a consideration of the postmodern mind in the next chapter. As we shall also see, the postmodern mind also starts to bring us full circle by reintroducing many of the elements we first observed with the mythic mind.

CHAPTER FIVE

Postmodernism and Meaning

The division between the modern and the postmodern is both simple and fundamental.

The modern world assumes that there is an objective world "out there" and that this world contains an inherent structure or order that is both permanent and discoverable. In contrast, the postmodern world assumes that the world is either unordered or pluralistic, and that any discernable order we discover in the world is constructed and imposed by human beings—to a greater or lesser extent—as an expression of their "subjective" intentions and desires, whether individual or collective. These subjective intentions and desires are necessarily particular, changing, and local, in contrast to the objective, universal, and timeless laws found in the nature of the modern world. In the modern world, truth is the correspondence between our ideas and objective reality; in the postmodern world, truth is more complicated, because there is no longer an unchanging objective reality to which our ideas can easily correspond. On the one hand, moderns characteristically argued about which among alternative beliefs are "true," deciding, for example, between science or religion, capitalism or communism. Postmoderns, on the other hand, characteristically argue about the nature and status of belief itself, whether *any* belief is warranted, or, alternatively, how a belief functions within a specific context. Less separates the modern scientist from the modern religious fundamentalist than separates the adherents of the modern from the postmodern perspective. With postmodernism, "epistemology joins the old family favorites—class, race, and nationality—as a source of political controversy."[1]

WE ARE ALL HEIRS OF KANT

The beginnings of postmodernism go back to the early days of the modern era. Empiricism had stressed that everything in the mind originates in the senses and, ultimately, in a plethora of chaotic impressions. Our concept or notion of a red flower, for example, originates in the sensations and impressions we receive from the real, empirical object we find growing in the garden. So far, so good; empiricism to this point seems straightforward and an expression of common sense. But what of the "objects" in our mind for which there is no corresponding sensory input, objects such as causality, time, and space? Whence do these come?

Kant argued that such ideas reveal the way the mind actively organizes, informs, or structures sensations. The mind does not passively mirror an order inherent in nature; rather, nature is ordered by the a priori ideas or categories inherent in the mind. We do not and cannot experience "things in themselves"—what he termed *noumena*—in all of their glorious, uninformed, pluralistic chaos. What we experience is *phenomena*, the representation of those sensations as they have been structured by human thought. All our thoughts and experiences are thus structured by the human mind's a priori categories. Again, without the categories that we bring to nature (including the categorical imperative we bring to the moral realm), human experience would be impossibly formless. Thus, in the case of causality, for example, the mind does not derive the ordering idea of cause and effect from sensations and habit—as the empiricists would claim—but, in the words of the historian of ideas Richard Tarnas, "already experiences its observations in a context in which cause and effect are presupposed realities; causality in human cognition is not derived from experience but is brought to experience."[2] In the act of human cognition, the mind does not conform to things; rather, things conform to the mind. Tarnas continues his summation of Kant's notion of a priori ideas this way:

> The order man perceives in his world is thus an order grounded not in that world but in his mind: the mind, as it were, forces the world to obey its own organization. All sensory experience has been channeled through the filter of human a priori structures. Man can attain certain knowledge of the world, not because he has the power to penetrate and grasp the world in itself, but because the world he perceives and understands is a world already saturated with the principles of his own mental organization. This organization is what is absolute, not that of the world in itself, which ultimately remains beyond human cognition. But because man's mental organization is absolute, Kant assumed, man can know with genuine certainty—know, that is, the only world he can experience, the phenomenal world.[3]

Three comments on Kant's revolutionary idea. First, the notion that nature conformed to the mind, rather than vice versa, remained largely submerged in Western culture until the twentieth century. Yes, a few madmen such as Nietzsche and the romantics maintained the family line, but the culture as a whole was ravished by the results emanating from science and the modern mind. Most people, most of the time, assumed that there was an inherent structure in nature—a natural law— because acting on that assumption was immensely fruitful.

Second, subsequent to Kant, various substitutes were proposed for the universal and eternal structures of the a priori categories. Indeed, after Kant, the task of philosophy very much became an attempt to understand and articulate how the mind structured experience. Thus, for example, Jung's archetypes were understood to be inherited structures or dispositions informing human experience. Others found the experience-informing structures in language (structuralism in all its guises); yet others looked to the shaping influences of historical epochs and "forms of life." Reminiscent of earlier Platonic notions, idealists traced the informing categories to inherent ideas. Regardless of their particular perspective and emphasis, all these movements share the postmodern assumption that order is a human product. From this perspective, the modern movement from metaphysics to physics terminates in a postmodern movement from physics to social and archetypal psychology. Postmodernism comes full circle by reintroducing the *telos* and purpose that science banished, only in this case the purpose does not reside in nature or God, Forms or sacred stories, but in human intentions, even if those intentions are often subconscious.

Finally, postmodernism eventually moved beyond Kant and his heirs in proclaiming that there is no universal or permanent order. For Kant, knowledge was still possible, because, if one could not discover the structure of nature, one could nevertheless continue to discover the structures inherent in the mind, or subsequently, in the structure of language or universal archetypes. The more radical postmodernists assert, however, that there is no universal or permanent structure anywhere, either in "objective" nature or in the "subjective" structures and categories of the mind. But I anticipate. More immediately, I examine how the "objectivity" of modern science was questioned by science itself.

MODERN SCIENCE UNDERMINED

Ironically, science itself made discoveries in the early twentieth century that called modernism's fundamental assumptions into question and, by so doing, contributed to the emergence of a postmodern perspective. The discoveries associated with the theories of relativity and quantum mechanics, in particular, helped undermine classical science and its assumptions.

First, relativity called into question the universality of the laws governing mass, time, and space. For Newton and classical science, these categories were constant and unchanging. An object had the same dimensions and mass whether it was located on earth or on the most distant planet; a clock measured the same unidirectional time regardless of its location in the universe. Relativity introduced us to a counterintuitive universe by saying that mass, time, and distance are "relative" to the frame of reference of the observer. Thus a person on a train traveling near the speed of light experiences time more slowly than one standing on the railroad platform. Similarly, a ruler on the train is shorter than an identical ruler resting on the platform, at least from the perspective of the person standing on the platform.

Relativity raises the question, Who is correct? Which observer more accurately describes the "real" time and the "real" dimensions and mass of an object, the person on the train traveling at the speed of light or the person standing on the platform? Relativity claims that there is no absolute, universal dimension of space, time, and mass, and that all of these are "relative" to the observer. The physicist and popular interpreter of science Brian Greene puts it this way: "It [the theory of special relativity] makes the strange claim that observers in relative motion will have different perceptions of distance and of time. . . . The most accurate measuring devices in the world confirm that space and time—as measured by distances and durations—are not experienced identically by everyone."[4]

The modernist assumption—questioned by relativity—that there is a single reality and order to which our ideas can truthfully correspond, without the contamination of subjective position and interests, was further eroded by quantum mechanics, in four ways.

First, the physicist Werner Heisenberg, with his now famous "uncertainty principle," stated and experimentally demonstrated that we could not simultaneously know both a particle's velocity and its position. The more we know about the velocity of a particle, the less we know about its position, and vice versa. It is not that we simply do not know; we can't know. Uncertainty is built into the universe as an epistemological limit. What's more, in the act of measuring and observing a particle, we apparently change the particle; that is, we cannot observe nature without disturbing it. Observing a particle knocks it off its course, and we cannot be certain about the extent to which our observations have changed the particle's momentum or position. The particle, or at least the particle we can know, does not exist as an autonomous object apart from our observation and measurements. In language reminiscent of Aristotle, the scientist and theologian John Polkinghorne argued that "Heisenberg believed that quantum entities do not possess precise positions and momentum but only potentialities for these properties, which then become actual when this is forced by an act of measurement."[5] In short, quantum theory, like relativity, blurs the classical modern distinction between subjects and autonomous objects.

Added to relativity and Heisenberg's uncertainty principle, Niels Bohr's principle of complementarity further undermined the assumptions of modern science. The principle of complementarity states that a single conceptual model or description may not be adequate to explain atomic or subatomic behavior. The most familiar example of this principle is the complementary theories that light consists either of waves or particles. Sometimes, matter behaves as though it consists of particles, whereas at other times it behaves as though it is a wave. This duality is absolute: when light is a wave, it is unarguably a wave; when it is a particle, it is unarguably a particle. Rather than trying to reconcile these two theories, Bohr argued that both theories are valid—not simultaneously but alternatively. The two concepts of waves and particles are complementary because both are required for a complete explanation of light, but they are mutually exclusive if applied at the same time. Complementarity reinforces relativity and uncertainty by saying that there is no single description of reality; all our descriptions are necessarily partial and informed by specific intentions and purposes.

Postmodern science has thus discovered that modern science, the classical science of Newton, is only "true for people-sized perceptions."[6] When twentieth-century physicists examined and tried to explain the world of the very large with relativity theory, or the very small with quantum theory, they found the universe a much stranger and uncertain place than they had imagined. What they had thought to be *the* world, was more accurately seen to be *a* world as perceived by people-sized, rational beings, a simplification and generalization that worked and fulfilled specific human purposes, but whose truth was neither universal nor guaranteed. Sounding very much like Kant distinguishing between *noumena* and *phenomena*, Bohr cautioned that we distinguish reality from our descriptions of reality. "It is wrong . . . to think that the task of physics is to find out how nature *is*," Bohr is reputed to have said. "Physics concerns what we can *say* about nature."[7]

SCIENCE AS A SOCIAL PRODUCT

The objectivity of modern science and the world it assumed was further undermined by historians of science, most notably by Thomas Kuhn's book *The Structure of Scientific Revolutions* (1962). Kuhn sought to explain how scientific practice and theories evolved. If scientific theories correspond to what is the case, to a permanent truth or structure inherent in nature, then how can one explain change and conflicting theories? William James anticipated this problem in the early twentieth century when he reacted to the plurality of scientific theories then emerging by observing that whereas "[u]p to about 1850 almost every one believed that sciences expressed truths that were exact copies of a definite code of non-human realities. But the enormously rapid multiplication of theories in these latter days has well-nigh upset the notion of any one of them being a more literally objective kind of thing than another."[8]

Kuhn explained scientific change by introducing the fruitful notion of the paradigm. As he uses it, the term *paradigm* has two meanings: "On the one hand, it stands for the entire constellation of beliefs, values, techniques, and so on shared by the members of a given community. On the other hand, it denotes one sort of element in that constellation, the concrete puzzle-solutions which, employed as models or examples, can replace explicit rules as a basis for the remaining puzzles of normal science."[9] According to Kuhn, a shared paradigm is what determines how scientists within a given community define the types of questions that can legitimately be asked and the types of solutions that are acceptable. Objective data are always seen from within an established paradigm of expectations and assumptions, which determines what data are collected, how they are collected, and the use to which they are applied. As a result, all data, as the philosopher of science N. R. Hanson succinctly put it, are "theory-laden."[10]

Normal science is conducted within, and according to the presumptions and examples of, the reigning paradigm. Anomalies, data that defy the reigning paradigm, are set aside or accommodated by ad hoc modifications, just as, for example, Ptolemaic astronomy added a succession of increasingly complex planetary epicycles to remove discrepancies, and defenders of the phlogiston theory of chemistry were driven to postulate negative chemical weights to maintain their paradigm. Eventually, however, the anomalies and ad hoc solutions introduced to save the reigning paradigm multiply to the point where the scientific community begins to question its assumptions and a simpler and more elegant alternative paradigm is proposed. Scientific revolutions occur whenever there is a shift from one paradigm to another.

Two points about paradigm shifts deserve emphasis. First, the shift is a genuine revolution, involving a total gestalt switch, rather than simply an accumulation of additional facts or ideas. It is not so much that there are new data as that the old data are seen and interpreted in an entirely new way because of the shift in paradigm. A paradigm shift does not occur one step a time, but involves a total and sudden conversion or reorientation, in which different features of the phenomena are selected for attention and new problems are identified as subjects of interest.

Second, the choice *between* paradigms—as the word *revolution* in Kuhn's title perhaps implies—is not entirely rational. The world is genuinely pluralistic, meaning that it can rationally or plausibly support many different conceptions of what the nature of ultimate reality is. There is no single answer. Each paradigm is largely self-validating, because it supplies the criteria that warrant its legitimization. As we have noted, all data are theory-laden. As a consequence, the decision to work within one paradigm rather than another is as dependent on custom, aesthetics, root metaphors, and sociological factors as it is on tests and arguments. Again, the historian Richard Tarnas provides a convenient summary:

> [R]ival paradigms are seldom genuinely comparable; they are selectively based on differing modes of interpretation and hence different sets of data. Each paradigm creates its own gestalt, so comprehensive that scientists working within different paradigms seem to be living in different worlds. Nor is

there any common measure, such as problem-solving ability or theoretical coherence or residence to falsification, that all scientists agree upon as a standard of comparison. What is an important problem for one group of scientists is not for another. Thus the history of science is not one of linear rational progress moving toward ever more accurate and complete knowledge of the objective truth, but is one of radical shifts of visions in which a multiple of nonrational and nonempirical factors play crucial roles.[11]

Another way of looking at the paradigm-dependency of our perceptions is to see how all knowledge claims or facts are only intelligible in their own context. This dependency on context is evident in everyday experience. The ballpoint pen with which I am writing, for example, cannot be understood apart from understanding alphabets and writing and paper. In isolation, the pen would be meaningless, as it is for a very young child. It remains an object, but, without context, it is not a "pen." Similarly, the meaning of being a "father" depends on the social context of the conventional family. Again, apart from that context, "fatherhood" is incomprehensible. When the context changes, as it has at the beginning of the twenty-first century, the meaning of fatherhood also changes. Postmodernism is distrustful of looking at "facts" in isolation and assuming that they either speak for themselves or mark the end of debate. Facts, as well as meaning, require contexts.

The study of different paradigms within science was eventually extended to science itself. That is, the objective, value-neutral world the scientific paradigm revealed and articulated was itself seen to be but one of many possible worlds, a social construction for specific and limited purposes. The question became, not which scientific paradigm is true, but whether the scientific paradigm itself reflects the way things are. Rather than a privileged or sacred road to truth, science is a specific choice, a decision to live in one world rather than another. Science is an interpretative structure that is itself variable, relative, and creatively employed for specific, largely pragmatic purposes. To fulfill these purposes, scientific explanations of the universe have been systematically denuded of all spiritual and human qualities, such as beauty, passion, and value. What we realize now from a postmodern perspective, in a way that we could not from the modern perspective, is that, again quoting Tarnas, "we cannot be certain that the world is in fact what these explanations suggest . . . only that the world is to an indeterminate extent *susceptible* to this way of interpretation."[12] Science may work, but pragmatism is no guarantee of truth. If one's purpose is to build a bridge or send a rocket into space, then science is the way to go. But if one's purpose is to decide whether to have an abortion or contribute to the Red Cross, then one needs a different world than the one science reveals. One does not have to go to an extreme constructionist position to acknowledge that by redefining the nature of scientific truth, as only one of many possible truths, postmodernism undermined the essential objective core of the modern mind and thus redefined the nature of truth and knowledge.

"TRUTH IS A KIND OF ERROR . . ."

Kuhn's work on the history of scientific revolutions is, of course, not uncontroversial. Moreover, for most working scientists, his theories are of little interest or consequence. Nevertheless, when combined with the theory of relativity, Heisenberg's uncertainty principle, and Bohr's complementarity, the cumulative effect is to undermine a naïve realism that assumes that scientific theories are literal descriptions of the world as it is.

As a central component of the modern mind, naïve realism, or the belief that we can literally describe the way nature is, makes two assumptions: one ontological and one epistemological. Ontologically, it assumes that there is a single, materially neutral objective universe; epistemologically, it assumes that we can know and describe this world in a way that corresponds to the way things are. In contrast, postmodern science argues that the universe is pluralistic, and that all we know is symbolic, theory-laden, and subject to the influence of socially constructed paradigms.

Pluralism and the influence of culturally constructed paradigms are dominant themes in postmodern thought, especially in the social sciences and humanities. To experience pluralism, one does not need to review relativity, quantum mechanics, and the history of science as I have done here. One only needs to read the morning newspaper's reports on conflicts between Christians and Muslims, modernity and fundamentalism, those who advocate the right to choose versus those who advocate the right to life. Perhaps the easiest way to articulate these themes is to return to Nietzsche—heir of Kant—and the central category of *interpretation.* According to the philosopher James C. Edwards, for Nietzsche, the "basic activity of consciousness is not spontaneous representation but *interpretation,* the willful imposition of structure and meaning on something—a text, a set of events, a sequence of sense-experiences—that demands it."[13] In a few short sentences, Edwards shows how a few excerpts from Nietzsche's *The Will to Power* redefine the meaning of knowledge, explanation, and truth in a way that anticipates the now familiar themes of postmodernism:

> Not "to know" but to schematize—to impose upon chaos as much regularity and form as our practical needs require.
>
> In the formation of reason, logic, the categories, it was *need* that was authoritative: the need, not to "know," but to subsume, to schematize, for the purpose of intelligibility and calculation.
>
> "Interpretation," the introduction of meaning—not "explanation." . . . There are no facts . . .
>
> The question "what is that?" is an imposition of meaning from some other viewpoint. "Essence," the "essential nature," is something perspective and already presupposes a multiplicity. At the bottom of it always lies "what is that for me?" (for us, for all that lives, etc.).
>
> Truth is the kind of error without which a certain species of life could not live.[14]

A corollary to this perspective is that all Truth, Truth with a capital T, is suspect or, worse, an expression of oppression, privilege and a will to power. If there is no objective way to determine right and wrong views, then only power remains for deciding whose perspective will prevail. Truth, theory, and rationality—that is, any story or system that denies a pluralistic universe—exhibits a "false consciousness" that inescapably conceals relationships of power (including violence and subordination) and masks the pluralistic reality as it is. A central category of postmodernism—*deconstruction*—is a methodology for "unmasking" or de-reifying what appear to be single, monolithic truths. The various social movements of the 1960s, for example, rebelled against the accepted truths of racial inequality, patriarchy, war, and acceptable forms of dress and sexual behavior. Singular truth is to be feared, because it marginalizes and ends the search for new truths. If we think we have the truth, we are not inclined to look further; if we are convinced that we know the truth, then we marginalize all those who disagree with us. The acceptance of complexity and the possibility of many possible meanings—whether we are speaking about a text, a society, a personality, a reemergent polytheism, or a history—is an antidote to totalitarianism and fundamentalism, and the blindness of a single vision, of whatever variety.

For the postmodernist, our ideas and symbols do not correspond to reality, they produce reality through an act of interpretation or construction, in which we select and reify one of many possible worlds according to our social and individual needs. The complexity and diversity of the sensations presented to the mind provide plausible support for many different conceptions of reality. By choosing one conception or viable option over another, we affect both reality and ourselves. Poverty, for example, casts a very different shadow if one interprets it as being caused by oppression and discrimination, rather than by lack of merit or initiative. From the perspective of postmodernism, reality is variously understood as an artifact, a human invention, a social construction, an expression of a sociohistorical horizon, a "form of life," or a set of "micropractices." Postmodernism abandons the search for a timeless, universal Truth in favor of becoming more self-conscious and transparent about our local motives and intentions. The modernist question, "Is it true?" transforms into the question, "How does it function?" or "What does it do?" No truth, just choices.

The strength of postmodernism is its acceptance, if not outright cultivation, of multiple perspectives and realities. Its associated methods focus on the local, the particular, the unsystematic, the episodic, the concrete, and the margins of conventional wisdom to highlight the enigmatic and unique. Correspondingly, postmodern methodologies multiply paradoxes and invent question upon question to undermine any settled assumption, in a way that encourages a range of alternative answers rather than a single solution. Positively, postmodernism unleashes the freedom to see and actively create new realities. Negatively, the fragmentation and incoherence it fosters, the existential burden of necessarily having to create one's own reality, and the knowledge that there is no decisive appeal, has social consequences that are still being played out. The social critic Walt Anderson observes about "alienation, anxiety, anomie" that "each term had something to do with what happens to people when they lose their certainty that social conviction is objective and permanent truth."[15] Furthermore, without objective appeal to "facts," conflicts cannot be consensually resolved, raising the specter of the interminable religious wars of the past.

FOUR QUESTIONS

Once again, we need to ask the four questions: (1) What do we know? (2) How do we know? (3) What does the postmodern mind emphasize and neglect? and (4) What does the postmodern mind contribute to the central question of meaning?

What Do We Know?

First, postmoderns know that the world is pluralistic. That is, reality possesses sufficient complexity, diversity, and fullness to plausibly support many different ways of being symbolically or categorically organized into a coherent world. There is no single or final world, nor is there a single or final Truth that corresponds to that world. Put another way, no single perspective is privileged over the alternative perspectives. Pluralism and diversity go all the way down; there is no foundation. There are multiple worlds and truths.

Second, the worlds we discover are, to a greater or lesser degree, created by what we bring to them, whether what we bring to them are a priori categories, language, archetypes, culturally and ritually sustained symbols, or the paradigms of scientific communities. For postmoderns, subjective and objective cannot be conveniently or easily distinguished. Reality is not objectively "out there" so much as it is a meeting between what's out there and what we bring to it. If the modern mind replaces metaphysics with physics, the postmodern mind replaces physics with psychology and the informing role of archetypes, symbols, and conceptual presumptions. In so doing, postmodernism goes beyond modernism by returning us to the intentional and literally informing power of myth and ideas. The meaning and teleological universe that were banished from a purposeful universe are returned to us in the form of our own desires and goals.

Third, although truth exists within each paradigm, world, or cultural system, determining what it is when worlds are being compared is problematic. Knowledge claims are debatable only within their respective contexts, paradigms, or communities. We can say, and have criteria for determining, what makes a good Christian or a good Muslim, a good architect or a good athlete, but we do not have a way of determining whether a Christian is better than a Muslim, or whether an architect is better than an athlete.

Truth exists within a paradigm but not between paradigms. The essential truth of pluralism and the inability to judge between paradigms exists despite the frequent observation that postmodernism contradicts itself in claiming that its own version of the truth is privileged. To be consistent, it would have to admit that postmodernism, too, is only one of many possible perspectives whose truth expresses specific interests and purposes.

Fourth, within the postmodern mind, truth is contextual or instrumental rather than representational. As William James articulated it, theories are "instruments, not answers to enigmas in which we can rest."[16] A scientific theory, a religious doctrine or symbol, or a philosophical conception is not to be judged according to whether it accurately mirrors reality, but according to whether it works more or less well, whether it is at least temporarily useful or edifying. The question is not "What does this mean?"; "Is it True?"; or "To what does this correspond?" but "How does it function in this specific context?"; "What does it do?"; "What social, psychological, political, or pragmatic need does it fulfill?" From this perspective, for example, we cannot say that religion is truer than science, or vice versa; we can only say that religion works in fulfilling some needs, while science works in fulfilling others. We cannot tell whether a story is sacred or authoritative because of what it is or because it refers to what actually happened, but only by observing how it functions. Thus, functionally, *Star Wars* may be more religious, because it presents us with authoritative and compelling examples of how to live, than the biblical story of Moses. Whereas the modern mind dismisses religion, stories, and history for not corresponding to the facts, or for being merely subjective, the postmodern mind accepts that they can remain true functionally. Or, as the popular biblical scholar Marcus Borg observes, "metaphors can be profoundly true, even though they are not literally true."[17] What we know is not the real or the true but how things work within specific contexts and for specific purposes.

Finally, the postmodern mind knows that the bleak, indifferent, meaningless world revealed to us by the modern scientific mind is not the real and only world. The appeal to objective facts does not end all discussion. Science is but one of many possible worlds or ways of organizing a coherent world. We organize the world "scientifically" for specific purposes, but those purposes are limited and do not comprehend all of human experience and needs. Whereas moral and religious questions are dismissed by the modern mind as metaphysical, and thus not a part of the real world, the postmodern mind has resurrected those questions as genuine and legitimate, albeit lying outside the concerns of the scientific paradigm and community. A pluralistic universe has undermined the single vision of the modern mind and, in so doing, has created an intellectual arena in which useless questions such as "What does life mean?" can once again flourish.

How Do We Know?

Because postmodernism acknowledges a plurality of worlds and functions, it exhibits a corresponding plurality of approaches or ways of knowing. Despite this plurality, certain themes are nevertheless evident.

The core approach is radical skepticism. If one assumes that in a pluralistic universe there are no universal truths, then *any* claim to the truth is by definition suspect, and anyone who presumes to speak of or for humankind, who declares specific values to be universal or timeless, or who claims to know *the* meaning of a text, is to be mistrusted. Indeed, more than skepticism, such persons are to be actively resisted, because such monolithic thinking inevitably leads to oppression and the marginalization or rejection of dissenting views. The absence of truth is not nihilistic; on the contrary, it is a positive, liberating activity whose acceptance of complexity, according to the postmodern icon Jacques Derrida, makes totalitarianism impossible "because totalitarianism depends so completely on its own version of truth."[18] If there are no objective means of distinguishing and choosing between one view or paradigm and another, then the decision as to which view will prevail depends on power, politics, or aesthetics. The rhetorical appeal to objective and disinterested truth so prized by moderns, the appeal even to the universal reason of the ancients, conceals relationships of power and influence. As a result, the road to wisdom travels along a path of skepticism, rather than that of trust and belief. The postmodernist's greatest fear is not of succumbing to nihilism but of being duped or seduced into blindly believing in something whose answers are both readily available and false. For postmodernists, totalitarianism is a greater threat than nihilism.

Postmodernism cultivates any method that deconstructs or exposes a multiplicity of viewpoints that are otherwise being concealed by a monolithic perspective. Truth is always plural. Truth (and meaning) is always followed by the question: true for whom, for what purpose, and in what context? Comparative and historical approaches that reveal that a historical or doctrinal truth, or a cultural norm, is only true from within a specific cultural, social, or class setting are common. Distrustful of the universal, postmodernism focuses on the particular, the eccentric, the marginal, the unrepeatable, and those aspects of experience that have hitherto been neglected, excluded, and deemed unacceptable because of the reigning paradigm and social group. Postmodernism is inherently anti-methodological, because no single method is or could be adequate to a pluralistic universe; truth cannot be articulated according to a single grammar, logic, or system of symbols. Postmodernism abandons the search for objective knowledge or finding the universal right answer in the modern sense of the term. Instead, it adopts a plurality of approaches and methods to avoid the modern mind's single vision and, in so doing, encourages evocation, intrinsically satisfying play, and openness to the diversity and richness of experience.

Approaches that cultivate skepticism and pluralism inevitably lead to a higher level of self-consciousness. The skeptic can no longer unself-consciously accept that monarchy or patriarchy or heterosexuality is simply the way "things are." Alienation, meaning the inability to unself-consciously accept the taken-for-granted world as it is, is an essential experience of the postmodern mind. Culturally, we thought we were rational, enlightened creatures until Freud made us more self-conscious about our unconscious desires and impulses. Similarly, Marx exposed, and made us more self-conscious about, how our values and outlook on life are determined by economics and social class. Again, reality for the postmodern is less "out there" than it is a human and cultural projection or imposition. In their classic text, descriptively entitled *The Social Construction of Reality*, the sociologists Peter Berger and Thomas Luckmann introduce the term *reification* to describe those instances when we mistakenly accept the products of human activity for the nonhuman and objective. In a central passage, they write: "[R]eification is the apprehension of the products of human activity *as if* they were something else than human products—such as facts of nature, results of cosmic laws, or manifestations of divine will. Reification implies that man is capable of forgetting his own authority of the human world, and further, that the dialectic between man, the producer, and his products is lost to consciousness. The reified world is, by definition, a dehumanized world. It is experienced by man as a strange facticity."[19]

Note that the thrust of reification is a "forgetting" and a "lost to consciousness" about the extent to which human activity—including the creation of religious and cultural symbols as well as scientific paradigms—creates what appears to be objective reality. Accordingly, our task as postmodernists is to "remember" and "to raise our consciousness" about how the world in which we live is constructed and imposed by human beings, as an expression of their personal and social—subjective—intentions and desires. Thus, for example, the sexual roles of men and women that once seemed a part of the objective structure of the world were undermined by the consciousness-raising of the women's movement. The women's movement de-reified those roles by saying that the traditional roles of men and women (men as the primary breadwinners and women staying home to raise children) were human constructs and not inherent in nature. Whenever we "remember" the human component of objective phenomena, we identify ourselves as members of the postmodern generation.

What Does Postmodernism Emphasize and What Does It Neglect?

Postmodernism is enormously liberating. Just consider: if nothing is inherent or inevitable, if reality is plural, if there is no ultimate "grounding," then no single viewpoint or perspective, whether doctrine or symbol, can have absolute authority. In line with a slogan from the 1960s, authority can always be questioned. There is no monolithic reality that can impose obedience or conformity; there are only choices of which culture, religion, or identity one wants to adopt. Postmodernism is an insistent antidote to religious fundamentalism, ideological fanaticism, social intolerance, and political totalitarianism alike. If any viewpoint is merely one of many possible interpretations, no single viewpoint should compel my allegiance or loyalty. What Phillip Rieff calls the "normality of disillusion" creates both the possibility and burden of existential choice.[20] Postmodernism reminds us that only God is God.

The liberation engendered by postmodernism nevertheless has a darker, more negative aspect. Postmodernism is by its nature subversive of all paradigms, for at its core is the proposition that reality is always multiple, local, and temporal. It proclaims that there are no universal and timeless truths. In this context, freedom easily slips into anarchy. The freedom to choose is absurd if no choice is worth making, "worth" in this case meaning a choice that is secured or legitimated by something that is not groundless or arbitrary. A tolerance of a plurality of viewpoints degenerates into indifference when all viewpoints are equally groundless and equally arbitrary. Nihilism results if no choice is better than any other. Thus, for example, Sartre's existential philosophy of commitment can be seen as a philosophy of despair, because it is based on the proposition that if all paths lead to nowhere then it's just as well to chose any of them. An uninhibited and unrestrained ability to choose, in its darker aspects, can lead to unspeakable horrors. We can choose to defy conventional prohibitions against murder, incest, and genocide, so long as it serves our purposes, because there is nothing inherent in nature or reason to restrain us. If God is dead, everything is permitted.

Two psychological consequences are neglected by postmodern enthusiasts. First, a culture, interpretative framework, or worldview protects us from the anxiety that facing the chaos of reality "as it is" elicits, including the reality of death and the experience of nothingness. Ernest Becker argues brilliantly in his classic book *The Denial of Death* that "it can't be overstressed . . . that to see the world as it really is is devastating and terrifying . . . it makes routine, automatic, secure, self-confident activity impossible."[21] From this perspective, postmodernism's efforts to demystify and deconstruct authoritative myths, symbols, and paradigms are misguided. Myths and symbols are necessary and essential ingredients of a human life. Repression and the limits imposed by culture are the necessary lies we tell ourselves in order to live in an otherwise miraculous but incomprehensible world, filled as it is with both beauty and death. Schizophrenia, according to Becker, occurs precisely when someone is unable to shut out the "terror" of life because he or she lacks the limits and structure provided by culture. Postmodernism, by insistently undermining the ontological status of any concept of reality or, as was said earlier, by being subversive of all paradigms, threatens to expose the "lie" and in so doing confront us with a truth with which we cannot live.

The second psychological consequence denied by postmodernism is motivational. How can one accept relativism without becoming a nihilist? How can I be receptive to pluralism and diversity without losing loyalty and commitment to my own vision of what is right and proper? This problem was anticipated at the beginning of the twentieth century by William James and his readers when they asked whether a belief can be whole-hearted when one knows that one is only acting *as if.* One of James's most famous essays is entitled "The Will to Believe." Again, in the pluralistic universe of postmodernism, my world is but one of many possible worlds, no more or less substantial or grounded in reality than any other; not the truth, but merely my truth. Knowing this, how far am I willing to go in imposing my vision on another or permitting others to impose their vision on me? Am I willing to die or sacrifice the future of my children to perpetuate the necessary lie I am living *as if* it were true? How much am I willing to give for what I believe, rather than what I know? To what extent is my commitment limited by the knowledge that what I know and believe is not grounded in the nature of reality but has been partially made by me? In short, can a life that is intentionally and self-consciously chosen ever be as compelling as one that feeds from the unknown, subterranean springs of faith? This is a question that postmodernism typically avoids.

Postmodernism and Meaning

What does postmodernism have to say about the central question of meaning?

Above all, postmodernism says that meaning is again a possibility. The modern world banished questions of meaning in favor of a value-neutral, objective, indifferent universe. It dismissed the questions "Why?" and "What for?" in favor of "How?" In contrast, postmodernism says that science, as the bedrock of the modern mind, is but one of many possible ways of organizing experience.

Science is enormously effective for specific purposes, but it does not describe the universe in all its complexity and diversity. Science has failed to recognize that something can—at one and the same time—be both true, in the sense of corresponding to what is the case, and utterly meaningless. What science leaves out is again a live option.

As a corollary to this first point, the postmodern universe is composed of multiple, self-consistent paradigms, interpretations, or worldviews. If the meaning of "it all" remains unclear, we can nevertheless find or create meaning within specific contexts and for specific moments while running, growing a business, or being a good parent, for example. No one questions whether life is meaningful when they are in love or their team scores the winning goal. To the extent that we are committed now to this world, now to that, we exhibit a form of serial monogamy that is reminiscent of the polytheism characteristic of the mythic mind examined earlier. In Christian theology and ethics, for example, Stanley Hauerwas has made much of abandoning the attempt to devise a universal ethic or the search for the meaning of the gospel in favor of an ethic and reading limited to specific Christian communities. Postmodernism thus offers two clues to the question of meaning: first, that there is a place for meaning when we are liberated from the monolithic thinking of scientism, and, second, that we are capable of finding or creating meaning within specific paradigms or worlds. If timeless meaning does not occur in the universe as a whole, it can nevertheless occur within the more limited communities in which we actively participate.

Even in the case of modern science, which assumes an otherwise meaningless universe, the working scientist finds meaning in the practice of discovery. The universe may be meaningless, but to the scientist, his or her work is not. The narrative of discovery, of finding the truth behind appearances, functions mythically by providing the scientist with purpose, orientation, and a sense of meaningful activity. Similarly, three additional myths function to motivate and provide meaning for postmodernists.

The first such myth is the postmodern's identification with the rebel or outsider. The outsider is an iconoclast who deconstructs and demystifies those who assert that they know or possess *the* answer. The outsider is brave and honest enough to say that the emperor has no clothes, and courageous enough to meet the challenge of living in a world without appeal or assurances. In so doing, the postmodernist undermines fanaticism and intolerance of whatever variety. Rebellion and the confrontation of pretension and inauthenticity constitute a heroic and meaningful story that provides direction and purpose, especially to the young and those tutored on the pioneering virtues of America.

The second mythic story informing postmodernism is that of the creator and artist. The mythic, philosophical, and modern minds discovered meaning in finding and conforming to the truths of myth, ideas, and nature, respectively. Deprived of the possibility of discovering an objective truth in the same way, postmodernism celebrates the ability to actively fabricate truth and meaning with new interpretations and ways of seeing. For postmodernism, truth is plastic. The story of the postmodern is the story of Nietzsche's Superman, the creator—whether artist, entrepreneur, politician, or some other—who does not passively accept the limitations of reality as it is but transforms and creates a meaningful reality through his own will and subjective efforts. Instead of asking "Why?" the postmodern asks "Why not?" Creating truth is itself a meaningful activity.

Finally, the third myth associated with postmodernism is that of the existentialist or polytheist who enjoys and finds meaning now in this world, now in that, without attempting to "get it all together" or find a more encompassing meaning. The message is to thoroughly enjoy and submit to the spell of the moment—of love, beauty, or happiness—without going outside the moment to think about its meaning or how it relates to a myth, idea, or extrinsic purpose. In the arresting phrase of the American philosopher George Santayana: "There is no cure for birth and death save to enjoy the interval."[22] The postmodernist is a tourist, not a pilgrim; a wayfarer, not a missionary. Having abandoned the search for *the* truth and *the* meaning, the point for postmodernism is the journey, not the end.

PART II

Contemporary Sources
of Meaning

CHAPTER SIX

Pragmatism and Meaning

Pessimism is essentially a religious disease.
William James, "The Will to Believe"

If I could invite any five Americans who had ever lived to dinner, William James would certainly be at my table. James wrote during an era in which American philosophy was not specialized and excessively academic, not, as he says, "a technical matter . . . [but] our more or less dumb sense of what life honestly and deeply means."[1] As a result, his writing consistently addresses questions or hypotheses that both arise from real life and are important, or, as he categorized them, hypotheses that are at once *live, forced,* and *momentous.* What's more, he writes in a style that is fluid, accessible, and filled with examples drawn from common life; indeed, this chapter includes an embarrassing number of direct excerpts simply because I found myself unable to paraphrase in a way that improves upon James's own words.

Another reason for my wanting to invite James to dinner is that he authored a classic description of the experience of meaninglessness. "[T]here fell upon me without any warning, just as if it came out of the darkness, a horrible fear of my own existence . . .

as if something hitherto solid within my breast gave way entirely, and I became a mass of quivering fear," he recalls. Reminiscent of Tolstoy's fearful awakening, James goes on to say that after the experience, "the universe was changed for me altogether. I awoke morning after morning with a horrible dread at the pit of my stomach, and with a sense of the insecurity of life. . . . In general I dreaded to be left alone. I remember wondering how other people could live, how I myself had ever lived, so unconscious of that pit of insecurity beneath the surface of life."[2]

James reflects on several occasions that philosophy begins with discontent. In a wonderful turn of phrase, he writes that our speculations would be quenched if the world were nothing but a "lubberland" of happiness. One can easily imagine that much of James's philosophy was an effort to comprehend, and move beyond, his fearful awakening. It both reflects themes already introduced in this study and anticipates others that figure in subsequent chapters. Three are especially germane.

THREE THEMES

Perhaps the most fundamental theme to James's thought is his advocacy of pluralism. On the question of whether the world is one or many, James always votes for the many. Pluralism means that the dumb, evanescent reality of sensations can be divided up into different "worlds," according to our own interests and perspectives. Reality is infinitely malleable and passively submits to our conceptions. "And why, after all," James asks, "may not the world be so complex as to consist of many interpenetrating spheres of reality, which can thus be approached in alternation by using different conceptions and assuming different attitudes, just as mathematicians handle the same numerical and spatial facts by geometry, by analytical geometry, by algebra, by calculus, or by quaternions, and each time come out right."[3] Genuine pluralism does not mean that there are many paths leading to the same destination; it means that there are many paths leading to many different destinations.

Sensations are an ideal limit to thought, always beyond our control, too concrete to be entirely manageable, entering our experience in a way "yet to be named." The way we see the world is always selective, and thus once removed from the raw facts. The facts associated with the battle of Waterloo, James notes, are the same, but for the English they spell "victory" while for the French they spell "defeat." Similarly, the healthy minded individual selects and notices the positive aspects of life—and thinks these are essential and universal—whereas the sick soul is persuaded that the real meaning of life is attained when we attend to the evil and negative aspects of life. Every way of conceiving the world emphasizes some aspects of the preexistent sensational realm and—necessarily—disregards others. No view or system of thought comprehends the whole; all views and systems are partial, incomplete, and ultimately false. "The whole drift of my education," James concludes, "goes to persuade me that the world of our present consciousness is only one out of many worlds of consciousness that exist, and that those other worlds must contain experiences which have a meaning for our life also."[4]

A corollary to pluralism is that we do not grasp reality directly. This constitutes the second theme to James's philosophy. Sounding very much like Kant, James argues that we do not grasp reality directly, but only through symbols or "some substitute for reality." In a discussion of "common sense," James insists that what appear to be intuitive or directly apperceived distinctions between thoughts and things, permanent subjects and changing attributes, space and time are "inductive generalizations like those more recent ones of the atom, of inertia, [or] of energy."[5] Even our most basic and fundamental categories—our common sense—are, he concludes, an accumulation of our own intellectual inventions. In short, to use a more contemporary expression, reality is socially constructed over time and within specific communities. Classical science was literalistic. Classical scientists—like all literalists—assumed that their thoughts directly corresponded with reality. With the breakdown of classical science, correspondence or conformity to a single reality was exchanged for a pluralism of partial worlds and what James describes as a "rich and active commerce" between our thoughts (symbols) and the universe of experience. The similarities between James's thinking and that of postmodernism on this point are apparent.

A third theme unifying James's philosophy addresses the question of how sensations and life in its concrete immediacy are transformed into a coherent "world." James answers this question in two ways. The first, and more common notion, as we have just seen, is that we create worlds through a process of selection and emphasis. In this connection, one thinks of examples from Psychology 101 where the answer depends on which perceptual clues one is attentive to, such as determining whether a glass is half-full or half-empty, or whether a figure is a duck or a rabbit. Earlier I cited James's observation that a healthy minded optimist and a sick-souled pessimist will select and highlight different sorts of experience. "What shall we call a 'thing' anyhow?" James asks. "It seems quite arbitrary for we carve out everything, just as we carve out constellations, to suit our human purposes."[6] From this perspective, reality is fixed, even singular perhaps, but nevertheless is susceptible to being carved out in many different ways depending on our purposes or predispositions.

More intriguing, and I think finally more important, than James's notion that we create worlds by a process of selection and emphasis is his notion that we actively contribute or add to reality through our own efforts, and in two ways.

James illustrates the first way we add to reality by citing the example of a constellation. The seven-star constellation known as the Big Dipper or the Great Bear, among other names, presents us with a quasi-paradox. On the one hand, the stars are "what and where they are." They dictate what we can add to them and our additions do not change their previous nature. "Never," James says, "could the number seven be questioned, *if the question once were raised.*" On the other hand, the act of counting and comparing, saying that there are seven stars and that they resemble a bear or a dipper, are "genuine additions made by our intellect to the world of fact"; "something comes by the counting that was not there before." These additions, James quickly adds, are not of "consciousness only, but additions of 'content.' They copy nothing that pre-existed, yet they agree with what pre-existed, fit it, amplify it, relate and connect it with a 'wain,' a number tally, or what not, and build it out." In counting the stars and finding a resemblance, we in one sense discover what was always there, but in another, by adding to it, create something entirely new.[7]

"Why," James asks in arguing against a correspondence view of truth, "may not thought's mission be to increase and elevate, rather than simply to imitate and reduplicate, existence? . . .

Rather is thought itself a most momentous part of fact, and the whole mission of the pre-existing and insufficient world of matter may simply be to provoke thought to produce its far more precious supplement."[8] A few pages later, James again emphasizes how thought adds to reality: "To a certain extent our ideas, being realities, are also independent variables, and, just as they follow other reality and fit it, so, in a measure, does other reality follow and fit them. When they add themselves to being they partly redetermine the existent, so that reality as a whole appears incompletely definable unless ideas also are kept account of."[9]

In some ways, James's notion that we complete reality is reminiscent of Aristotle. Only in this case, potential is actualized, not by the teleological end found in universal Forms, but by human thought. Whether we create worlds through selection or addition, however, James emphasizes that there is something solidly there, preexisting, to which we can add. In another context, however, he argues that we actually and more radically contribute to creating realities by collaborating with what is in situations where there is no preexisting, fixed referent.

This second, more radical way of adding to reality is a central theme of James's essays "The Will to Believe" and "Is Life Worth Living?" James offers an illuminating example. Imagine he says that you are climbing a mountain and that you have worked yourself into a position where the only means of escape involves making a great leap. Have faith that you can make the leap and you are "nerved" to accomplish it successfully. Doubt and mistrust your ability to make the leap and you will probably fall into the abyss: "Refuse to believe and you shall indeed be right, for you shall irretrievably perish. But believe, and again you shall be right, for you shall save yourself."[10]

What we might call self-fulfilling prophecies apply to situations where the outcome is genuinely in doubt, neither inevitable nor impossible. In personal relations, for example, how one answers the question "Do you like me or not?" helps determine whether you will be liked. Faith "on my part in your liking's existence is in such cases what makes your liking come. But if I stand aloof, and refuse to bulge an inch until I have objective evidence, until you have done something apt . . . ten to one your liking never comes."[11] Similarly, a train of passengers can be robbed by a single individual unless they believe themselves able to unite to resist. Given that social faith, the robbery would not even be attempted. There are then, James concludes, "cases where a fact cannot come at all unless a preliminary faith exists in its coming and where faith in a fact can help create the fact."[12]

The title of James's famous essay "Is Life Worth Living?" asks the question directly. Yes or no? Who is right about the universe as a whole, the optimist or the pessimist, the healthy minded or the sick soul? Both are, to the extent that this is an instance where belief contributes to fact. "Thoughts are things," James quotes a mind-cure proponent as saying. Live *as if* the world were meaningful and believe in the "efficiency of courage, hope, and trust" and your experience will corroborate your belief. Pessimism leads to weakness, but optimism leads to power. "If your thoughts are of health, youth, vigor, and success, before you know it these things will also be your outward position."[13] Think otherwise, and a different outward position will follow. Beliefs add to reality and, in so doing, yield practical fruits. Beliefs are real if they have real effects.

The ability to add to reality, especially in instances where our faith in a fact can help create the fact, requires courage, hardihood, and a willingness to live without assurances or guarantees. There are no certainties; the outcome is in doubt. Life, as James says, evoking the prototypical pioneering spirit of America, involves risk and feels like a "real fight, as if there were something really wild in the universe, which we, with all our idealities and faithfulness, are needed to redeem; and first of all to redeem our own hearts from atheisms and fears."[14] Whereas absolutist schemes appeal to the tender-minded and permit a "moral holiday" (a holiday because a certain or fixed universe, whether damned or redeemed, does not require our participation), the universe of maybes appeals to the hardy and brave, because the outcome remains both uncertain and dependent on our efforts.

We cannot know whether our faith is justified apart from our engaged acts and commitments. Regardless of how many objective calculations we might perform, we really cannot know whether we can successfully leap across the crevasse until we jump. As the old saying goes, you have to play the game in order to see who will win. The pragmatist, James observes, is "willing to live on a scheme of uncertified possibilities which he trusts; willing to pay with his own person, if need be, for the realization of the ideals which he frames."[15] Faced with his own crisis of meaningless, James chose to believe in free will and his ability to choose, without foundation, one thought and act rather than another.

CLARIFICATION AND TRUTH

"Realities are not true, they are; and beliefs are true of them."[16] Thus, James succinctly introduces us to the question of the relationship between our ideas, concepts, and words—what he often refers to as "notions"—and reality. Conventionally, that relationship has been understood as one of correspondence. The notion "truck" refers to the vehicle on the street corner and is true to the extent that it points to that vehicle and not to the motorcycle next to it. The notions of God and democracy likewise correspond to realities, albeit more complex ones than a truck. Pragmatism offers a more nuanced view of what a thing is because our notions both correspond to real things and "add to" that reality through our selections and commitments. More than that, however, pragmatism is a method for clarifying what words, concepts, and notions mean by grounding them in experience and, in so doing, protecting us from speaking nonsense, both literally and figuratively. Meaning does not stop with a notion's referent but extends to the notion's effect. The pragmatic method, James explains, "is to try to interpret each notion by tracing its respective practical consequences. What difference would it practically make to any one if this notion rather than that notion were true? If no practical difference whatever can be traced, then the alternatives mean practically the same thing, and all dispute is idle."[17]

Suppose you have to transport a heavy box of books to a friend's apartment. The notion of the truck proves itself true in experience because when I arrive on the street corner I have a vehicle in which to carry my box. Its meaning is different from the notion of a motorcycle because, guided by that notion, I would not have a means of carrying the box. The meanings of the notions *truck* and *motorcycle* thus differ according to the consequences they lead to in experience. It difficult to see in cases that deal with concrete objects, such as this one, that the meaning of a concept lies in its consequences and not in its referent, but it becomes clearer, I think, with more abstract notions in which the reference is neither so apparent nor self-evident.

Take the notion *God*, for example. What is the concept's referent; to what does it correspond? No one, not even the most extreme literalist, I think, could say that the referent of *God* is as concrete and self-evident as the referent of *truck*. James cautions that the intellect, "even with truth directly in its grasp, may have no infallible signal for knowing whether it be true or no."[18] Again, to understand the meaning of *God* we cannot stop with the referent for God but must proceed to ask what concrete difference God makes in someone's life? The meaning of *God* is not the object-referent (which in any event we cannot grasp or, as 1 Corinthians 13:12 puts it, see face to face) but its effects, its consequences in people's lives. Thus, James suggests, *God* means assurance and comfort that an ideal order, including a moral order, is permanent and that belief in the primacy of spirit and free will provide a basis for hope. Belief in "Absolute Mind," which for James is a synonym for *God*, enables us to enjoy a moral holiday, because we can trust that the world's fate is in better hands than our own. In contrast, materialism denies an eternal moral order, ensnares us in an inescapable determinism, or else—as with existentialism—places the world's fate entirely on our shoulders. The notions *God* and *materialism* are thus clarified and distinguished not by their referents or lack of referent, as the case may be, but by their consequences in actual lives.

Beyond a method for clarifying the meaning of a notion by grounding it in its effects, James also proposes a method for defining truth. If truth cannot be determined by establishing a correspondence between a notion and a thing, then on what basis can it be established? We have just seen that notions are distinguished by their consequences. James takes that thought one step

further by saying that the true notion is the one whose consequences are satisfactory, useful, or simply conducive to a better
life. Another way of saying this is to say that truth is an honorific
title or category. To say that a notion is true is to recognize,
honor, and acknowledge that it is useful: "True ideas would
never have been singled out as such, would never have acquired
a class-name, least of all a name suggesting value, unless they had
been useful from the outset."[19]

Again, James provides an illustrative example. Until about
1850 or so, he observes, people believed that scientific theories
expressed truths that were exact copies of nonhuman reality.
The proliferation of scientific theories since that era, however,
had undermined that belief. Instead, theories were treated as
"conceptual shorthand" and true "so far as they are useful but
no further." The superiority of one theory over another may
not consist so much in its literal objectivity, he adds, "as in subjective qualities like its usefulness, its 'elegance' or its congruity
with our residual beliefs."[20] Similarly, the pragmatist cannot
reject any hypothesis, including the God hypothesis, "if consequences useful to life flow from it."[21] If the God hypothesis
"works satisfactorily, in the widest sense of the word, it is
true."[22] Reflecting his pluralistic bias and sounding very much
like the postmodernists, of whom he is a precursor, James
acknowledges in a critical passage that various types of notions
have their respective uses and thus their respective truths.
"Common sense is *better* for one sphere of life, science for
another, philosophic criticism for a third, but whether either
be truer absolutely, Heaven only knows. . . . They are all but
ways of talking," he adds, "to be compared solely from the point
of view of their use."[23]

James's arguments concerning the definition and defense of his pragmatic conception of truth are subtle and wide-ranging, if not, on occasion, contradictory. If this were a study of James rather than a study of meaning, a more complete review and analysis of his arguments would be required. However, for our purposes, four points about a pragmatic conception of truth are sufficient.

First, truth must be *made*. Here James approvingly cites Henri Bergson's idea that notions are "made for the purpose of practice, and not for the purpose of insight."[24] Just as we cannot know whether we can successfully leap over the crevasse until we actually commit to and attempt the jump, so we cannot know whether a notion is useful, and thus true, until we commit to and employ it. Answering the question of whether the consequences of believing in this hypothesis will add value and prove more satisfactory in the long run than its alternative is not a matter for speculation but a matter of action and consequences. To anticipate, James would ask us: What leads to a more satisfactory life: a belief that life is meaningful or meaningless?

Second, to articulate what is perhaps obvious, truth for James is instrumental. It is not an end in itself, but only a "preliminary means towards other vital satisfactions. The practical value of true ideas is thus," he adds, "primarily derived from the practical importance of their objects to us."[25] Even the notion and truth of religion is to be judged, not by an intrinsic enjoyment of God, but by the extent to which it leads to a "larger, richer, more satisfying life."[26] This is what we might call a functional view of truth. Presumably, this view implies that alternative conceptions can be substituted for one another, and are equally true, so long as they have equally satisfying consequences. Also implied by this view is that truths can change, and become false, if they cease to be instrumental in providing satisfying consequences. What is true in one historical era or phase of an individual's life may be false in another.

Third, with his notions about what truth means *pragmatically,* James establishes a relationship between truth and the satisfaction of human purposes and desires. Truth is not disinterested or objective, nor can it be determined by observation or contemplation. On the contrary, truth is always connected with the satisfaction of desires and interests and determined by commitment and a willingness to act on beliefs. On this view, truth is inseparable from who we are, our particular circumstances and way of life. All truth is biographical. Does this mean that anything can be true so long as one finds it satisfying? Is truth that idiosyncratic? Or does that "one" entail social/historical/ cultural contexts and psychological archetypes that link the individual to a more universal self and community? What "one" finds satisfying is surely inexorably linked to the culture in which one lives.

James's thinking about pluralism and truth can be summarized and revealed with a final, commonplace example. What is truer: a screwdriver or a hammer? It depends, of course, on what you need to accomplish. If you need to drive a nail, the hammer is your tool, whereas if you need to set a screw, a screwdriver is what you want. Is the hammer "truer" than the screwdriver? Of course not. Both have their uses in a pluralistic world. How do we know that the hammer is "true"? Because it works in driving a nail. We know not because we determine rationally that the hammer is the better tool for driving a nail but because we act in pounding a nail into a two-by-four and, in so doing, verify that it works better for this purpose than a screwdriver. We verify its truth for that specific use or purpose. Furthermore, we cannot understand the meaning of a hammer apart from its use and the context of a world in which nails exist and pieces of lumber need to be attached to one another. James is saying that notions and concepts are tools or instruments, like hammers and screwdrivers. Like the tools of a carpenter, each notion has its instrumental use in satisfying particular needs, which we verify by acting to get things done.

Not surprisingly, James defends himself against the charge of solipsism by saying that a notion, and the actions that followed from commitment to that notion, would not be satisfactory if it were not in some degree congruent with reality. Satisfactions are "indispensable for truth building," he remarks, but then quickly adds, "but I have everywhere called them insufficient unless reality be also incidentally led to."[27] Furthermore, James holds that truth is not a single instance of what works best, but "fits every part of life best and combines with the collectivity of experience's demands, nothing being omitted."[28] That is to say, the satisfactions derived from one truth cannot be in conflict with those derived from other truths or vital benefits. Thus, perhaps despite himself, James's pragmatic conception of truth absorbs aspects of both the correspondence and coherence conceptions of truth.

Fourth, and most intriguingly, James provocatively speaks on occasion about the limits of knowing. The truth of notions or conceptual knowledge itself is to be judged—true or false—instrumentally by its usefulness and consequences. "'Knowing,' in short, may, for aught we can see beforehand to the contrary, be only one way of getting into fruitful relations with reality, whether copying be one of the relations or not."[29] We seek to know because we think that knowledge leads to a more satisfying life, but here, in yet another expression of a pluralistic spirit, James declares that knowing, even perhaps the knowing of self-consciousness, is only one way of getting in "fruitful relations" with reality.

James distinguishes between conceptual knowledge or knowledge *about* things, on the one hand, and the kind of knowledge that arises from "living or sympathetic acquaintance," on the other (cf. Wilfred Cantwell Smith's distinction between faith and belief, discussed in chapter 2). The superiority of intellectual knowledge is, he says, a "practical one." However, to gain "complete insight into reality," we must "fall back on raw unverbalized life as more of a revealer."[30] "Reality, life, experience, concreteness, immediacy, use what word you will, exceeds logic, overflows and surrounds it."[31] This is the form of engaged knowledge that is reflected in the biblical accounts of men "knowing" their wives. Thought, he says elsewhere, "deals . . . solely with surfaces. It can name the thickness of reality, but it cannot fathom it."[32] Whereas one path can lead to what James calls "conceptual decomposition," the other path, that of "the immediate experience of life," can solve the "problems which so baffle our conceptual intelligence."[33]

In contrast to his emphasis on an active engagement and struggle with reality in the instrumental value of all knowing, this alternative way of knowing is a "kind of passive and receptive listening."[34] Indeed, what divides the religious from merely the moralistic character is this capacity to surrender to passivity and relaxation. This becomes (or more accurately restates) a crucial theme in James's *Varieties of Religious Experience*, from which

I quote at some length below, followed immediately by another lengthy excerpt from his *A Pluralistic Universe:*

> Passivity, not activity; relaxation, not intentness, should be now the rule. Give up the feeling of responsibility, let go your hold, resign the care of your destiny to higher powers, be genuinely indifferent as to what becomes of it all, and you will find not only that you gain a perfect inward relief, but often also, in addition, the particular goods you sincerely thought you were renouncing. This is the salvation through self-despair, the dying to be truly born, of Lutheran theology, the passage into nothing of which Jacob Behmen [the German mystic Jakob Böhme] writes. To get to it, a critical point must usually be passed, a corner turned within one. Something must give way, a native hardness must break down and liquefy; and this event (as we shall abundantly see hereafter) is frequently sudden and automatic, and leaves on the Subject an impression that he has been wrought on by an external power. . . . With those who undergo it [religious experience] in its fullness, no criticism avails to cast doubt on its reality. They know; for they have actually felt the higher powers, in giving up the tension of their personal will.[35]

> As long as one continues *talking,* intellectualism remains in undisputed possession of the field. The return to life can't come about by talking. It is an *act;* to make you return to life, I must set an example for your imitation, I must deafen you to talk, or to the importance of talk, by showing you, as Bergson does, that the concepts we talk with are made for purposes of *practice* and not for purposes of insight. Or I must *point,* point to the mere *that* of life, and you by inner sympathy must fill out that *what* for yourselves. . . . An intellectual answer to the intellectualist's difficulties will never come . . . the real way out of them, far from consisting in the discovery of such an answer, consists in simply closing one's ears to the question.[36]

In these two passages, sounding now like a Zen monk, now like an existentialist, James guides us down an unexpected and intriguing path, far removed from his earlier emphasis on instrumental action. Along the way, he introduces us to several important themes, including the distinction between moralistic and religious perspectives, the need to act to verify our truths, the limitations inherent in conceptual knowledge, and the distinction between instrumental and intrinsically valuable experiences. I shall continue to explore these themes in later chapters. For the moment, however, I summarize James's contribution by asking my four questions: from James's perspective, what do we know, how do we know, what is emphasized and neglected, and what does he have to say about the question of meaning?

FOUR QUESTIONS
What Do We Know?

According to James we know at least three things.

First, we know that the world is pluralistic. Reality is not single but multiple; not static and finished but malleable and in process. Many religions, many cultures, many values, many languages, many ways of understanding the course of history, many theories and paradigms about the fundamental nature of the universe—all attest to a pluralistic universe. Men are from Mars; women are from Venus. What does philosophy have to do with faith? The differences between these divergent realities are both genuine and permanent. They cannot be explained away by saying that one reality is more fundamental, more advanced, or more primitive than another and that, eventually, we'll all agree on what is eternally and universally real and the good.

Genuine pluralism means that each reality is legitimate on its own terms and expressive of a way of life. Genuine pluralism means that in saying something is true, right, or real, we must always ask: true for whom? True in what context or under what circumstance; true for what purpose or to satisfy what need?

Second, we know that reality is mediated. We do not grasp or see reality face to face but only as it is mediated by notions, concepts, and symbols, including, especially, language. The mediated nature of reality makes pluralism possible. Even our commonsense knowledge of everyday life, apparently self-evident notions about the permanence of objects, time, and space, are cultural inventions. In stressing the mediated nature of reality, James both looked backward to Kant and anticipated Peter Berger and Thomas Luckmann's *The Social Construction of Reality* (1966). The observation that we categorize reality in different ways has by now become commonplace. Students of metaphors, the history of science, and literary tropics, among others, have shown how what we "see" is mediated by metaphors, paradigms, and cultural symbols. Reality is not something we "discover," but something we at least partially fabricate through the mediation of our cultural symbols.

Third, we know that reality is still in the making, and, in that making, we are active, contributing participants. We carve out constellations, ask, "How many stars are there?" and relate their shapes to bears and dippers. Furthermore, we make reality facts by acting on our beliefs for, as James reminds us, "faith in a fact can help create the fact." We believe in our ability to jump the crevasse, and we do; we doubt our ability, and we fail. In both instances, fact follows belief. Reality is not completed or actualized apart from our acts and commitments.

Last, we know the meaning of terms by their consequences. What we think has consequences, whether it involves jumping a crevasse or living in a meaningful universe. No matter how abstract categories may seem, notions have practical, concrete consequences. If terms do not have different consequences, they are functionally equivalent, and our discussions are nonsense. There is no difference of truth that doesn't make a difference of fact somewhere. Persons who place their faith in abstractions or ideals ("Absolutists" in James's vocabulary) live differently than persons who do not. They can, for instance, sanction anything and everything as expressions of the absolute, whereas those who place their faith in pluralism must be willing to live without assurances or guarantees. Similarly, those who believe in an absolute God have a guarantee that there is an ideal order, and that tragedy is only provisional and partial, whereas those without such a belief live in a more uncertain and genuinely tragic world.

How Do We Know?

We know by faithfully acting on our commitments and beliefs. We cannot know, or for that matter actualize, reality apart from acting. I cannot know what it means to jump a crevasse until I make the leap; I cannot know what a hammer means until I act to drive a nail or set a screw. I cannot know the meaning and consequences of believing in the absolute, or alternatively in pluralism, until I act *as if* it were true. Knowledge requires engagement and active verification. Truth is made, not discovered ready-made.

We thus know the meaning of one notion in contrast to another by observing the effect of our beliefs on the acts of our daily lives. But beyond meaning, how do we know whether our notions are true? In a word, we know their truth because they satisfy needs. Truth is proven and verified. Notions are true if they work, in the long run and in congruence with all our other truths. Does a belief work in satisfying some need? If so, the belief is true; if not, the belief is false.

What Does James's Thought Emphasize and What Does It Neglect?

James emphasizes that the world is both pluralist and malleable. We live in an unfinished universe, to which we can add our part. This is a universe that is inherently uncertain, thus requiring our vigorous and active engagement. What's more, the world we help create responds to or is an expression of our needs and interests. We invent a hammer because we need to drive a nail; we identify and name a constellation because it helps us orient ourselves and provides a sense of permanence and perfection in an uncertain and imperfect world. Because truth is determined by a notion's functional efficiency in satisfying needs, it is always contextual rather than absolute. Truth is always contingent and relative to the needs of specific persons, times, and places. The truth of a hammer is that it drives a nail, just as the truth of absolutism is that it provides a seemingly permanent and universal foundation for our notions. Truth is always followed by the questions: true for whom and from what context?

What does James neglect? A pluralistic viewpoint neglects permanence and universality. By emphasizing our ability to contribute and add to reality, pluralism neglects, and thus ill equips us to respond to, those aspects of reality that we cannot change. An optimistic outlook may help me jump a crevasse or form rewarding friendships, but it will not help me overcome death. In the end, I'll die. How does one determine what can be changed and what cannot? To that question, James provides no answer.

By emphasizing the instrumental and extrinsic usefulness of notions, James also neglects the question of what has *intrinsic* value. It is all very well to say that meaning is determined by consequences and truth is determined by the fulfillment of needs, but that does not tell me what needs should be met or how we go about choosing one need rather than another. Furthermore, if any notion—as we have seen even with the notion of God—is ultimately functional and instrumental, then other notions that satisfy those needs can be substituted for it. God is thus neither unique nor irreplaceable, merely functional in providing certain religious experiences. Instrumentalism implies that there is no meaning apart from "an end"; indeed, the meaning is the end in a way that collapses the distinction between meaning and purpose. Thus, for example, the purpose and meaning of school is the "end" of getting a better job; the meaning of work is obtaining money; and the meaning of this life is preparation for the next. This forward-looking quality of pragmatism is reminiscent of Aristotle's theory that meaning resides in the movement toward the fulfillment of a final Form or teleological end. In both instances, intrinsic, terminal value is exchanged for the extrinsic value of that to which a notion leads.

And, finally, James does not discuss the sources of our needs and satisfactions. Are they biological, social, cultural, psychological, or what? Truth cannot be established apart from answering that question, and yet, on that subject, James is largely silent.[37] From whence do those needs come, are they equally legitimate, and to what extent are they either idiosyncratic or universal and timeless? Furthermore, even when we are clear about our intentional goals, how do we decide *what* to choose when the pragmatic results of those choices may not become apparent for generations? The automobile satisfied a need for transportation, but will people generations from now look back on the resources we expended and the global warming to which we contributed and wonder: "What were they thinking!?" To the extent that understanding needs, and the choices that flow from the fulfillment of those needs, is the purview of psychology, James cannot address the philosophical question of truth apart from psychology.

Pragmatism and Meaning

What does James say about the question of meaning? In the first place, he says that it is an important (meaning a *live, forced,* and *momentous*) question, and for two reasons. First, meaning is neither impossible nor certain: we live in a world in which both are possible. Second, how it all turns out—whether our lives are meaningful or meaningless—may depend on us and on what we add to reality. What we add is not merely "subjective"; it is, James says, a "most momentous part of fact." The world may be "objectively" meaningless, but that does not condemn us to meaningless lives. Indeed, one gets the impression in reading James that the most important questions are precisely those that are melioristic or undetermined. James's world may be less certain but it is also more dramatic and meaningful because we have a stake in the outcome.

Regardless of how one answers the question of meaning, James also gives us a litmus test for determining whether, in talking about meaning, we are talking nonsense. Our talk is just that, empty talk, unless we are able to trace a path from our concepts and notions to real consequences in how we act and live. He reminds us that how we answer the meaning question will have consequences in how we perceive, and thus act in, the world. When Tolstoy lived in a meaningful world, he acted and felt one way; when he awoke to an apparently meaningless world, he lived and acted in a world transformed. Meaning takes us to a different place than meaninglessness. Pointedly, we believe *with*, not *in*, our notions. This has always been the case—whether life was meaningful because our lives appealed to myths, Forms, or nature—but here James makes the case that life can be meaningful in the absence of a direct correspondence with another, more real, more universal and eternal realm. Like other notions, meaning is an instrument for action, not an inert duplicate of corresponding realities. The hypothesis of a meaningful universe cannot be substantiated objectively; it must be verified by our commitments and actions. Tutored by James's perceptions, we are encouraged to ask: What sort of instrument is the notion of meaning? How does the question of meaning itself add to reality or function? What happens when we awake and ascribe either meaning or meaninglessness to experience? What is being spoken when we voluntarily break an unconscious silence to ask the question? I shall return to these questions in my Conclusion.

The question of meaning is not a question with a corresponding answer, but an instrument, a tool that directs us to specific realms of experience. In the absence of earlier correspondences (whether to mythic narratives, Forms, or nature), meaning—as a truth—becomes the more or less successful resolution of needs and interests and, in doing so, presses toward either particular biographies or archetypal individualizations in which those needs become manifest. Both the meaning and the truth of a hammer only become apparent in a world that both needs and is populated with nails. Pluralism suggests that there are many meanings that serve to satisfy a corresponding number of different needs and personalities. Implicitly, the "resolution of needs" raises the question of how needs and resolutions are related. For example: Are there many possible resolutions (truths) to the same "need," depending on specific contexts, or is there a plurality of needs as well as of resolutions? What need or interest does the question of meaning address? What is its function?

One way to see how people invest their lives with meaning is to see how meaning fails. For pragmatism, meaning fails in a number of ways. Primarily, it fails if we refuse to *add to* reality through our active, engaged participation. We must act *as if* and believe *with* our notion that the universe is meaningful in order to verify its truth. We can neither wait until all the evidence is in nor hesitate until assurances of formal proofs and objective correspondences to more eternal and universal realities are secured. James wonders at one point: How committed can we be to that which we know we have partially made? How much would you sacrifice if you were self-consciously living *as if* a notion were true? The answer is both momentous and forced. We must decide what to do and act, otherwise all possibility of meaning is lost. We must risk leaping over the crevasse, for it is only in making the attempt that we add our bit to reality and help *make* the truth of the beliefs in which we place our faith.

Lastly, James raises the issue of method. Perhaps the question of meaning cannot be resolved by thinking *about* it. The pragmatist asks: Has thinking *about* questions of meaning made life seem more meaningful? Can thinking about the question take one from meaninglessness to meaning, from darkness to light? If not, if thinking does not resolve the need and persistent urge for meaning, then the method is demonstrably false and untrue. Knowledge *about*, useful as it may be for certain purposes, may nevertheless be an impediment to obtaining wisdom. Instead of conscious thinking *about*, instead of manipulating abstract concepts to achieve instrumental ends, are there other, more intimate and concrete ways of satisfying the need that raising the question of meaning exposes? James suggests that there may be. "[K]nowing may be only one way of getting into fruitful relations with reality," he says. Instead of thinking *about*, instead of ceding "intellectualism undisputed possession of the field," we can—for example—point to examples of imitation, ritualistic participation, and orthopraxis. If so, philosophy and self-conscious, deliberate thought may need to give way to myth, story, and intrinsically satisfying experiences.

Imitation and praxis bring us to James's concluding, radical insight about method. The active pursuit of the question of meaning may reach an impasse. When it does, the world turns upside down, and a turning point is reached, he suggests, where we are saved, not through our own efforts, but through self-despair and a "kind of passive and receptive listening." Paradoxically, we achieve our goal by abandoning our efforts to obtain it. This is the point, I think, when notions, including the notion of meaning, are transformed from instrumental tools for satisfying "other" extrinsic needs and interests to something of intrinsic worth, pleasure, and value. We have been led to a destination beyond which we need not go.

William James is a pivotal figure in the history of meaning. On the one hand, he is representative of many aspects of the scientific age in which he lived, including the presumption of a meaningless universe and the instrumental value of thought in fulfilling human rather than teleological ends. On the other hand, he also anticipates the pluralism of postmodernism, including the coexistence of many possible worlds and the limitations of a scientific worldview. James was an early citizen of the postmodern world in which monotheism and the authority of science were being eroded by an emerging experience of pluralism and relativity. As such, he is particularly useful in introducing us to a host of intriguing questions and in setting the agenda for subsequent chapters.

Chapter 7 examines the work of another James, James Hillman, whose archetypal psychology is attentive to issues that James deals with only in passing. First, Hillman explores more thoroughly than William James the intimate connection between philosophy and psychology, highlighting things we do unself-consciously. William James assumed that we make a conscious decision about whether life has meaning. After all, the title of his famous essay is "The Will to Believe." In contrast, Hillman often speaks of those occasions when we are neither in control nor is our thought instrumental, but when our thought "thinks us," as awkward as this sounds. Archetypal psychology returns us to earlier, mythic ways of thinking, in which devotion, submission, and imitation are more important than rationality and self-conscious decisions, when meaning is granted or found rather than made. Our needs are subconscious as well as conscious. Hillman also presents a way of thinking that is at the same time both more universal and timeless than the pragmatic, contextual thinking of James, but, unlike philosophy, is concurrently nonconceptual, concrete, and imagistic.

Chapter 8 focuses on the work of Huston Smith and the reemergence of metaphysics. Like James, Smith responds to a perception of meaninglessness, but his response takes a very different turn. Beyond a pluralism of appearances and perceptions, Smith reasserts the ancient wisdom that there is an underlying, universal, and timeless truth that successfully responds to the questions James neglects about how one goes about choosing which of many possible worlds is better or worse. From a metaphysical perspective, there is a truth that is not relative or instrumental to my needs and my location in time and space, but that exists independently of whom I am and my circumstances. Smith reminds us that that all values are not instrumental; on the contrary, there are intrinsic values and pleasures that do not locate or deflect meaning forward to a distant "end" or express idiosyncratic or cultural needs.

Chapter 9 focuses on contemporary naturalists. Children of the modern, scientific age in which James wrote, naturalists accept that the universe is meaningless but nevertheless embrace those occasions of intrinsic meaning and celebration that are both entirely in this world and completely satisfying. Naturalists are receptive to spiritual experiences such as awe, humility, and a sense of connectiveness without needing to appeal to purpose, Forms, or teleological ends for meaning. Their spirituality can thrive apart from an association with the historical religions. Paradoxical as it may seem, life in a world without appeal is both miraculous and sufficient.

CHAPTER SEVEN

Archetypal Psychology and Meaning

In the middle of the night, I awake in response to an urgent, insistent demand to urinate. I get up, shuffle down a dark corridor to the bathroom, then return sleepily to bed. I try to get back to sleep, unsuccessfully. By no amount of effort can I will myself to sleep.

Fragments of thoughts and memories tumble over in my mind: a project at work, a snippet of a conversation, a memory of a long-ago trip, the image of a cameo locket. I fall into a restless sleep, dream chaotically and intermittently, and then return to my half-conscious thoughts until morning. The alarm goes off, and I begin the day.

To ask the question we've been asking—"What is the meaning of life?"—may be intelligible, but to ask the question—"What does it mean to awaken in the middle of the night?" seems ludicrous. The first impulse is to say, "It doesn't mean anything. It just *is*. If anything, it just means that my prostate is larger than when I was younger."

James Hillman—widely credited with being the founder of archetypal psychology—argues in his intriguing and representative book *The Force of Character* that getting up at night in fact does mean something; it cannot be explained away or dismissed as merely a biological impulse. "Suppose . . . that getting up from sleep awakens you not only *in* the night, but *to* the night," he says provocatively.[1] In a diminutive tour de force, he similarly claims that the meaning of other symptoms of getting older—memory loss, declining eroticism, and irritability, for example—are likewise not exhausted by either biological causality or prospects of inevitable decline. On the contrary, each is a presentation and embodiment of character, and thus an initiation into another way of life. "Can we entertain the idea," he asks, "that all along our earthly life has been phenomenal, a showing, a presentation?"[2] The insight of old age, he adds, is that it deliteralizes biology. To understand what Hillman means by these idiomatic expressions, we need to learn more about the archetypal psychology that he champions and the associated strategy for meaning it exemplifies. An archetypal strategy of meaning combines aspects of the mythic, scientific, and philosophical strategies examined earlier, while adding its own unique flavor.

THE ARCHETYPE

In his foundational work *Re-Visioning Psychology*, James Hillman variously describes archetypes as the "deepest patterns of psychic functioning," the "frames of our consciousness," the "root metaphors," and the psychic "premises" or "structures" that literally inform the perspectives we have of the world and ourselves. Archetypes are similar to the axiomatic, a priori self-evident images, categories, or first principles discussed earlier in connection with myth, Kant, and the models and paradigms of science. They are the psychic premises that make all knowledge and experience possible. Acting as human substitutes for the patterned, recurrent instincts guiding animal behavior, archetypes are, according to Hillman, manifested in the "the *genres* and *tropi* in literature; the recurring typicalities in history; the basic syndromes in psychiatry; the paradigmatic thought models in science; [and] the world-wide figures, rituals, and relationships in anthropology."[3] Archetypes, Hillman goes on to say, provide the "patterns of our thinking as well as our feeling and doing. They give all our psyche functions—whether thinking, feeling, perceiving, or remembering—their imaginal life, their internal coherence, their force, their necessity, and their ultimate intelligibility."[4]

Archetypes are ontologically fundamental, equivalent to Plato's Forms and Aristotle's universals. Human reality is *wholly* dependent on archetypal fantasies. They are, Hillman proclaims, the "only existents that are not reducible to something other than their imagery; only they are as they literally appear; only fantasies are utterly incontrovertibly real."[5] As such, they are prior to all other *apparent* realities and thus more real, powerful and valuable. This ontological priority means that archetypes are inescapable. Our choices and decisions *always* reflect archetypal or mythic stances and patterns. "We are always in one or another root-metaphor, archetypal fantasy, mythic perspective," Hillman asserts, "All things are determined by psyche images."[6] Our knowledge (including our scientific and profane knowledge), our actions, our emotions, even our sense of self all derive from the archetypes. Accordingly, we are not autonomous, willful egos but are in truth on loan from a more fundamental realm.

We do not have ideas or emotions, or even a self; on the contrary, informing archetypal fantasies have us. Or as Mircea Eliade succinctly stated it, turning the phrase of the existentialists upside down in discussing the archetypal role of myth, "the essential precedes existence."[7]

What this means in practice is an incarnational view of the universe. Behind, beneath, or above the material world is the world of archetypes. Causality has a source beyond what's apparent. The scholar of religion David Miller approvingly quotes his mentor and colleague Hillman as saying: "We cannot be in the physical world without at the same time and all the time demonstrating an archetypal structure."[8] Our task is to *see though* or *deliteralize* the material world in order to glimpse the archetypes that both structure our behavior and thought and lend them meaning, credibility, and authority. What Hillman calls *pathologizing* means turning something literal and common into something "unknown and deep." It means discovering that the psyche (expressed through archetypes) is speaking imaginatively in what we had been taking for granted as literal and one-dimensional. From this perspective, the material—as well as a materialistic philosophy—is itself a fantasy. Literal action— whether political, scientific, or personal—is always a metaphorical enactment or an incarnation of an archetypal fantasy. Our actions and thoughts today and at this moment are expressions of more universal and timeless archetypes.

Mircea Eliade calls the process of linking the day-to-day with a sacred, archetypal, or mythical realm a *hierophany*. A hierophany occurs whenever—through some detail of landscape, artifact, or behavior—the sacred is revealed or shows itself. Informed by this other realm, a material object is deliteralized and at the same time transformed into something sacred or mythological. A hierophany does not deny the material object but sees the material as an incarnation of another, more meaningful realm. Acts become rituals. Similarly, *pathologizing* (again to use Hillman's term) links or sees through events and ideas to their archetypal roots, to their "ultimate hidden value," and, in so doing, lifts otherwise barren facts from their literalness by giving them significance and meaning. Sounding very Platonic, Hillman concludes by saying that "all things desire to return to the archetypal origins of which they are copies and from which they proceed."[9]

The terms *archetype* and *myth* are virtually interchangeable here. We search for the significance of events, Hillman says, in their "archetypal or mythical patterns," looking for the "myths within the facts, the archetypal patterns that can broaden and deepen connections." A fundamental characteristic of archetypes— a characteristic that distinguishes them from abstract concepts— is their expression as images. All consciousness, feelings, and ideas, Hillman asserts, must present themselves as images. The most compelling of these images, in turn, are of persons. *Personifying* signifies a way of being in and experiencing the world, a way of knowing, in which vivid, compelling archetypes are perceived as persons. Our most fundamental ideas and root metaphors are expressions of persons, "Hero, Nymph, Mother, Senex, Child, trickster, Amazon, Puer, and many other specific prototypes bearing the names and stories of the Gods," according to Hillman, "keep our persons in order, holding into significant patterns the segments and fragments of behavior we call emotions, memories, attitudes, and motives."[10]

The stories of those persons who "keep our persons" in order are structured or fall into the narratives we call myths, which, unlike abstract concepts, communicate to us directly in ways that are emotional, dramatic, and sensuous. They speak to us of universals (like Platonic Forms), but they do so in specific, concrete images of figures, places, and events that paradoxically have never happened but always happen. The great myths, of which Greek myths are a subset, reveal the structure of our thoughts and emotions.[11] By acquainting ourselves with these myths, we are able see the imaginative patterns that articulate our actions. In so doing, we deliteralize our lives by grounding them in another ontological order. A mythic or archetypal perspective does not ask of an event "Why?" or "How?" It asks "Which?" archetype (or personifies by asking "Who?") or myth this event brings to light or reveals?

A CRITICAL DIFFERENCE

The difference between archetypes and either Forms or myths can be stated simply: unlike Forms and myths, archetypes do not depend on belief in either a supernatural or a metaphysical realm. The authority of archaic myth depends on a belief in the existence of mythic gods and stories; that is, on an ontologically different, eternal, and superior realm outside or above our day-to-day existence. The stories of the gods are exemplary and true precisely because they are narratives of the supernaturals. Thus, for example, the story of Jesus Christ is exemplary of how I should live, and revelatory of the nature of reality, because it is the story of a god, a transcendent supernatural being who is born of a virgin and is resurrected, unlike a mortal. Similarly, for Plato, the objects and ideas of the phenomenal world are imperfect imitations of an eternal and changeless metaphysical realm of Forms. Truth and justice, as well as perfect trees and flowers, are grounded in the metaphysical. We move from shadows projected against the wall of the cave to the light of day. This other, transcendent and changeless world, whether of gods or Forms, makes sense and gives significance to our impermanent and otherwise meaningless lives.

Both archaic myths and idealistic philosophy are thus sustained by a belief in a transcendent realm. When belief in the existence of this realm is eroded, so too the informing power and luminosity of the derivative myth or Idea is eroded. The myth becomes merely a primitive, quaint story—myth as a "false story" in the pejorative sense—or is subjected to allegorization. Bereft of a sustaining realm of eternal Forms, beauty and justice become merely names, convenient, pragmatic, or politicized categories and abstractions, without any corresponding substance. Secularization, if not cynicism, describes what happens when belief in the transcendent realm sustaining myth and idealism is eroded.

Like myth and idealism, archetypes also point to a different reality, but the reality to which they point is neither transcendently supernatural nor metaphysical; rather, it is "inside" and natural. Archetypes offer us the familiar division between the phenomenal world and another world of greater depth and eternal truth without requiring us to believe in either supernatural gods or metaphysical Forms and ideals. As such, they are able to satisfy a persistent hunger for escape and transcendence, for something more than this day-to-day existence, within a wholly secular or scientific framework. The process of sanctifying reality is the same—one of seeing through the veil of this transient world to the reality of another more permanent world—but the form and presumptions are entirely different.

Sir James Frazer, Carl Jung, Mircea Eliade, and Joseph Campbell discovered and documented recurring myths and images across cultures and generations, but they located these archetypes in the human psyche. Images and stories of virgin births, great floods, the separation of heaven from hell, and the death and resurrection of a god-man occur universally around the globe and in our dreams. Outside of local and historically conditioned variations, one can objectively, scientifically identify the same underlying images and stories. The first task of "any systematic comparison of the myths and religions of mankind should therefore be . . . to identify these universals," Campbell writes.[12] These recurring, apparently biologically innate, stories and images, have been associated inter alia as the German anthropologist and ethnologist Adolf Bastian's *Elementargedanken,* or "elementary ideas"; as Jung's archetypes of the "collective unconscious"; and as Aldous Huxley's "perennial philosophy." If modern Christians can no longer believe in a supernatural virgin birth, Christ's resurrection, or the heavenly Promised Land as mythic fact and literal truth, they can nevertheless believe that, beneath the apparent randomness of day-to-day living, there are life-sustaining patterns in the depths of the human unconscious. Again, the transcendence available with these archetypes does not require belief in an abstract, supernatural, or metaphysical realm; on the contrary, for Jung, Eliade, and their colleagues, their existence is objectively and scientifically established through the study of dreams and comparative anthropology and religion. The occurrence of widespread archetypes establishes an objective, disinterested foundation for realms that were formerly dismissed in the scientific era as being merely subjective, irrational, and arbitrary. I recall seeing a film some years ago of an interview with Jung who, when asked if he believed in God, faced the camera directly and replied slowly (and ambiguously) that he did not believe in God, he knew.

A second way archetypes are different from either archaic myths or idealism is their limited scope. Archetypes explain and deepen human motivation and behavior, but they neither attempt, like myths, to explain the origins of a sacred place or object nor try to provide a transcendent Form of "dogness," for example, that would explain how a boxer, spaniel, and shepherd can all be identified as dogs. By limiting themselves to specifically human acts and perceptions, archetypes retain their significance in the modern era by not challenging or violating the explanatory canons of science, including materialism and causality. Archetypes may provide insight into why I find this story rather than that compelling; they may contribute depth, hope, and meaning to my everyday life; they may even explain why I act the way I do. But they do not, and deliberately do not, seek to explain why the earth revolves around the sun or a wolf howls at the moon.

Finally, a third way archetypes are different from archaic myths is that the latter were local. That is to say, the believers in archaic myths generally did not know about the myths of other peoples or places. As a result, their locally conditioned myths were unchallenged as unique sources of orientation and explanation. In contrast, the contemporary study of mythology and archetypes is inherently comparative. This comparative perspective undermines the authority of any single mythology and acts as an impediment to seeing myths as either literally descriptive or unquestionable true. The comparative approach thus produces paradoxical results. On the one hand, it undermines the authority of any single or local myth, while on the other, it establishes the existence and authority of myths in general—as well as their underlying archetypes—by demonstrating mythology's widespread and recurring patterns.

Whether by limiting its scope, by presenting its findings as objective and disinterested, or by demonstrating the widespread occurrence of myths, archetypal psychology represents a creative accommodation of mythic and philosophical thought to the dictates of a scientific or modern mind that insistently rejects either supernaturalism or idealism. As such, it retains the significance of myth and idealism for an era beyond belief.

COGNITIVE SCIENCE AND ARCHETYPES

One question that archetypes elicit is this: how does one explain the reoccurrence of the "same" archetypal image and story in various places and times, both cross-culturally and in our dreams? What is the source of the widespread story of the solitary, somewhat mysterious hero for example? How can this archetypal story paradoxically be both very concrete and specific, yet universal and timeless?

One answer to that question is offered by the emerging field of cognitive science. Like all science, cognitive science seeks to explain all phenomena in terms of an exclusively materialistic causal sequence. Cognitive science attempts to demonstrate that the most basic of our concepts, including the concepts of time, essence, reason, mind, and causation—as well as friendship, failure, and lies—rely on concealed or unconsciously held metaphors. Metaphors, in turn, are derivative of our perceptual and motor systems, the neural structures of our brains, and the "specifics of our everyday functioning in the world."[13] Human bodily movement, manipulation of objects and perceptual interactions involve reoccurring patterns or "image schemata." These basic gestalts are progressively extended metaphorically and applied to increasingly abstract categories. This means that reason and idealistic categories are not a transcendent feature of the universe or of a disembodied mind; they are rooted in our physical bodies. Their universal, timeless quality is something we share as embodied human beings, rather than reflecting an ideal, Platonic realm.

For cognitive science, metaphors are functionally equivalent to myths and archetypes because they shape how we conceptualize all aspects of our experience, "how we think, what we experience, and what we do every day," as two founders of the discipline put it.[14] Whether intentional or not, it is appropriate that the title of George Lakoff and Mark Johnson's pioneering book on cognitive science, *Metaphors We Live By*, echoes the title of Joseph Campbell's book *Myths to Live By*. Like the familiar distinction myth draws between this day-to-day world and the more fundamental, informing world of myth, cognitive science speaks of the "hidden hand" of our conceptual and metaphorical systems that unself-consciously informs how we comprehend experience and defines our unreflective common sense and metaphysics. Reflecting the science in cognitive science, there is no disembodied mind, soul, or reason. All categories, including the most abstract and transcendent of categories, are attributable to an exclusively materialistic causal sequence, beginning with the capabilities and limitations of the human body. From the perspective of cognitive science, philosophy is in the flesh; the mind is always embodied; and meaning, imagination, and reason have a basis in bodily movement and perceptions.

Cognitive science deals largely with the meaning of terms and categories and not the larger question of life meaning. As a result, it does not speak to our concerns with the same immediacy as archetypes, with which it shares many characteristics. Nevertheless, it offers a provocative and fundamental reinterpretation of Western thought that may contribute to the question of meaning more generally. For those who are intrigued, the sources listed in the bibliography offer a starting point for further study.

THE CHARACTERISTICS OF ARCHETYPES

Archetypes exhibit two complexes of related characteristics.

1. Archetypes are autonomous, generative, and god-like.
   At one point during his extensive descriptions of archetypes, Hillman says that one thing is "absolutely essential" to the notion. What is that essential thing? Hillman says it is "their emotional possessive effect, their bedazzlement of consciousness, so that it becomes blind to its own stance."[15] What this means is that we do not choose or control archetypes; they control us. They do not serve us; we serve them. They are the "autonomous psychic contents," the "*a priori* element" in all our moods, reactions, thoughts, and actions. We do not project the archetypes of beauty or love or order onto the world from our subjective experience; on the contrary, we find beauty, love, and order in the world already and respond to them. Hillman evokes Aristotle's concept of Form to articulate the notion that archetypes, as an expression of soul, are the "active intelligence" that

forms and plots each person's fate. Noncorporal archetypes and fantasies define the final aims and purposes
behind our incarnated acts and thoughts. Archetypal
Forms are thus, Hillman concludes, the "shaping force
of the visible."[16] All experience begins in the "breath"
or "subtle" body of archetypal fantasies.

Both the autonomy and the bedazzling effect of
archetypes become apparent when we consider dreams,
emotions, symptoms, preferences, behaviors, and modes
of thought. In each case, reflection reveals that we are
compelled and constrained by forces we do not fully
control. Like Saint Paul, we symptomatically say and do
things we do not wish to say and do; we fall in and out
of love, we are subject to thoughts and prejudices that
seem beyond our conscious ability to change. Dreams
come to me during the night, and when I awake, I
cannot make myself go back to sleep. Hillman stresses
that our afflictions and emotions come and go, not by
our will or conscious intention, but by factors independent of our control. By so doing, they provide
insight into the autonomy and power of archetypal
Forms. In this connection, it is appropriate to recall
how Tolstoy spoke about the insistence of the questions "Why?" and "Why not?" in terms of contracting
a fatal disease.

The potency and autonomy of archetypes suggest
a comparison and establish a link between archetypes
and mythology. Hillman uses the term *personifying* to
indicate how we transform archetypes into persons
and narrative events that touch and move us in a way

that more abstract concepts cannot. The ability of these archetypal persons to structure our consciousness with such force and possession leads Hillman to say that we might as well call them gods, as people did in the past. In considering the similarly bedazzling effect of myth and archetype, recall the power of movies to fully arrest and engage our attention, discussed in chapter 2.

From a personifying perspective, the question "What archetype lies behind and structures my experience and actions?" becomes the question "Who?" "To which archetypal figure or god is my vision loyal? What god is at work when I do this rather than that, am compelled by an idea or symptom beyond my control?" For archetypal psychology, Hillman notes, there is "a God in every perspective. . . . All things present themselves to consciousness in the shapings of one or another divine perspective. Our vision is mimetic to one or another of the Gods."[17] We neither choose nor project our gods or goddesses; on the contrary, they manifest themselves in us and in our behavior or, as David Miller puts it, "The Gods grab us, and we play out their stories."[18]

Archetypes are like gods then, but with two qualifications. First, the gods of archetypes are limited in their potency to affecting human perspectives and meanings. They inform how we perceive and experience the world, and in turn our actions, but they cannot literally or naïvely explain the dividing of the Red Sea or feeding the five thousand with five loaves and two fishes. And second, as noted earlier, the gods of archetypal psychology are not located in heaven or on Mount Olympus, but in the human psyche.

2. Archetypes are symptomatic, impersonal, universal, and timeless.

The notion that we are not fully in control, that our actions and thoughts are informed by loyalties to a priori, hidden gods and goddesses is unsettling. To acknowledge the potency and existence of gods goes against everything we believe. We are accustomed to and comfortable with thinking that God is dead, and that there is a little ego in our heart or brain sitting at the controls, consciously deciding where to steer us. Indeed, the entire Enlightenment project—including a liberal education—can be seen as an effort to free us from the unconscious dictates of religion, culture, and society, to the point that we can make our own autonomous, rational decisions. We are repelled by "unthinking," irrational fanatics of all persuasions because of their unquestioning loyalty to the gods of nation, class, or race. From this perspective, we are less human and self-actualized the more we are subject to unconscious drives and directives.

Hillman asks us to consider the notion that the gods are still alive! Reflecting his clinical practice, Hillman points out that symptoms—like dreams, emotions, preferences, and modes of thought—highlight those occasions when we are compelled to acknowledge that there are forces in our lives (as well as our societies) that we cannot fully control. The gods force themselves symptomatically into awareness. Symptoms occur without, and often against, my deliberate intentions; their presence is an alien visitation. Whence they come I do not know. Symptoms end the rule of the heroic ego. The Enlightenment had it wrong. It said that we could choose between dark irrational impulses and the bright light of conscious, rational decisions. In contrast, Hillman wants us to consider the radical notion that our choice is not between darkness and light but between which of the gods to follow, since following one god or the other is inescapable.

If we are not in control, if, on the contrary, some archetype or god informs all our moods and actions, then "my" actions are, paradoxically, not "mine." To identify my actions with my "ego," with my individual and idiosyncratic personality is to literalize "me" and, in so doing, to fall victim to what Hillman calls the "personalistic fallacy,"[19] or, perhaps more accurately, the personalistic archetype or myth. From this perspective, our actions are oddly impersonal and dehumanized, because we can no longer speak so possessively about "my soul," "my feelings," "my emotions," "my afflictions," and "my dreams." Our feelings and thoughts are, paradoxically, not ours. Statements that express my deepest personhood, such as "I love you" or "I am afraid" are collective universals, whose value lies precisely in their impersonality, that they are said by everyone, everywhere. The old saw that no sin is original applies to the other emotions as well. Thinking archetypally means connecting concrete human events with their impersonal divine background in such a way that they become universal, transpersonal, and timeless. Myths give our unreality a significant context. We become more human, not through becoming more self-conscious and rational, but by identifying and connecting with the gods and archetypes we both imitate and serve. By connecting what goes on in my individual life with what goes on in the lives and dreams of all people, in all places and in all times, archetypes connect me to something essentially human.

IS THERE AN ARCHETYPE IN THE ARCHETYPE?

Archetypal psychology says that we cannot escape archetypes; they structure and inform *all* our thoughts, emotions, and consciousness. Ideas and narratives are compelling, seem so intrinsically familiar and certain, and carry weight and authority precisely because they embody or incarnate underlying archetypes. If this is true, what about the archetype of the archetype? If an archetypal perspective seems compelling, what archetype does it represent?

Throughout this study, we have seen a recurring pattern of division between the real and the more real. With myth, the profane world is a reflection of the sacred; with philosophy, the world of passing appearances imperfectly embodies a realm of eternal Forms; with science, objective, mathematically describable laws replace our subjective opinions and feelings; with postmodernism, a raised consciousness that reality is socially constructed dispels the idea that reality is singular and *is* as it appears to *us*. This same division between appearance and a hidden, greater reality is also expressed in the stories of our culture: the prince hidden in the frog, the clues to the detective story that are both concealed and in front of our eyes, and the bread and wine that are transubstantiated into the body and blood of Christ. In each of these instances, the taken-for-granted world of the everyday conceals a hidden, deeper reality. Archetypal psychology extends this pattern and fundamental division by seeing though the literalism of the everyday to reveal the recurring archetypes that structure and inform our acts, emotions, and thoughts. When seen though, the everyday has depths and shadows. The perception that another reality is hidden within our commonsense, taken-for-granted reality is a persistent archetype. It is the "archetype of the archetype" and a fundamental categorization of reality that is both extended once again by the perennial philosopher and challenged, though not defeated, by proponents of naturalism. Before proceeding to both that extension and challenge, however, let us conclude by asking our four summarizing questions.

FOUR QUESTIONS
What Do We Know?

We know three things.

First, as just noted, we know that the literal, taken-for-granted world of the everyday can be seen through to reveal recurring, archetypal symbols, narratives, and ideas. Largely subconscious archetypes structure and inform our thoughts, emotions, and actions and provide depth and coherence to our lives. In so doing, archetypes are comparable to the gods of old.

Second, the bedazzling effect and potency of archetypes suggest that we are not fully in control, meaning that our decisions and choices are not entirely our own. We cannot take our autonomous, self-directing ego literally, but must see that it, too, is one of many possible archetypes structuring our consciousness. Being in control and making rational choices is only one of many possible ways of being: archetypally, only one of many possibly gods.

Third, archetypes are not subjective and idiosyncratic either to individuals or societies; on the contrary, they are collective, fixed, eternal, and universal, recurring throughout the human species. The existence and identification of archetypes has been observed objectively in dream analysis and comparative studies in anthropology, mythology, and religion. More speculatively, cognitive science suggests that archetypes may arise from the universal limitations and capabilities of our human, material bodies.

How Do We Know?

We know about archetypes, first, because of the cross-cultural, historical, psychological, and anthropological studies that have revealed the existence or manifestation of a limited number of basic, recurring symbols, narratives, and ideas. The occurrence of these recurring patterns requires an explanation that the category of archetypes seeks to provide. That explanation does not depend on belief in a divinely sanctioned, sacred realm of archaic myths or Platonic Forms but rests squarely on human psychology and biology.

Second, we know the bedazzling potency of archetypes because it is revealed on those occasions when we are not fully in control, when our ability to act on the basis of fully conscious, rational decisions is compromised. We cannot make ourselves fall in and out of love, the Middle East is perpetually caught up in a seemingly unending cycle of violence, we act out prejudices and presumptions about class, race, and beauty, we symptomatically do the things we don't want to do and don't do the things we wish we would, and—paradigmatically—our dreams come and go autonomously during the one-third of our lives we spend sleeping. As Jung observed, the gods have become our "diseases," manifesting themselves in our symptomatic obsessions and addictions. Archetypes are an explanatory category for helping us understand our human limitations and inability to be fully intentional.

What Do Archetypes Emphasize and What Do They Neglect?

By emphasizing that we are *inescapably and always* serving and imitating hidden archetypes, archetypal psychology radically challenges the Enlightenment ideal (or more accurately the Enlightenment archetype) of the fully conscious, autonomous, rational individual. Our first impulse is to deny the autonomous reality, and often irrationality, of the archetypal gods. Easier to say that archetypes are representative allegories, instrumental symbols, colorful metaphors, or educational homilies or conceits than to admit their autonomous existence and power. Twenty-five years after the fact, I still recall the moment during a Hillman lecture when I was shocked to realize that he really believed in the autonomy and power of archetypes. They weren't just the fruit of humankind's ability to create metaphors and symbols but were active, independent agents in their own right.

Archetypes, like archaic myths, emphasize continuity and conformity to a corpus of timeless, universal emotions, images, and narratives. Paradoxically, our deepest emotions and most heartfelt acts are impersonal and unoriginal. By establishing a link to archetypal myths, our most personal, concrete experiences become universalized—the poetical concrete universals that express events that have never happened but have always happened. Through archetypes, we participate in a different ontological order. Act becomes ritual. Archetypes emphasize the necessity and inevitability of grounding our day-to-day lives in a deeper, more universal and eternal context.

Principally, archetypes neglect our ability to make autonomous, self-conscious, rational, and intentional decisions. They compromise our ability to make genuine choices. In contrast, think back for a moment to our discussion of William James and his emphasis on the power of choosing, of deliberately deciding even in those situations when not all of the evidence on which to make a decision is available. The "will" in William James's "The Will to Believe" is not ours but a manifestation of a deeper archetype. Paradoxically, archetypes deny, or at least deemphasize, the ideals of the Enlightenment, while concurrently accepting the notion that they are nevertheless established by scientific methodologies as being both real and objective.

Second, archetypes deemphasize the emergence of the genuinely new, whether new behaviors or new ways of constituting the world. Seeing through contemporary life by linking my actions with archetypal Greek myths strains credibility when my life is cluttered with e-mail and the virtual reality of video games.

Is there nothing—no technology, social arrangement, or level of consciousness—that is genuinely new? Whether or how new gods or archetypes emerge on the scene is a question that archetypal psychology largely ignores.

Archetypal Psychology and Meaning

Archetypal psychology is an immensely rich area for investigating the question of meaning. Its success in reintroducing a sense of life-meaning to a nominally scientific age is attested to by the popularity of contemporary works such as Thomas Moore's *The Care of the Soul* and Hillman's *The Force of Character*, in addition to the classic texts of Jung.

Archetypal psychology speaks to the question of meaning in at least four ways.

First, meaning occurs whenever events, emotions, and thoughts in everyday life are connected to their informing archetypes. Soul, which is not a thing or object but a perspective, signals a seeing though the ordinary in a way that connects what is evident to otherwise hidden archetypes that are at once more real, powerful, and valuable. The most fundamental significance of events rests in the archetypal or mythical patterns they manifest. Archetypes give ordinary life depth, value, and meaning. They are the foundation of our lives, the gods of nation, ideology, culture, and religion on which we, as David Miller says arrestingly, "depend for deliverance from sheer nothingness and the utter inconsequence of existence."[20]

To say this in another way, a lack of life-meaning occurs whenever we fail to connect the everyday to its archetypal foundations or footings. Symptoms such as meaninglessness, emptiness, and a vague yearning for personal and spiritual fulfillment reflect this failure. What are the causes of this failure? One is literalization—that is, failing to see through the day-to-day and either denying or simply not knowing about the enormous corpus of available myths and archetypes for giving our lives depth and shadow. Life seems meaningless, is without depth, whenever we try to skate only on its evident surface. We live in secular time, ignorant of the mythic patterns and eternal time in which we live and from which we cannot escape. "We do not see," as Hillman says, "that the new is the old come round again, and that to understand the new we must return to the old."[21]

A second way archetypes offer a strategy for meaning is their ability to provide—like Forms—an end, purpose, or intelligence. Thus Hillman argues that the symptoms of our later years change in their significance when we find their purpose to be a manifestation or embodiment of character. Our otherwise random acts and thoughts gain in meaning and intelligence to the extent that we see them as unconscious imitations of mythic patterns and structures. Perhaps I'm floundering in my job search, or as a parent, until I discover my direction and purpose by seeing myself as a warrior, magician, or craftsman. Inspired by the archetypal stories of what it means to be a soldier, young men courageously and stoically go into battle. Inflamed by the rags-to-riches archetype of the successful entrepreneur, young workers are motivated to sacrifice themselves for the prospect of future riches. Paradoxically, by becoming more aware of these archetypal patterns, we are also liberated from the compulsion to unwittingly serve them. If the devil's wiliest trick is to convince us he does not exist, myths that we do not know we have have us.

A third way archetypes are related to meaning involves not taking "meaninglessness" literally but symptomatically. We need to see through meaninglessness itself by asking: "What is the myth or archetype within meaninglessness?" Rather than trying to deny or solve the problem of meaninglessness, we need to ask "What is its depth?" and "Of what is it a manifestation?" The experiences of Tolstoy and William James, the existential novels of Albert Camus, and the plays of Samuel Beckett all reflect recurring archetypal patterns. Our experience of meaninglessness can itself be given depth and intelligence by connecting it to these archetypes. The experience of meaninglessness can evoke thoughts and feelings that are otherwise not available in our sunnier moments. As such, the sense of meaninglessness and the insistent questions "Why?" and "What for?" are neither good nor bad but manifestations of a different, albeit darker god. Speaking as a therapist, the archetypal psychologist Thomas Moore links depression, a close companion of meaninglessness, to mythologies about Saturn and a necessary witnessing to the death of our old assumptions and ways of life so that a new life can be born.[22] It's an old story: birth and death are inscrutably paired. Saturn adds weight, depth, and substance to our experience. From an archetypal perspective, meaninglessness is not the menacing phantom that shadowed James and Tolstoy but a gift and portal to a less naïve, less fanatical form of faith.

Fourth, and finally, archetypal psychology advances the disturbing notion that we do not find or create meaning, but that meaning finds us, or fails to find us, as *it* wills. We are alternatively inspired or abandoned by the gods in a way that is beyond our conscious will and intentions. We inescapably live symptomatic lives. Theologically, we are reminded that salvation is through grace rather than works. We cannot force inspiration, love, or passion; we can only wait patiently with expectation, preparation, and hope.

Archetypal psychology combines aspects of myth, philosophy, science, and postmodernism. In so doing, it has proven a compelling source of meaning for many. Nevertheless, its reliance on seemingly archaic myths, and its expression in the language of gods and goddesses, remains a stumbling block. Belief in autonomous, invisible archetypes that are compelling, universal, and timeless is often no easier than believing in a conventional God or a realm of transcendent Forms. In chapter 9, we examine a source of meaning that insistently proclaims the adequacy of living in this world and this world only. Seeing though or transcending daily life—whether to myth, Forms, or archetypes—is both unsustainable and unnecessary for living a meaningful life. Before examining that alternative, however, in the next chapter we see another example of how people invest their lives with meaning by appealing to a metaphysical realm beyond our day-to-day, taken-for-granted experience.

CHAPTER EIGHT

Metaphysics and Meaning

... to be properly human, you must go beyond the merely
human.

E. F. Schumacher, *A Guide for the Perplexed*

Is there another, transcendent dimension beyond which we and
our instruments cannot count, measure, or weigh? Is there a metaphysics beyond the exclusively materialistic physics on which
science and the modern outlook are based? How we answer that
question is fundamental. For what's at stake is how we answer a
host of associated questions, such as the possibility of life after
death, the intrinsic value of human life and nature, and—for
many—the very concept of a meaningful life.

Historically, the rejection of metaphysics separates us from
previous ages, and perhaps even today from the majority of
humankind. For moderns who accept the tenets of empirical science, the question of whether there is anything beyond the physical seemed settled long ago, and for good reason. The benefits
of science and of deliberately limiting ourselves to physics are
that it works spectacularly well. Penicillin is more effective than
prayer; telephones are more effective than smoke signals. Every
day we make decisions based on publicly available evidence,

predictability, and reason, rather than the less certain guidance of tradition, feelings, and intuition. As a modern, I want objective facts, not subjective impressions or opinions. I want to discover a sequential, causal connection that I can ultimately control, rather than relying on unpredictable divine—that is, metaphysical—intervention. Because of the effectiveness of science, it is easy to dismiss those who cling to a belief in metaphysics, whether in previous ages or our own, as primitive, underdeveloped, or simply nostalgic. Like a belief in Santa Claus, metaphysics is something we leave behind as we individually and collectively mature.

Progress and the associated movement from superstition and magic to science is a familiar and triumphant story. Nevertheless, persistent critics of science, or, more accurately, of scientism and the dismissal of metaphysics on which it rests, point to at least two deficiencies.

First, critics argue that scientism excludes a good part of what makes life human, including beauty, love, values, and life-meanings. Transcendence or positing the existence of a realm beyond a singular ontological plane is excluded as literally "immaterial," meaning for us irrelevant. The material plane is all that there is. All that matters is matter. The most complex phenomena, such as human consciousness, values, love, and religion can be reduced to, and explained by, exclusively material causes. Nonmaterial causes are excluded on principle. To speak of a better world, or a truer world, or a world that is intrinsically valuable—that is, a world that suggests a different ontological plane—is literally to speak non-sense. Science deals with questions of means, not ends. The excluded questions of ends—"What should I do with my life?"; "Why is there evil?"; "Does Life have meaning?"—are ones that science cannot answer—indeed, it seems strange even to raise them. Science does not have a vocabulary in which these questions can be articulated. But what is sacrificed or left out when we indulge in what Huston Smith has called "ontological strip mining"? Simply, the world of values and purposes in which people had thought themselves to be living.

The dismissal of metaphysics has a second deficiency: it fails on pragmatic grounds, that is, it does not lead to a better life. Alienation, anomie, nihilism, meaninglessness, a pervasive spiritual malaise—these have become a recurring theme as the age of reason has given way to the age of anxiety. Commenting on a dramatic drop in European birthrates, one observer has said, in an arresting phrase, that Christian Europe's loss of faith has resulted in the "loss [of] the biological will to live."[1]

Critically, the negative, unintentional consequences of a scientific perspective were present in its materialistic ontology from the start. Protected by faith and cultural traditions from the barren, material world that science reveals, it is only now that we can clearly see the darker side of science: that its constricted worldview has brought alienation. Modernization forces upon us a world that is denuded of all humanly recognizable qualities, including beauty and ugliness, love and hate, passion and fulfillment, sin and redemption. A person who restricts his or her attention to only what can be counted, measured, and weighed lives, *necessarily*, in a very poor world. We are thus trying to live fulfilling lives in an incomplete, inferior world. "Our own age," the Elizabethan scholar E. M. W. Tillyard says in passing, "need not begin congratulating itself on its freedom from superstition till it defeats a more dangerous temptation to despair."[2]

Paul Tillich is famous for defining religion as the "ultimate concern." This can be taken either psychologically or ontologically. In the former, more typical reading, "ultimate concern" means whatever happens to concern the person the most, whether it be sex, ambition, sports, popular culture, keeping up with the Joneses, or whatever. This is to define religion functionally. In this view, religion is an honorific title, and we can easily and unself-consciously talk about golf being a man's religion. In contrast, an ontological reading of ultimate concern suggests that religion is concerned with what is in fact ontologically ultimate. In this view, reality is graduated into different levels. Some levels are more real than others; correspondingly, some concerns are more ultimate than others. Religion is an ultimate concern because it is concerned with that which is ultimate, meaning that which is most real, or most true. In this view, our world is meaningless because we are concerned with a level of reality where meaning cannot flourish or be sustained.

To speak about what is most true and most real goes against the pervasive assumptions of the world in which we live. For us, viewing the world as exclusively material is just common sense. As a result, we have difficulty with describing something as more or less real than something else. Science tutors us that there is one and only one ontological level, and that level is exclusively materialistic and value-neutral. At best, we have "subjective" or "community-based" values. To understand the world in which phrases such as more Real and more True make sense requires two steps. First, I shall briefly revisit the material introduced in chapter 4 to understand more clearly the relationship between science and metaphysics. And second, I shall describe in some detail the metaphysical, hierarchical view of the universe whose qualitative ordering principle is directly opposed to the quantitative ordering principle of a materialistic physics. The terms *greater* or *lesser* have entirely different meanings when understood qualitatively and quantitatively. Seeing the world metaphysically is nothing short of an invitation to live in another world.

BE CAREFUL WHAT YOU WISH FOR

The heart of science, and the materialism on which it rests, is the motivation to control. Science has made a Promethean bargain with knowing the world: x counts as knowledge if it leads to prediction and control.[3] What leads to control? Control is facilitated by focusing on primary qualities (size, weight, and measure) and an analytic, experiential method that reduces complex phenomena to simpler, atomistic units arranged in causal sequences. If a quality does not demonstrably contribute to prediction and control, it is ignored. Science is thus selective about that to which it is attentive. It is concerned primarily only with those aspects of truth or reality that are useful for manipulation or to achieve pragmatic ends. The rocket scientist—as a scientist—does not care, and thus ignores, whether the missile is carrying an American or Chinese flag to the moon. The laws of physics do not recognize national boundaries. The scientist cares only that the rocket is escaping the earth's atmosphere on a predictable trajectory. Eventually, indifference to the secondary qualities (taste, smell, color, and touch residing with the human subjects) becomes denial, and science becomes scientism. Science begins by saying it can answer only pragmatic and instrumental questions, but it ends by claiming that these questions are the only questions that can be legitimately asked.

Scientism equates the absence of evidence with evidence of absence, as Smith arrestingly puts it.[4] Within the conditions defined by the Promethean contract, all truth is pragmatic or instrumental; that is, truth is limited to that which leads to desired ends.

The control motive thus leads to empiricism (epistemology), which in turn leads to naturalism (ontology). The end of this sequence is a particular form of consciousness or anthropology, in short, a particular form of being human. Our "will-to-control," Huston Smith reminds us, "has cut our consciousness to fit its needs—tailored our awareness to fit its imperatives."[5] The awareness that science fosters is ultimately alienating, to the extent that it reduces the colorful world we had thought ourselves to be living in to a mechanistic world of cold, hard, indifferent facts. The world thus presents itself to us in a particular, partial guise when we approach it with the intention to control. If we accept this proposition, it follows that if we were to approach the world with a different intention, it would show us a different face altogether. What does the world look like if our beginning point is not a desire for control but a passion to know the whole versus a partial truth?

> The slenderest knowledge that may be obtained of the highest things is more desirable than the most certain knowledge obtained of lesser things.
>
> St. Thomas Aquinas[6]

The dominance of the naturalistic, materialistic ontology underlying science and the modern mind makes imagining an alternative ontology—a genuine metaphysics—difficult. How do we describe an alternative world that contains objects that are not only quantitatively different in size and weight but different in the degree to which they are real or true? What does it mean to say something is more Real or more True? This all sounds like mumbo-jumbo.

Modernity is an outlook in which this world, existing as it does on a single ontological plane, is the only one that is genuinely countenanced and affirmed. The alternative view claims that the world is structured hierarchically in a way that makes it possible to distinguish between higher and lower levels of being. This is absolutely critical. Understanding hierarchical structure is a prerequisite to wisdom, that is, for seeing the world as it is, rather than the truncated, partial world we see when we approach it for our limited, instrumental purposes. But having said that, what am I saying in referring just now to levels of being?[7]

To answer that question, consider the animal, vegetable, and mineral categories we first learned about in elementary school. Holding an object, the teacher asked: "Is this animal, vegetable, or mineral?" In this way, we learned a rudimentary way of categorizing the objects in our world. But go further now and ask: "What separates the vegetable from the mineral?" None of us would deny that there is an astonishing difference between inanimate minerals and living plants, nor can we ignore the departure of "something"—let us call it life or x—when the plant on our windowsill dies. If we call the mineral level m, vegetable life is $m + x$. Consider the mystery of x: we can neither create nor fully explain it but we can easily destroy it. Fail to water your plants or place them in the sun and they die; that is, the mysterious x disappears, leaving only the minerals behind. We are forced to admit then that x is "something quite new and additional, and the more deeply we contemplate it, the clearer it becomes that we are faced here with what might be called an ontological discontinuity, or, more simply, a jump in the Level of Being."[8]

Similarly, there is an ontological jump, and an addition of powers, when we move from plants to animals. Animals can do things that are entirely outside the capabilities of plants. We may designate these mysterious powers as y and speak of them in terms of consciousness. I can recognize consciousness in my cat Gypsy, if for no other reason than she can be knocked unconscious. In this event, she will remain alive—like a plant— but her unique animal powers of consciousness will have been lost. If vegetables or plants can be represented by $m + x$, animals are represented by $m + x + y$. Again, this y factor represents an ontological discontinuity and another jump in the Level of Being. We can neither create nor explain consciousness entirely by m and x, but we can easily destroy it. Indeed, the factors that separate the various levels remain essentially mysterious, and our explanations do little more than reduce the higher levels to the lower.

So we move through the elementary categories, then, from mineral to vegetable to animal. But there is more to this than we learned in elementary school. For who can deny that as we move from the animal to the human level we make another jump? Humans possess the minerals comprising their bodies (m), the powers of life (x), and consciousness (y), but also something more, a mysterious power, which we might call z. Unlike animals, humans are capable of self-consciousness or self-awareness, the ability not only to think but to be aware that they are thinking. "There is something able to say 'I' and to direct consciousness itself," according to Schumacher. "This power z, consciousness recoiling upon itself, opens up unlimited possibilities of purposeful learning, investigating, exploring, and of formulating and accumulating knowledge."[9] Humans are qualitatively more than animals, just as animals are qualitatively more than plants or minerals.

A hierarchy thus exists, consisting of four levels of being. Although higher and lower forms exist on each level, and the precise demarcation between levels may be at times in dispute, the respective levels of being are nevertheless different in kind, not just in degree. Minerals undeniably possess fewer powers than plants, just as plants undeniably possess fewer powers than humans. No accumulation of minerals will become a plant, just as no profusion of plants will become an animal. Again, there is a mysterious "jump" between each ontological level. Does this hierarchical trajectory suggest the possibility of a level, or levels, above the human, $m + x + y + z + $? We shall return to that critical question after we have examined the hierarchical levels of being in more detail.

PROGRESSIONS

From lower to higher, the levels of being exhibit an infinite number of progressions.

Reflect again on the progression from mineral to vegetable, to animal and human. As we move to from lower to higher, we also move from the more common to the rarer. Minerals are universal; they are the indestructible building blocks on which everything that exists in our world rests. Plants, although virtually universal on earth, are rarer than minerals; think of deserts and rocky summits above the timberline, for example. Animals are rarer still than plants, requiring as they do a particular environment in which to thrive and reproduce. And finally, humans and self-consciousness are on the rarest level of all, representing as they do only the tiniest sliver of living organisms.

Increasing rarity also reflects increasing vulnerability. Progressing this time from the highest to the lowest, humans can all too easily lose the z-factor of self-awareness and self-consciousness and, in doing so, revert to their instinctive "animal natures." It's hard to remain self-conscious and fully human on a Friday evening drinking beer while watching a ball game on TV. Similarly, the removal of the y-factor—consciousness—reduces an animal to something less than an animal, a living being still, but without the ability to adapt deliberately to an environment. Patients lapse into comas and people are knocked unconscious in accidents in a way that reveals how vulnerable and fragile consciousness is. Consciousness is more vulnerable than life, simply because we can lose consciousness without losing life, although when medical patients do so, for example, they are tellingly referred to as being in a "vegetative state." Plant or vegetative life, jumping to another level lower, is clearly less vulnerable than animal life, as the tenacity of the weeds in my garden attests. Nevertheless, plant life is itself more vulnerable and fragile than the lowest level of being, the m-factor, to which all the other levels are eventually reduced.

Note in the movement from lower to higher, that there is also a progression from visible and outward to invisible and inward. Only the m-factor is entirely visible and predictable. The x-factor that separates matter from life remains "invisible" and mysterious, something that we can take away or destroy easily, but cannot create. Likewise, the y and z factors—consciousness and self-awareness—are wholly invisible, without or beyond sight, sound, touch, smell, taste, extension, or weight. At the highest level, it comes as a shock to acknowledge that we humans are invisible, ghostlike creatures whose personhood—constituted by our thoughts, emotions, feelings, ambitions, speculations, day-dreams, fantasies, loves, desires, and hates—cannot be directly grasped. In light of the increasing rarity, vulnerability, and invisibility of the higher levels, it is hardly surprising that knowledge of these levels is correspondingly less common and more subtle.

Another way to describe the progression to greater and greater invisibility and inwardness is to reflect on the "world" suggested by each level. On the lowest level, there is no self-contained, autonomous "world." Inanimate matter is totally passive and subject to a rigid connection between cause and effect. All action is initiated externally; we skip a rock across a pond and mix chemicals in our laboratories. In contrast, plants have a limited world, requiring a patch of soil, light, and water. Causality is not entirely external, because the plant can react and adapt to different stimuli, bending toward the sun and strengthening its resistance to bugs, for example. For our part, we have less control over plants than over rocks. Without a "green thumb," I can kill the healthiest of plants. Progressing to the next level, an animal's world is incomparably greater than a plant's, possessing as it does an "inner space" for the creation of greater freedom and autonomy. An animal can be pushed around like a stone, can be stimulated like a plant, but it also possesses internal *motives* such as instinctive drives, attractions, and compulsions. Animals can adapt behaviors to their environments in a way that plants cannot, and, again, from our perspective, they are less controllable, as cantankerous mules and barking dogs will attest. A pet dog will be internally, invisibly motivated to please its master in a way that a plant will not. Finally, on the highest level, humans possess the largest autonomous world, a power or *will* to move and act even when there is no physical compulsion, stimulus, or motivating force present. Humans, unlike animals, can anticipate and act on future goals, and not only react to but also create behavior-orienting symbols. In starkest contrast to the mineral level, human causality is immensely complex and mysterious. No animal climbs Mount Everest, and no animal would have survived the death camps of Nazi Germany. There is thus a qualitative difference between the highest and lowest levels of being.

The progression from passive to active and the movement toward an autonomous world can also be expressed as a progression from necessity to freedom. Again, at the material level, there is no freedom. Matter is locked into a rigid sequence of cause and effect. In contrast, animals—though largely driven by instincts—have a larger area of freedom. Gypsy the cat can choose to curl up on the sofa next to me or to sleep contentedly by herself on a chair. At the highest level, of course, self-conscious humans have an enormous degree of freedom and are capable of a bewildering number of genuine choices, from what they will eat to where they will live. Action on the material level is initiated by others, whereas action on the human level comes from "inside" and with deliberate intention.

One final progression: the higher does not merely possess powers and capabilities that exceed the lower, it also has, as Schumacher explains, "power over the lower; it has the power to organize the lower and use the lower and use it for its own purposes."[10] There is a paradox here, of course. That which is rare, fragile, and invisible is also the most powerful. Recall how Platonic Forms and archetypes have the power to organize uninformed potentiality into actualities. That is to say, causality rests with ends rather than beginnings. Thus, for example, daily work is organized and directed by goals established by strategic "higher level" thinking, just as our lives and emotions are directed by our invisible, informing ideas and ambitions. Living organisms have the power to organize inanimate matter, animals utilize the plants of the forest, and self-consciousness—as present in human beings—organizes all the levels beneath it to achieve its own purposes. In contrast to the modern view that explains and reduces the higher to the lower, the drift of a hierarchical view is always to explain the lesser by the more, the lower by the higher. It insistently asks: what is informing and directing the lower, of what is the lower an expression? In the hierarchical world, the lower is always leading to and being informed by the higher.

KNOWING ALSO REQUIRES A HIERARCHY

As without, so within—the isomorphism of man and the cosmos is a basic premise of the traditional outlook.

Huston Smith, *Forgotten Truth: The Primordial Tradition*

Humankind, as the highest level of Being, contains the lower levels. In the simple formulation outlined above, mankind is the sum of $m + x + y + z$. As a result, it is not surprising that certain aspects of humankind can be elucidated by studying the lower levels. Thus, for example, knowledge of chemistry is essential to understanding physiology, just as studying animals offers insights into human behavior. The existence of the higher levels does not mean that the lower levels are unimportant or can be neglected; on the contrary, a perfect understanding of m, x, and y would explain everything about humankind, *except that which makes humankind human.* We can understand and to a large extent control minerals, plants, and animals because they are *inferior* to us, meaning that they exist on lower levels of being. However, to understand another being on our own, human level of being, to understand that mysterious *z*-factor of self-consciousness, we need another instrument of cognition; we in fact need to be on the same level of being as that which we are studying. "Knowing demands the organ fitted to the object," Schumacher quotes Plotinus approvingly, before adding "nothing can be known without there being an appropriate 'instrument' in the makeup of the knower . . . the understanding of the knower must be *adequate* to the thing to be known."[11] I can understand the inner, fragile, and invisible world of my neighbor, however imperfectly, only if I can understand my own emotions, fears, and aspirations. Trying to understand my neighbor by staying exclusively on the lower level of materialism is like trying to appreciate gourmet cooking by studying chemistry.

I characterized science earlier by saying that it is an insistently pragmatic method informed by the motivation to control. A hierarchical view characterizes science ontologically by saying that it studies the lowest, material levels of being, and indeed attempts to understand—and reduce—everything on the higher levels exclusively from the perspective of the lowest. From the viewpoint of science, what we have called the *x, y,* and *z* factors— and the qualitatively different levels of reality they suggest—are merely epiphenomena or subjective. Again, the hallmark of science is that it operates on a single ontological level, whose focus is on the most external and material aspects of the universe. The instrument for understanding this lowest level of being correspondingly draws on the lowest level within us. For cognition at the mineral level, man's primary instruments are his five senses and the apparatus through which those sense are extended and reinforced. A great strength of scientific knowledge is that its truths are publicly, intrasubjectively available and objectively verifiable, because it is based on the lowest and thus most common and widely distributed level of being.

In contrast, wisdom can be attained only by bringing into play the higher powers and levels of self-consciousness. "Just as the world is a hierarchic structure with regard to which it is meaningful to speak of 'higher' and 'lower,'" Schumacher observes, "so the sense organs, powers, and other 'instruments' by which the human being perceives and gains knowledge of the world form a hierarchic structure of 'higher' and 'lower.'"[12] In this connection, Schumacher makes a helpful distinction between *experience*—which tells us about sensible things—and *illumination*, which tells us about what things mean, what they could be, and what they perhaps ought to be. Only by cultivating the higher levels in ourselves, traditionally through religious practices, can we hope to understand that which is equal or higher to us. In language that is reminiscent of a sentiment expressed by William James, Huston Smith advises us that "understanding proceeds through living what one is trying to understand."[13] Knowledge of the higher levels requires personal transformation, not seeing different things but seeing things differently.

What this means in practice is that higher knowledge— wisdom—is not available to everyone; we are not entitled to assume that we are necessarily adequate to knowing everything at all times and in all circumstances. A correspondence obtains between the level of being on which I live (my level of self-consciousness, for example) and my ability to see the subtle, invisible levels of reality. The ability to see is not a birthright but an achievement, an achievement we might quickly add, that some will attain but most will not. We should not dismiss the higher levels of reality as nonexistent, or merely subjective fantasies, simply because they are not accessible to us or because our glimpses of that reality are fleeting and uncertain. The fact that I—like most of us—cannot follow the intricacies of quantum physics doesn't mean that it is unreal or not true. It only means that I have an inadequate instrument of understanding. Genuine achievement is always undemocratic and elitist. Fewer people are adequate to the task of climbing Everest than Stone Mountain on the outskirts of Atlanta.

A PROSCRIPTIVE HIERARCHY

The hierarchically arranged levels of being briefly described above are not only descriptive; they are also prescriptive. That is to say, the hierarchy contains an ethical imperative to move from lower to higher, because the higher is also better, truer, and more eternal. Thus, for example, humans are better than animals and freedom and self-directed action is better than living passively, that is, mechanically, according to the dictates of biological or cultural impulses. To say that one object or behavior is categorically better than another runs counter to the philosophical and social relativism characteristic of postmodernism, for which "there is no truth only choices" and "no better or worse, only differences." In starkest contrast, a hierarchical perspective that posits that one level of reality and being is ontologically higher and better than another returns the question of truth to its original ontological base. Without such a base, how does one know in which direction to move or act, all directions being equal? In a world without qualitative hierarchies, the only measurement for advancement is quantitative, meaning more of this one thing or another. In many instances, of course, the measure of all value is reduced to greater or lesser amounts of money.

The imperative to move from lower to high redefines conventional ethics. Ethics is not—as we normally think of it—primarily a moralistic exercise of distinguishing right from wrong; it is more fundamentally an exercise in self-transformation during which we move from lower to higher levels of being.[14] Whereas modernity's touchstone and appeal is to generic and objective experiences that are familiar to us all, a primordial or hierarchical outlook aligns the components of the soul so that we can experience the world in a new, ontologically higher and more accurate way. The hierarchy from lower to higher provides both a life orientation and a method for achieving happiness. Humankind's happiness lies in developing its highest faculties, gaining knowledge of the highest things, and, if possible, seeing God or the Good. In contrast, if persons develop only their lower faculties—which they share with the animals—and correspondingly gain knowledge of only the lowest levels of reality, they will fail to reach their highest human potential. Meaning does not reside in the lower but in the highest levels of reality.

An example from Hinduism of an idealized movement from lower to higher is illustrative. What do people want? According to Hinduism, in Huston Smith's account, people first of all want pleasure. They want to hedonistically indulge their senses and lower impulses. There is nothing wrong with such indulgence, but eventually satisfying private pleasures comes to seem trivial and unfulfilling. When this happens, people begin to want worldly success, including wealth, fame, and power. Because these goals are social in nature, they last longer than the private goals of pleasure. Nevertheless, these, too, eventually fail to fulfill human nature, because their achievement is precarious, insatiable, and ephemeral. Together, the goals of pleasure and success constitute the path of desire. These goals are not "bad," but Hinduism regards the objects of the path of desire as if they were toys. "If we ask ourselves whether there is anything wrong with toys," Smith explains, "our answer must be: On the contrary, the thought of children without them is sad. Even sadder, however, is the prospect of adults who fail to develop interests more significant than dolls and trains."[15]

Eventually, the toys are put aside when the objects of the path of desire fail to bring happiness and meaning. When this occurs, the pilgrim begins the path of renunciation, renunciation in the sense of an athlete renouncing junk food and leisure to run a marathon. The lower is renounced in favor of the higher. In this instance, pleasure and a hunger for worldly success are renounced for duty, the desire to give and serve a higher purpose and acquit oneself responsibly toward a community. The rewards of serving others are many, but these, too, eventually become unfulfilling and meaningless, because all communities too will pass away.

"There comes a time when one asks even of Shakespeare, even of Beethoven, is this all?" Aldous Huxley observes, echoing the lyrics of Peggy Lee's 1950s hit song "Is That All There Is?"

When that time comes, Hinduism proclaims, we turn to higher things and the level of being that fulfills our truest natures. What do people *really* want? We want being, knowledge, and joy—infinitely. In short, what we really want is liberation (*moksha*) and release from the impediments separating us from the limitless being, consciousness, and bliss our hearts desire. That is to say, we renounce the finite and lower levels of being for the higher. If the lower levels of pleasure, success, and duty are emptied of meaning, then our hope rests in the infinite.

The hierarchical foundations of Hinduism provide a guide for what its adherents should want and that for which life is worth living. In addition, Hinduism highlights one other aspect of hierarchies: at the highest level of being, the motivation of action and belief is intrinsic. The goals of science are pragmatic or instrumental. This orientation limits what we notice and accept as real and important. What is meaningful is limited to what is useful. In contrast, at the highest levels of a hierarchy, our motivation is intrinsic and our vision is correspondingly whole. There is nothing higher or better with which it can be justified. Truth, with a capital T, is finally like love. If one loves for any reason other than the beloved's intrinsic lovableness, it is not love. No longer constricted by extrinsic, pragmatic purposes, we can be and see reality whole; we can see things as they are.

HOW MANY LEVELS?

Are there only four levels of being or are there more? Can the hierarchy of mineral, vegetable, animal, and human be extended or projected to higher realms that are progressively more invisible, rare, and real? The adepts of the mystical traditions universally answer that question in the affirmative. Humankind is "open-ended," Schumacher reports, "not at the highest level but with a potential that might indeed lead to perfection."[16]

But having said that, we must quickly remind ourselves that the higher we go on the hierarchy, the more our own inadequacies are exposed, and the more difficult it becomes to understand and articulate the higher levels of being. The lower can not understand the higher, just as a dog is limited in its understanding of its master.

Numerous hierarchical schemes describing levels of being above the human are available. Huston Smith's proposal, which he identifies as the "Wisdom tradition" at the core of the world's religions, is illustrative. Progressing from lower to higher, he distinguishes four levels of reality: terrestrial, intermediary, celestial, and the infinite. The terrestrial and the lower intermediary levels encompass the now familiar mineral, vegetable, animal, and human levels; the celestial and infinite levels surpass them.

The terrestrial level is the easiest to understand and articulate. This is the level of the visible and material world, whose distinctive categories are space, time, and matter/energy. It is the level of the empirical sciences and corresponds to our lowest level of being. The intermediate level, in contrast, rests between the natural, terrestrial level and the celestial world. Though still firmly rooted in the terrestrial level, the intermediate level becomes apparent when we reflect on such phenomena as the effectiveness of prayer, parapsychology, and demonic or divine possession. Smith locates the informing capabilities of archetypes in this realm, saying that archetypes not only pattern our thoughts and emotions but can also shape matter. In Christian theology, the intermediate level is represented by the incarnation of Christ, who is both wholly human and wholly divine. The intermediate is the terrestrial level as it is literally informed and shaped by the celestial. Recall, in this context, our earlier discussion of Aristotle's notions about the informing qualities of the Forms and James Hillman's discussion of archetypes.

Above this intermediate level, we find the celestial. On this level, the archetypes are unalloyed and pure. This is the level corresponding to Plato's Forms. Whereas terrestrial objects are ephemeral and fragile, objects on the celestial level are eternal and undiluted. The roses lining my sidewalk are both attenuations of and less real than the transcendent Form of Roseness. Theologically, this is the realm of God in his knowable or manifest aspects, whose omnipotence and omniscience speak to our soul and attest to a fullness beyond his creation. On this level, we worship and stand apart from God as Other—as One "like us" but of *infinite* freedom, power, and compassion.

Terrestrial, intermediate, celestial. Is there anything still higher? Theologically, is there anything higher than our conventional notions of God? Smith evokes the mystical currents of the world's religions in answering in the affirmative: "Theism is not the final truth. . . . The final reality is unlimited, for it is infinite; to put the point in an aphorism, nothing *finite* can be final."[17] The infinite goes beyond and transcends our conceptual categories. The finite cannot encompass the infinite. The wisdom tradition recognizes and attests to a level of being that goes beyond the inadequate instruments of our language and concepts to perceive it. Finite creatures, we are nevertheless urged on by the infinite. Whereas the celestial realm speaks to our soul, the infinite realm speaks to our spirit during those mystical moments when the God beyond comprehension (the Godhead, the God-beyond-God) and the "I" of my distinct ego dissolve into One. We are heirs to infinite being, infinite awareness, infinite bliss.

At this highest realm, descriptive words—because they are limited, whereas what they attempt to describe is not—*must* fail. In Buddhism, this is the point where the adept silently points to the moon and abandons the craft that enables us to cross the river. "There are some who mistake this point as the end of the world," Smith cautions; "whatever can be neither imaged nor coherently conceived, they argue, does not exist. But the Truth does not need us and is in no way dependent upon our powers of conceptualization. There are regions of being—the unimaginable perfection of totality is at the moment the case in point—that are quite unrelated to the contours of the human mind. The mind is comfortable with facts and fictions. It is not made for grasping ultimates."[18] Let's be frank: understanding this highest level beyond words and images is difficult in the extreme and is reserved for the very, very few mystics and adepts whose instruments of perception match the level of being they seek to understand and with which they hope to merge (or—in a moment of awakening— they know they have been merged with all along). Because the ability to perceive this highest level of reality is rare and fragile, it is little wonder that the rest of us can easily dismiss it as illusory and subjective.

The highest levels of the hierarchy of being that Smith describes are important for two reasons. First, they point to experiences that reveal the inadequacy of words, images, and consciousness. Schumacher, Smith's co-conspirator in resurrecting metaphysics for our time, says it this way: "Reality, Truth, God, Nirvana cannot be found by thought, because thought belongs to the Level of Being established by consciousness and not to that higher Level which is established by self-awareness. At the latter, thought has its legitimate place, but it is a subservient one. Thoughts cannot lead to awakening because the whole point is to awaken from thinking into seeing."[19]

So, to anticipate, we must ask whether the question of meaning and meaningless is an instance of a vain thought that must be overcome by nonthinking or paradoxically a thinking-beyond-thinking. Moreover, the motivation for "seeing" or knowledge of this highest level of being must finally be intrinsic. It is good in itself and self-justifying; no appeal is necessary. We do not seek enlightenment because it will calm our minds and lower our blood pressure, improve our productivity, or make us more attractive to the opposite sex. By definition, it cannot lead to, or be a sacrifice for, anything higher or greater. Creating a better world or saving the one we have is secondary to seeing the ways things are more clearly.

"O God!" the eighth-century female Sufi saint Rabi'a al-'Adawiyya of Basra is said to have prayed, "If I worship thee in fear of Hell, burn me in Hell; and if I worship Thee in hope of Paradise, exclude me from Paradise; but if I worship Thee for Thine own sake, withhold not Thine Everlasting Beauty."[20]

FOUR QUESTIONS
What Do We Know?

Like postmodernists, we know that what we know is an expression of our motivation. The dominant, sacral mode of knowing in the modern era—science—is an expression of our motivation to control. Knowledge is defined as that which contributes to that control. If knowledge does not lead to control and pragmatic results, then its status as knowledge is suspect or dismissed altogether.

The world we see through the instrument of science is thus restricted and limited, a partial truth that reflects but one of many possible motivations. Change the motivation and you change the world.

What do we know about the world that is revealed when we are motivated by a desire for truth rather than control? We know that it is qualitatively arranged into a hierarchy that progresses from less to more freedom, autonomy, universality, and permanence. We know that there is an ontological difference between mineral, vegetable, animal, and the human that precludes higher levels being reduced to and explained by lower. This same ontological hierarchy provides a basis for a corresponding moral hierarchy. Our ethical imperative is to move from lower to higher. In radical contrast to the moral and ontological relativism that is revealed by science—in which there is no better or worse but only differences—the traditional hierarchical view supplies a genuine life orientation by saying this way or direction is better and qualitatively more desirable than that. The point and meaning of life is to become truly human by developing our higher faculties.

Thirdly, we know that there is Truth with a capital T. In contrast to modernism and postmodernism, truth is not relative to perspective or historical context, nor is it an expression of class, race, or gender. The titles of Huston Smith's books *Forgotten Truth* and *The Way Things Are* highlight the unchanging, transpersonal nature of that Truth and the hierarchical foundation on which it is based. We may vary, according to our abilities, in our *perception* of it, but the Truth itself remains universal and eternal. The routes may be different, but all paths converge on a single summit.

How Do We Know?

We know because such a view is virtually universal in human history, extending across both time and cultures. The adepts of the world's religions testify to its truth, for example, and it is verified in the ecstatic experience of mystics. "It is," Smith succinctly says, "the vision philosophers have dreamed, mystics have seen, and prophets have transmitted."[21] But having said that, we must also acknowledge that we know only by aligning ourselves with that which we are studying. Wisdom requires personal transformation. We can only know the higher reaches of reality and truth by cultivating the higher qualities and capabilities within ourselves. Knowledge of the higher truths—wisdom—is neither available to everyone nor common. On the contrary, the higher we move, the more rare and more subtle the truth becomes. We come to know by persisting in the vision and by practicing the disciplines conveyed to us by mystical adepts. Even when we do not see what they see initially, we need to persist under their tutelage until the "Ah hah!" experience occurs, and we exclaim: "Oh, yes, now I see what you have been saying all along." Wisdom relies on faith and commitment rather than skepticism and doubt. We know by seeing with the eyes of faith rather than by discerning causal sequences and producing pragmatic results.

What Does a Metaphysical View Emphasize and What Does It Neglect?

Three things primarily. First, it emphasizes a form of knowledge and experience that is nonpragmatic. Whatever value traditional metaphysical knowledge has is not immediately useful in the conventional meaning of that term. Being a metaphysician is not a good career choice. The emphasis placed on achieving higher states of being and knowledge correspondingly deemphasizes, sometimes to the point of neglect, the material and practical aspects of life. Mystics do not make good car mechanics. Focusing on Roseness rather than the red rose in front of me can make me immune to the transcendent beauty of *this* world. Articulating what it's like to live on the highest levels of being can sound vague, "mystical," and otherworldly in a way that is hard to translate into our day-to-day categories of experience.

To say this in a slightly different way, a metaphysical view stresses the intrinsic value of wisdom. The point of wisdom is wisdom itself; it is its own reward. It does not lead to goals or purposes beyond itself; nothing is higher or better. In this it resembles, albeit on a higher ontological level, other intrinsically valuable activities that have no "purpose," such as love or play or sports. It is its own purpose. Smith succinctly points to the intrinsic value of wisdom, saying: "The only thing that is unqualified good is extended vision, the enlargement of one's understanding of the ultimate nature of things."[22] My skeptical colleagues at the engineering firm were correct in being suspicious of my interest in metaphysical questions, including the question of meaning, because it is supremely impractical and "good for nothing," as the old expression puts it. Achieving the highest states of knowledge, experience, and being is seductively addictive, in a way that can overwhelm other legitimate, albeit more mundane, concerns.

Third, the metaphysical view proclaims and emphasizes a largely static, unchanging reality and truth and neglects the ephemeral and transitory. This means that we discover truth and align ourselves with that truth rather than living under the existential burden of having to create truth. We do not create meaning; we discover it, or it discovers us. We can never relax and come to rest when the universe depends on our efforts, whereas in a metaphysical world, we are reassured that beneath the randomness and pluralism of the world, there is stability, order, and direction. This is a world that emphasizes what's repeated and the same, rather than what's new and innovative. In this respect, at least, it resembles the recurring, eternal motifs of myth.

What does a hierarchical, metaphysical view neglect? Principally, it neglects the local, particular, temporal, and relative. That is not surprising. Metaphysics exchanges truths for the Truth and deemphasizes the experiences and transitory joys of this world. From the perspective of the West, it also contradicts the social values of egalitarianism and equality. Because there is a hierarchy, because some know and are living on a higher level than others, some persons are correspondingly more important and valued than others. As a result, in India, for example, Hindu metaphysics supports a hierarchical caste system that, from our perspective, is inherently unjust and discriminatory. All ways of investing life with meaning have their darker aspects.

Metaphysics and Meaning

What is the metaphysical mind's contribution to the question of meaning? How does meaning enter our lives when understood from a metaphysical perspective?

First, the new metaphysicians—if I may categorize Smith and Schumacher in that way—address the question of meaning directly. Indeed, their principal argument and motivation for reintroducing metaphysics is to counter what they see as a pervasive sense of meaninglessness in modern life. Metaphysics is an antidote to meaninglessness. As we have seen, Smith and Schumacher attribute meaninglessness to two sources. First, life is meaningless because we have been bedazzled by scientism and its claim that the only thing that matters is matter. As a result, we are left with a world that has been flattened and drained of transcendence, value, beauty, and meaning. No wonder it seems as though we are living in a wasteland.

Second, in a move that returns the question of truth and meaning to its original ontological base, the world is perceived as meaningless because we focus on the lower levels of a hierarchy of being and, in the process, neglect the higher. Tillich admonishes that religion's "ultimate concern" must be understood ontologically, that is, as a concern for the ultimate things. Humankind's happiness rests in moving from lower to higher, developing our highest faculties and gaining wisdom about the highest things. Advertisers tell us that happiness and meaning depend on the acquisition of things; whereas the metaphysician tells us that happiness and meaning depend on the perception of higher things. This is a message that the modern mind will be reluctant to accept, based as it is on presuppositions that many of us cannot comprehend. Nevertheless, the wisdom tradition asserts that humankind can achieve both happiness and redemption by focusing on acquiring knowledge of the good, the true, and the beautiful. Meaning is, by definition, transcendent of the material and thus literally "metaphysical." As such, it is not reducible to social, psychological, or material circumstance.

One more thing about how meaning enters our lives: our ability to "see" meaning is not commonly available and interpersonally demonstrable like the experiments of science. The metaphysician reminds us that the perception of meaning depends on our achieving a certain higher level of consciousness, which depends, in turn, on a way of life. Schumacher's aphorism says it all: "Your level of Being attracts your life."[23] We cannot assume or presume that meaning is readily available; that it is something the perception of which is lost, rather than achieved. What this means in practice is that we cannot see meaning and purpose apart from a disciplined, attentive focus, based on faith and commitment. The exclusivity of the achievement flatters our need to feel special and to be a member of an elite group. As metaphysical novices, we live by trust and under the tutelage of someone who sees the hope and promise that the final vision will be achieved. Once attained, that vision will be self-justifying and intrinsically fulfilling in a way that will dissolve the question of meaning altogether and return us to a renewed innocence before the question was asked. Fleeting though they are, brief moments lived on the summit are more real, revelatory, and eternal than the life we live in the valley.

Meaning thus requires becoming a certain type of person. Not surprisingly, then, it enters our lives when we see ourselves as being on a type of journey. In the example from Hinduism, life is meaningful to the extent that people identify with the story of those who progress from searching after pleasure and success to a quest to know one's duty and infinite being. The story of the journey is a story of self-transformation. Such identification is isometric to the way meaning enters the lives of those who identify with a particular mythic story. By accepting the story as our own, we cease being alienated outsiders and become members of a deliberate, selective tribe of "seekers." The quest myth provides a narrative pattern and orientation to the question "What do I do to make my life meaningful?"

The question of meaning for the metaphysical mind comes down to this: (1) Are there worlds that transcend or go beyond the material world? and (2) Is meaning located in those worlds? Beyond the details of whatever illustrative hierarchy we might cite, mystical adepts and the majority of humankind answer both of those questions in the affirmative. When we are in search of meaning, we need to look "higher" in both ourselves and in the world. As was noted earlier, the question of meaning is often equivalent to the question of purposeful ends. The meaning of a watch, for example, is to keep time. Science and modernity stripped life of its purposeful ends and in so doing stripped life of its meaning as well. Metaphysics reintroduces a life-affirming orientation to purposeful ends and thus establishes the basis for a meaningful life.

CHAPTER NINE

Naturalism and Meaning

I will not apologize, therefore, for an activity that makes me
a child. An activity that takes me away from women and business, pleasure and passion. An activity that is its own meaning.
An activity without purpose.

George Sheehan, M.D., *Running and Being: The
Total Experience*

Are the delights and joys available in *this* world a sufficient
answer to the question of meaning? The naturalist inhabits the
same world as the existentialist. But whereas the existentialist
finds living in an indifferent world without appeal absurd and
angst-filled, the naturalist finds it sufficiently joyful and intrinsically meaningful. For the naturalist, life does not acquire meaning because it corresponds to an external myth or philosophical
idea, nor does it acquire meaning because it leads to or embodies
a pragmatic purpose or teleological end, whether in this world or
the next. On the contrary, the meaning of life is simply "life
itself." The answer to the question of meaning has been right in
front of us from the start. The apparent pointlessness—that is,
meaninglessness—of life, the biologist and naturalist Ursula
Goodenough testifies is "deflected . . . by realizing that I don't

have to seek a point. In any of it."[1] Realizing that she didn't have to answer, or even seek to answer what she calls the "big questions" came, Goodenough says, as an epiphany. The naturalist does not escape the question of meaning in drugs, conformity, or mindless activity; paradoxical as it may sound, she finds meaning by becoming more attentive to an otherwise meaningless world.

NATURALIZING THE DIVINE

Naturalism rests on three basic assumptions: materialism, reductionism, and causality. I examined these assumptions in more detail in chapter 4, so their description here can be brief. First, naturalism denies that there are any supernatural or spiritual realities. Nothing transcends the physical world described by chemistry and physics. There are no realities independent of physical realities; literally, no metaphysics. Even independent mental states, such as emotions and consciousness, can be understood as very complex combinations of material elements. Closely allied with materialism, the analytic, for us commonsense, process of reducing complex phenomena to relatively simpler parts—emotions to organic chemistry, for example—expresses the second foundation of naturalism: reductionism. Complex phenomena, including, for example, "spiritual experiences" can be analyzed into increasingly simpler material components. We quickly progress from God to psychology to chemical reactions in the body. Third, a naturalistic understanding of causality ties materialism and reductionism together by saying that all phenomena are caused by a sequence of exclusively material events, from the simple to the more complex, without supernatural, metaphysical, or divine intervention.

What this means in practice is that we cannot call on God, mental states, or anything outside a material causal sequence to explain either how or why an event or reality occurs. There is no supernatural agency or teleological purpose, nor for that matter a physically autonomous mind or human spirit. Naturalism accepts the fact, as do the existentialists, that we are living exclusively in a material, finite, closed world.

The history of science can be understood as a record of naturalizing (others would say secularizing) one phenomenon after another. *Naturalizing* describes a process whereby things that used to be explained by and attributed to supernatural agency, special powers, or immaterial stuff are understood to be the result of entirely empirical, material processes. The biblical narrative of creation is naturalized into the Big Bang, just as the origin of humankind, formerly held to be created in God's image, was naturalized by Darwin into a sequence of biological adaptations and random selections, albeit a very long one. Closer to our own interests perhaps, Freud and Feuerbach naturalized religion by tracing its origins to psychological or anthropological needs; similarly, Marx and Durkheim traced religion's origin to social relationships. Of course, the naturalizing project continues. More and more, we explain our own behavior, consciousness, and self-consciousness alike without recourse to the inner, supervising agency of mind or spirit. In short, the naturalist replaces the soul with DNA.

As exhibited by angst-burdened existentialists, the worldview of the naturalist, at least initially, is likely to elicit alienation and nihilism. Nevertheless, at least some naturalists acknowledge that the emotions associated with traditional religions and spirituality are useful, even necessary. Useful and necessary, we may add, even in the absence of their metaphysical or transcendent underpinnings. Humankind is inescapably *Homo religiosus.* The need for self-transcendence, for a sense of connection with something larger and more enduring than ourselves, for a sense of wonder, reverence, and awe, and for acceptance and gratitude, remains compelling even if we inhabit a naturalized, indifferent universe. For the naturalist, spiritual or religious responses—such as awe, reverence, and gratitude—can be elicited by natural reality. These responses are both intrinsically satisfying and valuable resources for getting us through tough times. Spirituality, Robert Solomon asserts, is "a kind of philosophical beacon, to remind us of what it is that really counts, not fidelity to any God or gods but *living well.*"[2]

The naturalist asks the simple question: Is it possible to feel emotions and be thoughtful in the ways formerly associated with religion and spirituality in the context of a fully modern, up-to-the-minute, exclusively materialistic understanding of nature? Spiritual experiences are understood to be legitimate and real in *this* world; their "reality" is not dependent on or substantiated by a transcendent, metaphysical world. If the naturalist is not nostalgic for a transcendent God, she is nevertheless nostalgic for the emotions and comforts associated with that God. Put differently, the naturalist abandons the idea of God, but not the experiences, emotions, and thoughts formerly elicited by a belief in God. Naturalized transcendence means a transformation *in* and *of* this world, a reawakening or redemption of perception, attention, and emotion from the alienating effects of lethargy, habit, and experiencing life secondhand. Spirituality, if not salvation, is available without metaphysics, entirely in this world.

THE SPIRITUALITY OF THIS WORLD

There is a kind of poetry, even a kind of truth, in the simple fact.

Chet Raymo, *Honey from Stone:*
A Naturalist's Search for God [3]

When you gaze up at the night sky in the high desert, the firmament is filled with stars innumerable. The facts of the universe are as familiar as they are incomprehensible. All the stars that I can see are part of but one galaxy and there are 100 billion galaxies in the universe, each containing perhaps 100 billion stars. While I recline at rest on a hillside looking up, the earth itself carries me along at a thousand miles an hour toward the constellation Orion. The orbital motion of the earth about the sun in turn whisks me along at 68,000 miles an hour toward Aldebaran in Taurus, while the motion of the sun, itself not fixed, adds another 34,000 miles an hour. How do human beings comprehend such space and distance?

The problem of comprehending the bare facts of the cosmos does not become easier if we stay closer to home. The earth is said to be 4.5 billion years old. The Antarctic, that barren icebox of our planet, was once covered in lush tropical forests. How long did it take to form the Grand Canyon? The scale of such vast periods of time and evolution defies the human imagination. In comparison, human history is less than a blink of the eye. The pyramids of Egypt are only some 4,000 years old. Additional facts are no less astonishing. We share our genes and ancestry not only with human-like gorillas but with mushrooms and trees and single-celled amoebas. We are thus, as Ursula Goodenough concludes, "connected all the way down." We are deeply embedded in nature, not apart from it. What's more, we are also connected all the way up, if you will. We are made of the same elements that propagate the stars. We are, literally, creatures of the intersteller dust. Amino acids, the organic building blocks of protein that are the chemical substrate for all life on earth, have been found on meteorites. Some speculate that the first living organisms arrived on earth as passengers on rocks falling from the sky. If so, all of us are descendents of aliens. Such discoveries, the naturalist Chet Raymo argues, affirm our unity with the universe. All of us belong to an immense vastness of space, time, and matter.

The most astonishing and wondrous thing of all? Naturalists celebrate the great and profound mystery that life emerged from the nonliving and, infinitely more, that matter achieved self-consciousness with the emergence of human beings. Could anything be more wondrous than the ability of matter to transcend itself, become aware of its own history and development, create culture, imagine worlds it has never seen, calculate the courses of the stars, and direct its own future? Could any deity be more profound or awe-inspiring than this?[4]

The existentialists heroically confronted a cold, indifferent universe, but they drew a mistaken conclusion. They interpreted the absence of meaning as meaninglessness and, in so doing, failed to see the poetry of bright surfaces and the simple fact. Facts. "What else is there?" asks the naturalist Edward Abbey. "What else do we need?"[5] Reading contemporary religious naturalists like Goodenough and Raymo provokes the same emotions that have been traditionally associated with devotion. Like the devout, contemplative naturalists experience a connectiveness with something more eternal and greater than themselves and are both awestruck and humbled by the universal mystery and wonder of Being. For the naturalist, there is no God, but spirituality remains. Chet Raymo's book *Honey from Stone* is subtitled *A Naturalist's Search for God*. Does his search involve speculation and theological discussions or reflection on a transcendent spirit? Absolutely not. Instead, we witness his attentive, detailed observations of the Irish landscape as he travels from Brandon Mountain to Caherard Hill. If we can no longer pray, Raymo says, we can nevertheless still praise.

TAKING DELIGHT IN WHAT IS

There is no cure for birth and death save to enjoy the interval.

George Santayana

Taking delight and finding intrinsic meaning in *this* world requires overcoming a complex of tightly associated ideologies. No matter how hard we try, simply enjoying idle leisure seems decadent in a world sufficiently wretched to demand responsibility, judgement, and decision.

The first ideological impediment to finding intrinsic delight in this world is the notion of usefulness. An experience gains value to the extent that it is instrumental or because it leads to something of value. What this means in practice is that the value of an experience is not seen as intrinsic but extrinsic. Thus, if my thoughts and actions are not adding value by contributing to greater wealth, personal improvement, or social justice, they are perceived as a waste of time. Children go to baseball camp to improve their skills rather than playing a pick-up game in the park.

The distinction between instrumental and intrinsic purposes is a muddle whenever we confuse religion with morality. Religion is well-being and the intrinsic activity of praising God and his creation, as one loves another for no purpose, Religion is intrinsically meaningful. In contrast, morality is the instrumental duty to live for something else, whether that be to fulfill a moral command or to achieve eternal rewards in the hereafter. The world is filled with injustice, poverty, and environmental degradations, and we have a responsibility and duty to work toward the restoration of Eden. The denial of that responsibility in acts of wonderment and praise seems self-indulgent. Moralists dictate that we willingly dismiss and sacrifice the intrinsic pleasures and satisfactions of this life for others. For the moralist, meaning is always meaning delayed.

Capitalism, too, impedes our taking intrinsic delight in this life by indoctrinating us with the proposition that value and desirability can be reduced to monetary value. We are seduced into confusing wealth with money, and a person's work is judged, not in terms of its intrinsic rewards, but by its value in the marketplace. The work of engineers is deemed more valuable because they are paid more than social workers and artists. Our perception and intrinsic delight in the world is reduced and exchanged for activities and perceptions that are useful or profitable. Our self-worth is bound to our worth in the marketplace rather than our ability to take delight. In confusing intrinsic value with what can be measured and exchanged, we forget the adage that the best climber is not the one who climbs the hardest mountains but the one who has the most fun.

Both pragmatism and postmodernism argue that what we see is influenced by our intentions. We see or carve out of reality only that portion of it that contributes to achieving our purposes and ignore the rest. Scientists, for example, focus on primary qualities rather than secondary ones, because those quantifiable qualities are critical to their ability to predict and control. They ignore the secondary qualities of color and smell, because such secondary qualities are not useful to their purposes. As a consequence, the world they and, by extension, we all know is both partial and limited to our "subjective" activity or intentions, and we ourselves are reduced to those same useful purposes. The medievals used the term *ratio* for this way of mediated knowing by logical abstraction from and reasoning about empirical data, as distinguished from intuitive knowing, or *intellectus*.

In contrast, to see things as they *are*, entire and apart from how they may be useful to us, we must see them without any intention. The antidote to our blindness or inability to see things as they are is thus a form of "practical irresponsibility" or aesthetic disinterest. Paradoxically, to achieve the goal we must renounce it. "Spiritual life is necessarily irresponsible" according to Henry Levinson's reading of the American philosopher George Santayana, "because its function is to cure the blindness that social, economic, and political responsibilities, intelligence, and vitality bring about."[6] We are alienated and find the world meaningless because we are not sufficiently and disinterestedly attentive to the delight and intrinsic rewards of what is, or as William Blake famously said, "if the doors of perception were cleansed every thing would appear to man as it is, infinite."

The naturalist does not attempt to add supernatural matters of fact to natural ones, but rather to infuse meaning into the natural—meaning contingent, material, and finite—lives people have been given to live. "There is," Santayana says, "only one world, the natural world, and only one truth about it, but this world has a spiritual life possible in it, which looks not to another world but to the beauty and perfection that this world suggests, approaches and misses."[7] The naturalist does not seek to transcend this contingent, fleeting world in favor of another more permanent and universal world, nor does she use this world as a portal or instrument of metaphysical disclosure. The world has no mythical depth, nor does it point to anything transcendent. This world is all we have, but this world is sufficient. "A naturalist no longer haunted by supernaturalism," Levinson writes, "can find the promise of the world enchanting, without grasping at the straws held out by supernaturalism or metaphysics."[8]

Cultural forms and institutions—such as art and literature, as well as sport and idle conversation, for example—create sufficient space for being attentive to and celebrating this world. As such, they are considered as forms of serious play. Play—activities done spontaneously and for their own sake—may ironically be our most useful occupation, because it makes life something more than an endless response to obligations and servile labor. Spirituality, understood as essentially comic, playful, and festive is distinguished from normal social and moral responsibilities and from life in the workaday world. "Only your mystic, your dreamer, your insolent loafer or tramp can afford so sympathetic an occupation," Levinson quotes William James as writing, for only in these useless occupations can we catch a glimpse of the things that make life worth living.[9] A naturalistic spirituality offers the possibility of achieving moments of happiness and joy in the midst of an utterly contingent and transitory world.

Spiritual activity—including genuine leisure—is an end in itself, to be pursued for its own sake. As such, it stands in sharpest contrast to the world of work, broadly understood to mean activity, including our intellectual activity, that is legitimated by an external purpose or social function. Aristotle categorized any activity performed for some utility among the *servile arts*. Work is the means of life; leisure the end. Without the intrinsic end, work is meaningless—a means to a means to a means. At the end of all extrinsic or instrumental acts, the final act must be intrinsically valuable.

In contrast to the *servile arts* and *ratio*, we have the liberal arts and *intellectus*. The liberal arts are free, at liberty from and not subordinate to, the workaday world of purposes and intentions. They are thus vehicles of transcendence. The paradigmatic examples of festivity, worship, and love are joyfully celebrated in a way that affirms the basic meaning and sufficiency of this world. In contrast to *ratio*, an active reduction of reality to suit our purposes, *intellectus* is the more passive, receptive "ability of simply looking (*simplex intuitus*), to which the truth presents itself as a landscape presents itself to the eyes," Josef Pieper writes.[10] It expresses an attitude not of someone who seizes but of one who lets go and by letting go can be receptive to and contemplative of the real in its wholeness. We are seized or captured by the real in such a way that it, and not our limiting intentions, is determinative. Spirituality, contemplation, intellection—call it what you will—is not distinguished by its immateriality but by this ability to relate and be open to the totality of being. Pieper summarizes the importance of leisure and *intellectus* this way: "The real wealth of man lies not in the satisfaction of his necessities, nor, again, in 'becoming lords and masters of nature,' but rather in being able to understand what is—the whole of what is. Ancient philosophy says that this is the utmost fulfillment to which we can attain; that the whole order of real things be registered in our soul—a conception which in the Christian tradition was taken up into the concept of the beatific vision."[11]

Liberated from the workaday world, we are free to enjoy and contemplate the world as it is: entire, wondrous, and full of grace. There is, as Hegel reminded us, not only use but also blessing.

NATURAL SUPERNATURALISM

Although denying the possibility of transcendence and metaphysics on the one hand, religious naturalism nevertheless expresses a secularized, this-worldly transcendence on the other. What's transcended in naturalism is not this world but the blinding influence of custom, inattention, and pragmatic usefulness that impedes our perception of the joy and wonder of what is. The theme of awakening to nature by transcending the blindness of custom and inattention offers a form of salvation that affronts neither our reason nor our humanity.

"How much virtue there is in simply seeing!" The romantic notion that lifeless, alien nature can be humanized and redeemed is rooted in what the literary critic M. H. Abrams identifies as "biblical and theological commonplaces."[12] The biblical pattern of paradise lost and paradise regained is repeated in a new, entirely naturalistic expression that excites a feeling analogous to those we feel when encountering the divine. As children, everything is new and wondrous and the question of meaning does not arise. As we grow older, however, custom and habit insidiously and relentlessly seduce us into too quickly assimilating new and fresh experiences into familiar, stereotypical categories of perception. We are alienated from nature, and find the world meaningless as a consequence, because of a failure of perception. We fall from the innocent grace of childhood whenever we substitute habitual modes of perception for the ecstasy of our sensuous existence.

In this context the romantic poet Coleridge in *Biographia Literaria* declared his wish to "give the charm of novelty to things of every day, and to excite a feeling analogous to the supernatural, by awakening the mind's attention from the lethargy of custom, and directing it to the loveliness and the wonders of the world before us; an inexhaustible treasure, but for which, in consequence of the film of familiarity and selfish solicitude we have eyes, yet see not, ears that hear not, and hearts that neither feel nor understand."[13]

In the Bible, the grand pattern of fall and redemption is external and historical. The expulsion of Adam and Eve from paradise is balanced by the appearance of a restorative new heaven and new earth at the end of time. What's more, the arrival of this new world will be abrupt or apocalyptic, an overwhelming revelation, rather than a slow, self-directed, or intentional realization. According to Abrams, the romantics reinterpreted and internalized this external history by "transferring the theatre of events from the outer earth and heaven to the spirit of the single believer."[14] Internalized, the location of the Apocalypse is not outside in the world but within. The new world is not another, transcendent world but this world transformed and seen in a new light, not the end of time but the time of the end. The destruction and passing of the old world expresses an internal movement in us, from the familiar to the wondrous, from a secondhand existence to a direct, unmediated (prototypically Protestant) encounter with what is. In this scheme, alienation is replaced by a sacred marriage between ourselves and a redeemed nature, a marriage that is both without purpose and sufficient unto itself.

The alienated hero, who—living in a meaningless universe— is nevertheless haunted by a sense of exile and loss, is thus the latest incarnation of a very old story. The romantics, in reaction to the emergence of science and the modern world, retained the paradigm and values of their Christian heritage by internalizing and demythologizing the biblical narrative. They thus naturalized the supernatural. The sufficiency, self-validating experience of directly encountering God—and the wonder, humility, and awe that ensures—is a prototype of the wonder, humility, and awe we experience in our direct encounter with what is when the glorified senses of our earlier and more innocent existence are restored and redeemed.

Before moving on to our four summarizing questions, a final comment about naturalism. Naturalism is understandably associated with nature. The English romantics glorified the Lake District, and closer to home, Thoreau retreated to the woods of Massachusetts. Though the solace of wild places is thus a central component of the naturalist tradition, the attention and reawakening of the senses that is celebrated in the unmediated encounter between humankind and nature should be extended to those occasions when we are singularly attentive and perceptive to what is, regardless of whether that occasion is in the nature of woods and streams. Redemption can occur, for example, in the attentive polishing of silver, the perfection of a tennis stroke, or the cleaning of one's room. Robert Solomon recounts how his fascination with bugs and critters provided a means for escaping his insecurities and painful self-consciousness. "My fascination with nature," he says, "transported me into a larger universe."[15] In such apocalyptic moments, we overcome ourselves and our alienation from this world by becoming lost in the attentive act itself, an act that at the time—need I add—is at once self-sufficient, meaningful, and timeless in a way that precludes raising the question of meaning altogether. We do not, in short, need to be in nature to be naturalists; we simply need to be attentive (as immensely difficult as that is) to what is here and now. Zen Buddhism has been telling us this all along. Spirituality is not fidelity to a transcendent God but living well and attentively in this world. Spirituality is living each day as though it were both the first and the last. "We ought to dance with rapture," D. H. Lawrence joyously proclaimed, "that we should be alive and in the flesh, and part of the living incarnate cosmos."[16]

FOUR QUESTIONS
What Do We Know?

From the perspective of religious naturalism, we know that the universe is composed exclusively of matter in a space-time continuum. Everything, the most complex idea or feeling, even what people call their souls, can be attributed to material causes. No dualism exists between matter and spirit, profane and sacred. The universe is not a portal to, or symbol of, a transcendent, metaphysical realm, whether that realm is conceptualized as referring to an eternal myth, universal Forms, or an omniscient and omnipresent God. What's more, the universe is value-neutral or entirely indifferent: it simply is. Neither good nor bad, neither ontologically higher nor lower, our one-dimensional universe is utterly without meaning, depth, or purposeful end. Humans are not made in God's image, nor are they moving toward a new heaven and earth. The *why* question presumes an intention that is not there.

Second, the universe that we know is immensely large and complex. Its extension in time and space is beyond human scale and comprehension. There are 100 billion galaxies, each with 100 billion stars. The universe is 15 billion years old; our sun is 4.5 billion years old. In contrast, our human species appeared only 130,00 years ago and the first cave paintings only 35,000–50,000 years ago. The numbers alone enforce both a sense of perspective and humility. Humbling, too, is the knowledge that we are intimately connected with the universe "all the way up and all the way down," because we know that chemically and biologically we share a common ancestry with both the stars and the simplest life forms.

Third, we know that the more we know and perceive, the more we apprehend and appreciate the countless miracles and improbabilities surrounding us. The biologist walking in the forest experiences a richer, more complex and wondrous place than I do. Her ability to identify and know the ecology of the plants and animals fosters a particular kind of attention and contact with the real that is unavailable to me. Ignorance is impoverishing. I see a "tree"; she sees a white oak of a certain age, growing in a particular soil, in a specific climate, populated by a unique species of squirrel. The person who is trained in music is in closer, more attentive contact with a symphony than I am, who knows only that it's stereotypically "beautiful music." Naturalism points to freshness of perception and thought, but not necessarily to unmediated or naïve experience.

Fourth, the romantics taught us that routine and inattention dull our perception and sense of wonder, compromising our ability to see as though for the first time. We see or smell or touch only as long as it is necessary to identify the object with which we are dealing. We eat breakfast while reading the newspaper; we look at a picture of the Grand Canyon even when the

Grand Canyon is before us. Furthermore, we are attentive to and account for only those portions of reality that satisfy our particular needs and intentions, ignoring the rest. As a result, our view of the universe is partial and constricted. We seldom see reality from a disinterested perspective, as it *is;* we see only how it can serve our limited needs. The miracle of flight, electricity, heart surgery, or a leaf is hidden by familiarity. What a miracle it would be for Thomas Jefferson if he were given a ride in an airplane!

And, finally, we know that we can experience awe, wonder, and transcendence beyond our own time and place in response to what *is,* in a way that does not rely on metaphysics. We know that a direct encounter with nature can elicit the same response as an encounter with the divine. Spirituality is available within a scientific worldview. With the same bowing of the head, the same bending of the knee that was formerly associated with the religiously devout, Goodenough can say, "What is, is" and "Blessed be to what is."[17] Most of us have had moments of natural mysticism when we were transported by the spectacle of an alpine glow on high peaks or the haunting sound of flocks of migrating geese. If we can hang on to those moments, no matter how fleeting, we can reject metaphysics without rejecting or dismissing experiences traditionally associated with religious devotion. Such experiences are not illusory or merely subjective. We know that they are genuine spiritual experiences, grounded, not in the supernatural, but in an attentive perception and knowledge of what is.

How Do We Know?

Naturalists accept the universe bequeathed to them by science. The nature they know and revere is empirical and entirely material.

There is no portal to or knowledge of "higher" things. Mysticism and insight are naturalized into their psychological and chemical components. Nonmaterial entities and causes—as well as those without economic benefit—are dismissed as either irrelevant (tellingly, we say "immaterial") or merely subjective and illusory.

A pragmatic encounter with nature is self-limiting and reductionistic. Whereas postmodernism and pragmatism argue that what we see is informed by our extrinsic purposes, naturalism highlights the occasions that have intrinsic value. Moments of festivity, celebration, and awe do not lead to other, more valuable moments or ends; they are ends in themselves, with intrinsic value that needs neither legitimization nor justification. Because our encounter with nature is not motivated by a desire to control, we can see nature as it is, entire rather than in part. Play—broadly understood as a disinterested if not aesthetic encounter with nature—is a form of epistemology, no less so than pragmatism.

What Does Naturalism Emphasize and What Does It Neglect?

Naturalism emphasizes occasions of intrinsic value. The experiences of wonder, humility, joy, and grace associated with a direct encounter with nature need no justification. Within this encounter, our stance is largely passive. We are overcome or stand in awe. We let go, like someone who in going to bed permits herself or himself to *fall* asleep. It is not we who act but something acting on us. Nature is bigger than our petty intentions.

In stressing positive, intrinsically valuable encounters, naturalists tend to neglect our negative encounters with nature.

The indifferent world upon which the naturalists look can be beautiful and awe-inspiring but it can also be cruel and unjust. It is easy to see how we would all like to linger while experiencing nature in her more benign moments; it is less so when we encounter in nature unspeakable cruelty, suffering, and injustice. Accepting the *is* with thanksgiving is difficult in circumstances of need, whether economic or emotional. Celebrating the sufficiency of the *is* is unlikely to be found among those who mine coal underground or single mothers waiting tables. A certain kind of passivity is acceptable only in otherwise happy circumstances. Furthermore, naturalists do not have the consolations that are available by transcending *this* world. The meaning of this transitory, fleeting world of sickness and death cannot be displaced and located in the eternal world of myth, Forms, or teleological ends. Naturalists do not console themselves that loved ones have passed away to another world or that they have sacrificed their lives for God, country, or family; they have simply died. Their bodies rot beneath the ground in a dark casket. If life beyond the grave exists, it does so only in the minds, thoughts, and achievements of others.

"Be it life or death, we crave only reality," Thoreau writes in *Walden*. Naturalists tend to emphasis direct, face-to-face encounters with nature. In doing so, however, they neglect the cultural, mediated component of our experience. Protestantism proclaims that we can have a direct encounter with God, without the mediating intervention of priests or the Church. Similarly, religious naturalists tend to think that we directly encounter nature and festivity. They recognize that culture can create festivals, religious rituals, and art that are intrinsically rewarding, but, within those occasions, they assume that experiences of joy and awe "simply" happen without mediation. The mediating role of language, images, and ideas in forming experience is neglected. Without culturally informing language, how would we recognize when awe or humility occurs? As paradoxical as it may seem, nature is never natural; our encounters with it are always mediated by language and prior experience. Because of language and culture, we live in a garden rather than a virgin wilderness.

Naturalism and Meaning

Naturalism highlights experiences that are intrinsically fulfilling, and that thus require no justification, much like myth. The question of meaning never arises, because one is unself-consciously caught up in the experience, which is its own reward. To ask of such occasions, "What does it mean?" is already to move outside full engagement with and in the moment, severing the intimacy that answers the question *before it is asked.* In practice, this means that thought can self-consciously raise the question of meaning but it cannot necessarily carry us over to an experience of unself-conscious engagement or return us to a point before the question of meaning arose or was necessary. By locating meaning in intrinsically meaningful occasions, naturalism suggests that we cannot ascribe meaning to an occasion by reference to an eternal myth, universal Form, or desired end. A meaningful experience in this sense is not a portal to an extrinsically more "real" and therefore more meaningful realm; it is what it is, sufficient unto itself. For naturalists, *spirituality* is an honorific term, signifying intrinsically valuable experiences, however fleeting, which evoke feelings such as awe, humility, and joy.

Robert Solomon summarizes the inability to articulate meaning, though not the impossibility of experiencing it, this way:

> So long as the question of the meaning of life is posed
> in its abstract form, "Why anything?", it will escape
> every attempted answer within our experience. To every
> such attempted answer, there will be a further question,
> "Why that?" This "absurd reasoning" is either hopeless or a
> mere excuse to slip in a bit of religious proselytizing. . . .
> What gives our lives meaning is not anything beyond our
> lives, but the richness of our lives. And that richness is pre-
> dominantly a product of the passions, which thereby become
> our answer to the problem of the meaning of life.[18]

Naturalism thus expresses two themes. First, transcendence
does not mean escape to another world; it means seeing this
world more clearly and in its entirety. What is transcended is our
habitual and stereotypical perception of the world in which we
live. The assumption is that contact with reality—putting aside
stereotypes, opinions, and prejudices—will always be satisfying
and conducive to living a fuller, more meaningful life. Reflecting
both Protestantism and the American frontier experience, we
transcend our customary, secondhand engagements with the
world to encounter this world directly, face to face, as it were, for
the first time. Naturalism is spirituality fully embodied.

Second, religious naturalism embodies the theme of exile and
return, or, speaking theologically, of fall and redemption.
Once—as children—we saw everything as alive and interesting
and new. As we grew older, however, we fell or were exiled from
this Eden-like state because of habit and custom. Instead of
seeing everything as new, we saw only the stereotypical and con-
sequentially "dead" perceptions of our predecessors. No wonder

life feels meaningless. We're eating fast food instead of slow cooking. Redemption and a return to a second innocence occur whenever we become—once again—fully and unself-consciously engaged in the moment. Naturalism emphasizes an active, intimate dancing out of faith, rather than a self-conscious reflection on and articulation of beliefs. Meaning is prior to and more fundamental than the question of meaning; once the question of meaning is raised, it may be impossible to get back to meaning itself.

Consider for a moment the example of the tennis player. Playing tennis is not a natural, instinctive activity. It requires a form of knowledge that, initially at least, is awkwardly self-conscious and deliberate. Eventually, however, the best tennis players become unself-conscious and fluid in their playing. While engaged in the play, the question of meaning does not arise, and, if it were to arise, the meaning of the game would most likely be lost. The athlete who plays primarily because of instrumental or extrinsic rewards, such as financial gain or pleasing parents or weight reduction, ascribes a meaning to playing that is a step removed from the intrinsic rewards of the game itself. We do not "believe" in tennis; we play tennis, and it is in playing, and only in playing, that we discover its intrinsic meaning.

Consistent naturalists, because of their allegiance to a scientific outlook, are unable to discriminate between occasions that are better or worse. There are disciplines and criteria for determining excellences within the game, but no way to determine whether tennis or golf is preferable. Naturalists can say of an occasion only whether it is meaningful or meaningless, compelling or dull. In saying that there is no depth, and that one can say only which god or "game" is more compelling, naturalism recalls aspects of the mythic mind with which we began. Like existentialism and Buddhism, naturalism reminds us that the meaning of life is life, nothing more, nothing less. Paradoxically, raising the question of meaning signals a failure of meaning when thinking serves, as Solomon notes, to "deprive me of the very meaning which it demanded."[19] Thoreau expressed both the fear of a life lost and the hope of a life redeemed in explaining that he moved to Walden because he wished to live deliberately and "to front only the essential facts of life, and see if I could not learn what it had to teach, and not, when I came to die, discover that I had not lived."[20]

CHAPTER TEN

Conclusion

This, then, is the ultimate paradox of thought. I want to
discover something that thought itself cannot think.
        Søren Kierkegaard, *Philosophical Fragments*

DIFFERENCE AND COMMONALITIES

A review of the eight strategies we have studied for investing life
with meaning reveals six fault lines or differences between the
respective approaches and five themes in common.[1]

First, the motivation and reward for the pursuit of meaning
differs among the approaches.

This is fundamental and colors all that follows. Among the
classic sources of meaning, the mythic mind searches for orientation and identity; the philosophical mind for permanence
and stability; the scientific mind for predictability and control;
and the postmodern mind seeks to undermine fanaticism and
monolithic forms of thought and experience. The contemporary sources of meaning discussed in Part II reflect more
complex sources of meaning but, provisionally at least, we can
say that religious naturalism seeks a renewed sense of wonder
entirely in *this* world; metaphysics a timeless and universal basis

for value and orientation beyond relativism; archetypal psychology a human, universal source of meaning, identity, and stability; while pragmatism seeks a way to accommodate pluralism and the limitations of intentional, instrumental thought. What we find is often a product of what we are looking for.

Second, the approaches differ according to how they answer the question of whether the apprehension of meaning is directly sensual or requires abstraction and seeing with the mind's eye? Naturalism, science, myth, and pragmatism all tend to find meaning in the directly or derivatively sensual, whereas philosophy, archetypal psychology, and postmodernism tend to find meaning through a process of seeing through the immediate and sensory to another dimension, however that other dimension is understood. Is meaning on the surface or an aspect of depth; is it in front of us or somehow hidden? The debate between philosophers and poets is ancient.

Third, is the world one-dimensional—meaning, in this case, exclusively material—or is there a multistoried universe that includes a nonphysical or metaphysical plane? Myth, archetypal psychology, and classical philosophy derive meaning from another ontological dimension, variously defined, whereas science, pragmatism, postmodernism, and naturalism apprehend meaning on a single plane.

Fourth, is meaning inherent in the universe, including a teleological end, or do we create it in an otherwise meaningless or meaning-neutral universe? Meaning is inherent in the universes of myth, archetypal psychology, philosophy, and metaphysics and, ironically, in naturalism, whereas meaning in the universe of science, postmodernism, and pragmatism is humanly created.

Closely aligned with the question of whether meaning is made or discovered is the question of whether it can be fully self-conscious and deliberate, often understood as an unencumbered choice, or whether we find it only so long as we do not step back into self-consciousness. Theologically, this is the question of whether we are redeemed through works or by grace. This question is complicated by the imperialism of both psychology and science. For the psychologist, we are always motivated by unconscious impulses and archetypes; for the scientist, all our thoughts and motivations are reduced to material causes. Can we choose to have meaning or does meaning choose us? Is meaning meaningful only so long as it is chosen (for most, the act of choosing itself invests an act with meaning) or can we accept meaning on faith and the authority of others?

Finally, is meaning an attribute of changing the world or does it change how we see or interpret the world? When we encounter evil or disease, is meaning more a question of actively working to change those conditions or is it seeing evil, for example, in a larger or new context? Huston Smith offers the example of a child losing an ice cream cone. For the child, it is a great tragedy. But for an adult, it is trivial. The tragedy for the child is transformed by the larger perspective of the adult. For the scientist and the pragmatist, meaning is the ability to change things for the better, and they therefore tend to ask "How?" rather than "Why?" In contrast, myth and philosophy focus on apprehending meaning in situations that are comparatively not susceptible to change. They neither ask for a causal explanation nor anticipate a different future. What they seek is an interpretation of what something means and a perspective or context to which it can be related. Meaning is once again discovered, not made.

A misfortune becomes meaningful when it is interpreted as ret-
ribution, a test of faith, or simply bad luck. Above all, the biblical Job wants an explanation. A familiar Zen Buddhist saying
highlights how changing one's perspective—paradoxically—
changes both everything and nothing: before enlightenment, we
chop wood, carry water; after enlightenment, we chop wood,
carry water. In contrast, the engineer would install a water pump
and a hydraulic wood-splitter.

If these are the fault lines that divide and distinguish the eight
approaches, there are nevertheless themes that expose commonalities between them.

First, regardless of approach, the question of meaning is the
price we pay for self-consciousness. The question does not
arise as long as we are unself-consciously and fully engaged in
the act of living, that is, when we take the world for granted.
We do not ask whether a movie, career, or love affair has
"meaning" as long as we are fully involved in the moment and
our expectations and actions flow unimpeded, guided by the
sure and secondary instincts of cultural myths. Our natural
state is one of faith rather than belief. For most of us, the question of meaning never arises; we never reach the point of self-
consciously asking, "What does life mean?" Most of us, most of
the time, live comfortably and unself-consciously following our
cultural instincts.

Whereas meaning has often been understood to be related to
purpose or correspondence, William James and postmodernists
encourage us to ask the pragmatic, functional question of meaning: What does raising the question of meaning "do"? What is its
function? What motive or interest do we seek to satisfy when
we ask "Why"? Beyond the very different motives for each of

the meaning strategies we've examined, the common trait is a fundamental dissatisfaction with the ways things are. Whether the source of this dissatisfaction is inherent in human nature or signals a failure of culture is less important than the recognition that the question of meaning happens when we suddenly STOP, look around, and say to ourselves, "Something's wrong here!" One's unimpeded, unself-conscious journey through life (that happy, drunken life that Tolstoy fondly remembered having lived before the *why* and *what for* questions became insistent) is being challenged and confronted in a way that leaves one unsatisfied and wanting. Recall in this instance James's observation that philosophical speculation would be quenched if the world were nothing but a "lubberland" of happiness.

Whenever our journey through life is impeded, that is, whenever we suddenly stop living unself-consciously because of death or cultural differences, wonder, or a thousand other reasons and frustrations, a separation occurs. We suddenly step back and become self-conscious. We become an outsider or spectator in a way that signals our ability to think *about* our circumstances. We begin to ask "Why?" In asking why, the myth becomes visible, the acceptance of "is" is challenged by "ought" or "could be," the transitory is questioned by the eternal and we compare the world as we find it to the world we imagine or create. Animals never ask these questions, nor—one imagines— do people living in primitive, isolated cultures. Because humans live in a symbolic as well as a physical world, stepping back in a way that makes us self-conscious—and paradoxically an object of our own thought—may be inevitable. Both the privilege and burden of transcendence are part of our inheritance as human beings.

The separation that occurs with the emergence of self-consciousness establishes a duality between the real and the more real, classically expressed as a distinction between appearances and reality. This is the third commonality among the approaches. For the mythic and archetypal minds, the eternal and universal mythic realm is more real than our day-to-day life, just as for the philosophic mind, the real is located in the realm of timeless Forms. For the scientist, the real is the objective world of hard facts and natural laws, expressible in mathematics and distinguished from subjective opinions, beneath seemingly random events. For postmodernists and pragmatists, what's real is the malleability of nature and its subjection to human interests. Reality is a human artifact or, as we have seen, socially constructed. Even naturalism, though firmly in a one-dimensional universe, finds a division between dull habit and a more genuine fresh encounter with the natural world. In each instance, the division that occurs with self-consciousness at the point where the meaning question arises reflects a division between the real and the more real and the associated desire or imperative to move from the one to the other.

Fourth, the dualism between the real and the more real implies a corollary. Meaning is located in or derived from a more real realm. There is not only a division between the real and the more real; there is a hierarchy. The real is dependent on the more real for meaning. In this book, this is most clearly expressed in chapter 7, on archetypal psychology and meaning, and chapter 8, on metaphysics and meaning, but implicit hierarchies exist in the other approaches as well. Thus, the meaning of my life—if I am thinking mythically—is derivative of the mythic stories. Recall Hillman's argument that character is informed by archetypes. Similarly, meaning for a Platonist is derived from the Forms; the Form is more real than the appearances of this world. Scientists find life meaningful to the extent that they are discovering and working in conformity with the laws of nature and progressively moving toward pragmatic human goals such as curing cancer or traveling at the speed of sound. For postmodernists, meaning is derivative of the liberty they obtain in seeing that reality is socially constructed, whereas naturalists find meaning in a direct encounter with nature that goes beyond our customary dulled perceptions. Although each approach defines what is real and more real differently, the underlying pattern remains consistent: the meaning of the less real derives from the more real.

Resolving the question of meaning contains the most fundamental form of transcendence. Our otherwise meaningless day-to-day existence is transcended through a connection to something that is at once more real and more meaningful. Motivations to transcend this world and the nature of that transcendence vary. Nevertheless, each of the strategies we have examined exhibits a form of transcendence. Classically, transcendence was articulated in terms of the metaphysical, as distinguished from the physical, as we have seen in the chapters on myth, philosophy, and metaphysics. But, as we have also seen, even those who reject metaphysical transcendence retain a form of transcendence. Transcendence of our natural, taken-for-granted world occurs whenever we step back and self-consciously ask, "Why?" Motivated by discontent, the scientist and postmodernist, for example, both wish to transcend the "given" of their physical and social circumstances, just as the naturalist wants to transcend a dull, stereotypical experience of nature for one that is available to us when we set aside our more immediate, instrumental intentions.

Just as doubt rests on a foundation of faith, so meaninglessness rests on a foundation of meaning.

Fifth, each of the strategies we've examined for investing life with meaning displays a movement from extrinsic to intrinsically meaningful experiences. Meaning's association with either correspondence or a purposeful end must give way to an experience of meaning that is intrinsically satisfying in a way that makes explanation or justification superfluous. Ironically, science was telling us this all along when it dismissed teleological ends from the universe. Meaning can no longer be delayed or located in the future; if it is to be found, it must be found in the here and now in a way that is self-justifying. Recall the prayer of the Sufi saint Rabi'a al-'Adawiyya quoted in chapter 8 that advised that one should praise God not because in so doing we earn favor and rewards in this world or the next but because it is intrinsically rewarding. Magic and purposeful ends must give way to celebration without reason or justification. The pragmatist and the scientist, who derive meaning from the achievement of human, materialistic goals, must face the necessity of choosing which goals are most intrinsically worthwhile. Working scientists find intrinsic pleasure in solving puzzles and knowing the secrets of nature, regardless of their application. We participate through ritual in archetypes and myth because it is intrinsically rewarding, because in so doing we become in a sense who we are and have always been, not because of their magical effect. Albert Camus was correct in saying that we finally live without appeal, but in saying that, Camus failed to emphasize the pleasures of enjoying intrinsically fulfilling experiences, experiences, that is, that need neither justification nor explanation. The movement from instrumental meaning to intrinsic meaning is present in each of the approaches we have examined, perhaps most clearly in naturalism and its Zen-like experience of nature and life. Tolstoy's succession of childlike questions "Why?" must finally reach the point of "Just because." In this connection, recall the naturalist Ursula Goodenough's epiphany when she realized that she didn't have to ask "Why?" The achievement of intrinsically rewarding experiences signals the point at which the dissatisfactions that elicited stepping back into self-consciousness and division are overcome or transcended. Regardless of how we invest life with meaning and purpose, the attempt to resolve the question of meaning displays how humans make themselves comfortable in a hostile and wondrous world.

How do we go about achieving or knowing these intrinsically worthwhile experiences? As we have seen, the answer to this question varies, too, among the eight approaches we've studied. But beneath that variety, there is a common thread. Knowledge in all of them requires participation and active engagement, whether that engagement is seen as ritualistic identification, iconoclastic deconstruction, intellectual contemplation, or socialization to a paradigm. Objectivity, which maintains separation between the knower and the known, must give way to reintegration and tacit knowledge. "Why?" must give way to acceptance. Thinking *about* becomes thinking *with;* belief becomes faith. Seeing requires us to become new persons. In this connection, William James's contention that our commitments and practice of acting "as if" can add to reality is especially important, especially when one is sensitive to unconscious as well as conscious forms of the will. In his *Pensés*, Pascal ponders whether we perform the Christian ritual because we believe or whether we believe because we perform the ritual. It is, of course, a false dichotomy, because thought and participation always go together, as the postmodernists in particular have taught us. The insistent abstract questions "Why?" and "What does it mean?" are muted when we return to the bright particulars of compelling surfaces that require neither explanation nor justification, when—fully engaged—we unself-consciously practice science or philosophy, participate in ritualistic identifications, or act out our iconoclastic fantasies.[2]

This movement from innocence to self-consciousness to what's been called a second innocence or naïveté finds a familiar example in the acquisition of other skills, such as learning a foreign language. The process of learning how to speak Spanish, for example, is very self-conscious and deliberate. Its feels unnatural and awkward, and one struggles to remember the correct word and verb tense. Eventually, however, the new skill becomes more and more unconscious and instinctive, less deliberate and more instinctual. We no longer have to self-consciously translate Spanish word by word; we simply and unself-consciously begin to understand and speak Spanish without translation. We begin to dream in Spanish. Thinking self-consciously at this point is an impediment. Analogously, I wish to say something about the question of meaning. Answering the question of meaning is like acquiring a new skill. We act *as if*, we self-consciously *try out* and *practice* new ways of living and being in response to frustration and meaninglessness until we acquire the *skill of meaning* at a new level. At this new level, meaning once again becomes less self-conscious, self-justifying, and sufficient, as it was before we asked the question.

Does the movement from original innocence—at the point before the question was asked—to a more self-conscious and halting exile, to an eventual "second innocence" in which we again act faithfully and less self-consciously sound familiar? To anyone of Western culture, it must. The movement is isomorphic to the mythical pattern of Eden, exile, and return to a second Eden. So in asking the question of meaning, we have uncovered the archetypal pattern of our search. Beneath self-conscious thought, we encounter the unself-conscious, informing archetype *The Search for Meaning: A Short History* has exposed. As with all archetypes, the insistent question "Why?" is symptomatic, as Tolstoy understood: we neither invite nor can deliberately silence the question. It comes or is revealed to us, apart from our intentions, and its satisfactions are finally intrinsic rather than instrumental. What's more, though the question of meaning—and the threat or experience of meaninglessness with which it is associated—is experienced individually, it is nevertheless impersonal, universal, and timeless. Within that archetype, what appears negative—the experience of meaninglessness, self-consciousness, and exile—becomes a reoccurring interlude in a larger, more positive narrative of innocence, fall, and redemption. Meaninglessness, which feels like a loss and a fall from natural grace, is the prelude to an eventual gain. Is the experience of meaninglessness disheartening and frustrating? Absolutely. But so too are the halting attempts to speak a new language. But neither experience is terminal. Meaninglessness is an instrumental experience that motivates us to go forward until we arrive at a new integration at a different point on the spiral of faith. This is not to deny that people get stranded in the wilderness. There are those who courageously start on the journey but never return home. All journeys involve risk. But, normatively, the archetype encourages us to have faith that exile will bring us to the Promised Land. Indeed, it is saying more than that; it is saying that the Promised Land can only be reached by leaving our homes and becoming pilgrims.

HOW MEANING AFFECTS OUR SENSE OF RIGHT AND WRONG

This book examines how we invest our lives with meaning. Normally, the question of meaning becomes most visible when people ask the question "Why?" in response to loss or pluralism. However, another way the question of meaning becomes visible occurs in ethical conflicts. Beneath explicit disagreements over issues such as abortion and economic justice, there are largely unspoken and less consciously held assumptions about what is real and true. The sociologist James Davison Hunter argues that the deep divisions between the antagonists in what he has dubbed "culture wars"—whether the issue is poverty, war, euthanasia, or capital punishment—reveal fundamentally different "commitments and beliefs that provide a source of identity, purpose, and togetherness for the people who live by them."[1] Thus, how one goes about deciding the issue of abortion, for example, says much about how one goes about investing life with meaning. The pragmatist and scientist, who live in a one-dimensional, value-neutral universe, tend to see abortion as a regrettable but nevertheless expedient remedy to an unwanted pregnancy, whereas the person living deeply within a myth that maintains the sacredness of life beginning with conception tends to see abortion as always unacceptable. We decide this way rather than that because one decision seems more meaningful than its alternative. Within this perspective, conventional questions of right and wrong become questions of meaning and meaninglessness. We may decide that abortion is "wrong" because abortion leads to a sense of meaninglessness (because nothing is sacred and fixed, not even life), whereas saving the life of the unborn is "right" because it provides a sense of meaning and purpose. Or, alternatively, we may decide that exercising the right to choose according to what is pragmatically best for the woman is "right" because it is more meaningful than bearing an unwanted child. Women have the right to choose, and violating that right goes against the freedom and self-determination that makes life meaningful.

Seeing through right and wrong to a more fundamental division between meaning and meaninglessness helps explain how people can deliberately commit "wrong" acts, how we can all, like Saint Paul, do the very thing we hate. Adultery, the petty crimes of teenagers—including drug use—and the indifference of the affluent to the poor illustrate how ethically wrong acts are nevertheless committed because they invest life with a sense of meaning and purpose. Actions can be both "right" and meaningless. The bored, "good" teenager will explore walking on the wild side because walking on the straight-and-narrow has become meaningless. Exploiting immigrant labor for the sake of lower costs and higher profits—or economic survival—seems more meaningful in an exclusively materialistic culture than preserving the more "metaphysical" dignity and justice embodied by the concept of a living wage. Meaning and purpose are stronger and more fundamental attractions than right and wrong.

Because it is more fundamental than specific decisions between right and wrong, how one invests life with meaning also explains how ethical decisions are related and form a complex. In his book *Culture Wars: The Struggle to Define America* Hunter distinguishes among various groups according to whether they are orthodox or progressive. The orthodox invest their lives with meaning and make their ethical decisions based on what they see as an external, autonomous sacred truth—whether that truth is located in an ideology, myth, scripture, tradition, or natural law. The orthodox Protestant who finds meaning in Scripture and makes decisions based on what it seems to prescribe and the philosopher who finds meaning in and bases decisions on an abstract concept of justice are formally the same in this respect. Both appeal to an external, unchanging, objective authority. In contrast, progressives invest their lives with meaning in terms of rationalism or pragmatism. They see themselves achieving humanly created goals and aspirations in an otherwise value-neutral universe by employing rationalism or pragmatism, whether or not these are held in conversation with particular religions or cultural traditions.[2] For the progressive, making decisions based on pragmatic consequences, without any inherent, rational, or sacred limitations, is more meaningful than adhering to an inviolable principle or standard. Culture wars and the ethical conflicts they engender are interminable and passionate because each side brings to the table fundamental commitments to what it sees as real, true, and good. Hunter summarizes the link between meaning and cultural/ethical conflicts this way: "What is ultimately at issue, then, are not just disagreements about 'values' or 'opinions.' Such language misconstrues the nature of moral commitment . . . [and] reduces morality to preferences and moral whim. What is ultimately at issue are deeply rooted and fundamental different understandings of being and purpose."[3]

A final, cautionary comment on the relationship between ethics and meaning. People may make the same ethical decision but nevertheless reach that decision by different routes. Advocates of restricting greenhouse gases, for example, may reach that decision because of very this-worldly reasons. In contrast, orthodox Protestants have reached that same decision by confessing that we have not been good stewards of the gifts God has given us. We have despoiled the garden in ways that violate the sacred quality of that trust. Similarly, those who are committed to reducing poverty may find meaning in, and base their decisions on, pragmatic considerations (poverty contributes to unstable societies and markets), the myths and stories of social justice found in Scripture, or the more abstract principle or concept of social justice. In each instance, the ethical decision is the same, although the basis for it varies. Cultural and ethical conflicts expose the way people invest their lives with meaning, but people who invest their lives with meaning in different ways can nevertheless reach the same ethical decision. Meaning is thus more fundamental than ethics.

NOTES

PREFACE

1. Colin Wilson, *The Outsider* (Boston: Houghton Mifflin, 1956).

2. In addition, I thank Kalicia Pivirotto, Marilyn Schwartz, and the staff of University of California Press; in particular, I wish to thank the acquisitions editor, Reed Malcolm, for his interest in and support of this project from the start.

3. Gaston Rébuffat, *On Snow and Rock*, trans. Eleanor Brockett, with technical assistance from J. E. B. Wright (1963; New York: Oxford University Press, 1968), 190.

1. INTRODUCTION

Epigraph: Maurice Friedman, *To Deny Our Nothingness: Contemporary Images of Man* (New York: Delacorte, 1967), 19.

1. Leo Tolstoy, *Confession*, trans. David Patterson (New York: Norton, 1983, 1996), 26–33. Also see the summary of Tolstoy, including excerpts, in William James's *The Varieties of Religious Experience* (New York: Longmans, Green, 1903), 152ff.

2. See Colin Wilson, *The Outsider* (Boston: Houghton Mifflin, 1956).

3. Robert C. Solomon, *The Passions: Emotions and the Meaning of Life* (Indianapolis: Hackett, 1993), 19.

4. When Martin Luther broke away from the culture and authority of the Catholic Church, he looked to his own direct contact with God and divinely inspired scripture for guidance. In so doing, he established the Protestant principle of an individual's right to question authority and the superiority of the individual conscience. Whenever we turn inward for guidance, we are heirs of the Protestant revolution Luther helped to instigate. On this point, see Peter L. Berger, *The Heretical Imperative* (Garden City, N.Y.: Anchor Books, 1980), and Reinhold Niebuhr, *The Nature and Destiny of Man* (New York: Scribner, 1941–43). For a more detailed description of how culture provides a surreality, see Peter L. Berger and Thomas Luckmann, *The Social Construction of Reality: A Treatise in the Sociology of Knowledge* (1966; Garden City, N.Y.: Doubleday, 1967).

5. Michael Novak, *The Experience of Nothingness* (New York: Harper & Row, 1970).

6. Bruno Bettelheim, *The Uses of Enchantment* (New York: Knopf, 1978), 3.

7. Novak, *Experience of Nothingness*, 14.

8. Solomon, *Passions*, 28.

9. James E. Edwards, *The Plain Sense of Things: The Fate of Religion in an Age of Normal Nihilism* (University Park: Pennsylvania State University Press, 1997), 43.

10. Wilfred Cantwell Smith, *Faith and Belief* (Oxford: Oneworld Publications, 1998), 155.

11. Viktor E. Frankl, *Man's Search for Ultimate Meaning* (Cambridge: Perseus Publishing, 2000), 112.

12. Richard Tarnas, *The Passion of the Western Mind* (New York: Ballantine Books, 1993), 420.

13. Erich Fromm, *Man for Himself: An Inquiry into the Psychology of Ethics* (1947; Greenwich, Conn.: Fawcett, 1965), 201.

14. Erich Fromm, *Escape from Freedom* (1941; New York: Avon Books, 1965), 97.

15. Friedman, *To Deny Our Nothingness,* 275. See also Paul Tillich, *The Courage to Be* (New Haven: Yale University Press, 1952).

16. Mark Jenkins, "The Hard Way," *Outside* 28, no. 11 (November 2003): 55.

17. For a fascinating update on this theme, see Benjamin R. Barber's *Jihad vs. McWorld* (New York: Ballantine Books, 1995).

18. Lionel Trilling, *A Gathering of Fugitives* (Boston: Beacon Press, 1956), 162–63, quoted in Samuel Levinson, *Santayana: Pragmatism, and the Spiritual Life* (Chapel Hill: University of North Carolina Press, 1992), 296.

19. Erich Fromm, *The Sane Society* (Greenwich, Conn.: Fawcett, 1955), 32ff.

20. Solomon, *Passions,* 28.

21. Iris Murdoch, *Metaphysics as a Guide to Morals* (New York: Penguin Books, 1993), 262.

22. Wayne Dyer: see www.drwaynedyer.com (accessed November 25, 2006).

2. MYTH AND MEANING

1. John H. Finley Jr., *Four Stages of Greek Thought* (Stanford: Stanford University Press, 1966), 3.

2. Eric A. Havelock, *Preface to Plato* (Cambridge, Mass.: Harvard University Press, 1982), 30.

3. Mircea Eliade, *The Sacred and the Profane* (New York: Harcourt, Brace & World, 1959), 12.

4. Wilfred Cantwell Smith, *Faith and Belief* (1979; Boston: Oneworld Publications, 1998), 36. The section epigraph is from ibid., 63.

5. Ibid., 146.

6. Joseph Campbell, with Bill Moyers, *The Power of Myth,* ed. Betty Sue Flowers (New York: Doubleday, 1988), 5.

7. Smith, *Faith and Belief,* 15.

8. Ibid., 42–43.

9. Northrop Frye, *The Great Code* (New York: Harcourt Brace Jovanovich, 1982), 171.

10. Joseph Campbell, *Myths to Live By* (New York: Bantam Books, 1978), i.

11. Lawrence G. Boldt, *Zen and the Art of Making a Living* (New York: Penguin Books, 1999).

12. David L. Miller, *The New Polytheism: Rebirth of the Gods and Goddesses* (New York: Harper & Row, 1974), 30.

13. James C. Edwards, *The Plain Sense of Things* (University Park: Pennsylvania State University Press, 1997), 17.

14. Mircea Eliade, *Myth and Reality*, trans. Willard R. Trask (New York: Harper & Row, 1963), 2.

15. Eliade, *The Sacred and the Profane*, 209.

16. Ibid., 206–7.

17. Hayden White, *Tropics of Discourse* (Baltimore: Johns Hopkins University Press, 1985), 2; emphasis added.

18. Ibid., 86.

19. See F. M. Cornford's *From Religion to Philosophy: A Study in the Origins of Western Speculation* (1912; Princeton: Princeton University Press, 1991) on the relationship between mythology and scientific concepts.

20. Robert C. Solomon, *The Passions: Emotions and the Meaning of Life* (1976; Indianapolis: Hackett, 1993), 27–28.

3. PHILOSOPHY AND MEANING

1. Plato, *The Dialogues* (New York: Bantam Books, 1986), 196.

2. Plato, *The Republic*, trans. and ed. F. M. Cornford (Oxford: Oxford University Press, 1945), 183.

3. John H. Finley Jr., *Four Stages of Greek Thought* (Stanford: Stanford University Press, 1966), 72.

4. Eric A. Havelock, *Preface to Plato* (1963; Cambridge, Mass.: Belknap Press, Harvard University Press, 1982), 264–65.

5. I speak here of discontent, but philosophy is also a reaction to wonder as expressed in Heidegger's question, Why is there something rather than nothing? In either case, the taken-for-granted, everyday life becomes a question.

6. Richard Tarnas, *The Passion of the Western Mind* (New York: Ballantine Books, 1993), 69.

7. Havelock, *Preface to Plato*, 241.

8. Tarnas, *Passion of the Western Mind*, 8.

9. James C. Edwards, *The Plain Sense of Things* (University Park: Pennsylvania State University Press, 1997), 23.

10. For examples of this resurgence, see Lou Marinoff, *The Big Questions: How Philosophy Can Change Your Life* (New York: Bloomsbury, 2003) and Christopher Phillips, *Socrates Café: A Fresh Taste of Philosophy* (New York: Norton, 2001), as well as books by Alain de Botton, such as *How Proust Can Change Your Life: Not a Novel* (New York: Pantheon Books, 1997) and *The Consolations of Philosophy* (New York: Pantheon Books, 2000).

11. Havelock, *Preface to Plato*, 200.

12. Nietzsche's remark about Christianity having become "Platonism for the people" is from the Preface to *Beyond Good and Evil*, trans. Helen Zimmern in *The Complete Works of Friedrich Nietzsche* (1909–13); see www.readeasily.com/friedrich-nietzsche/00172/index.php (accessed December 1, 2006). I do not go into the fascinating question of why the change from the mythic to the Platonic mind. Havelock and Finley, among others, attribute the change to a shift from oral to written forms of communication. Many see our own age as becoming more mythic because of a shift from written to electronic forms of communication.

4. SCIENCE AND MEANING

1. Richard Tarnas, *The Passion of the Western Mind: Understanding the Ideas That Have Shaped Our World View* (1991; reprint, New York: Ballantine Books, 1993), 57.

2. E. A. Burtt, *The Metaphysical Foundations of Modern Science* (Mineola, N.Y.: Dover Publications, 2003), 83.

3. Floyd W. Matson, *The Broken Image: Man, Science and Society* (New York: George Braziller, 1964), 27.

4. Bryan Appleyard, *Understanding the Present: Science and the Soul of Modern Man* (New York: Doubleday, 1994), 25.

5. Huston Smith, *Beyond the Post-modern Mind* (Wheaton, Ill.: Theosophical Pub. House, 2003), 198.

6. Franklin L. Baumer, *Religion and the Rise of Skepticism* (New York: Harcourt, Brace & World, 1960), 80–81; emphasis added.

7. Appleyard, *Understanding the Present*, 32.

8. Ibid., 3.

9. Ibid., 140.

10. Spinoza quoted in Matson, *Broken Image*, 24.

11. Smith, *Beyond the Post-modern Mind*, 180.

12. Tarnas, *Passion of the Western Mind*, 420.

13. Burtt, *Metaphysical Foundations*, 239.

14. Gerald Holton quoted in Robert Nisbet, *History of the Idea of Progress* (New Brunswick, N.J.: Transaction Publishers, 1994), 346.

15. The roots of the idea of progress in Christian eschatology or expectations of the redemption of history are deep. Indeed, Tarnas states simply that, with the notion of progress, "[t]he original Judaeo-Christian eschatological expectation had here been transformed into a secular faith" (*Passion of the Western Mind*, 321).

16. Christopher Dawson as quoted by Christopher Lasch, *The True and Only Heaven: Progress and Its Critics.* (New York: Norton, 1991), 43.

17. Appleyard, *Understanding the Present*, 233–34.

18. Ibid., 126.

19. M. H. Abrams, *Natural Supernaturalism: Tradition and Revolution in Romantic Literature* (New York: Norton, 1971).

20. On this point, see, e.g., David L. Miller, *Gods and Games: Toward a Theology of Play* (New York: Harper & Row, 1974).

5. POSTMODERNISM AND MEANING

1. Walt Anderson, *Reality Isn't What It Used To Be: Theatrical Politics, Ready-to-Wear Religion, Global Myths, Primitive Chic, and Other Wonders of the Postmodern World* (New York: Harper & Row, 1990), 6.

2. Richard Tarnas, *The Passion of the Western Mind: Understanding the Ideas That Have Shaped Our World View* (1991; reprint, New York: Ballantine Books, 1993), 344.

3. Ibid., 345.

4. Brian Greene, *The Elegant Universe: Superstrings, Hidden Dimensions, and the Quest for the Ultimate Theory* (1999; New York: Vintage Books, 2000), 25ff.

5. John Polkinghorne, *Science and Theology* (Minneapolis: Fortress Press, 1998), 31.

6. Bryan Appleyard, *Understanding the Present: Science and the Soul of Modern Man* (New York: Doubleday, 1993), 144.

7. Niels Bohr quoted ibid., 145.

8. William James, *The Meaning of Truth* (1911; reprint, Amherst, N.Y.: Prometheus Books, 1997), 58.

9. Thomas S. Kuhn, *The Structure of Scientific Revolutions* (1962; 3d ed., Chicago: University of Chicago Press, 1996), 175.

10. N. R. Hanson quoted in Ian G. Barbour's *Myths, Models, and Paradigms: A Comparative Study in Science and Religion* (New York: Harper & Row, 1974), 103. Those familiar with this title will recognize my indebtedness to Barbour's outstanding work.

11. Tarnas, *Passion of the Western Mind*, 361.

12. Ibid., 421.

13. James C. Edwards, *The Plain Sense of Things: The Fate of Religion in an Age of Normal Nihilism* (University Park: Pennsylvania State University Press, 1997), 34.

14. Ibid., 34–35, quoting Friedrich Nietzsche, *The Will to Power*, ed. Walter Kaufmann, trans. Walter Kaufmann and R. J. Hollingdale (New York: Random House, 1967), 515, 604, 556, 493.

15. Anderson, *Reality Isn't What It Used To Be*, 37.

16. William James quoted ibid., 258.

17. Marcus J. Borg, *Reading the Bible Again for the First Time: Taking the Bible Seriously but Not Literally* (2001; San Francisco: HarperSanFrancisco, 2002), 41.

18. Jacques Derrida quoted in Pauline Marie Rosenau, *Post-Modernism and the Social Sciences: Insights, Inroads, and Intrusions* (Princeton: Princeton University Press, 1992), 90.

19. Peter L. Berger and Thomas Luckmann, *The Social Construction of Reality: A Treatise in the Sociology of Knowledge* (1966; Garden City, N.Y.: Doubleday, 1967), 89.

20. The phrase is Philip Rieff's. For his insightful discussion of the mechanism of liberating oneself from cultural constraints and dictates, see his *The Triumph of the Therapeutic: Uses of Faith after Freud* (1966; Chicago: University of Chicago Press, 1987), 43.

21. Ernest Becker, *The Denial of Death* (New York: Free Press, 1973), 60.

22. George Santayana, "War Shrines," in *Soliloquies in England and Later Soliloquies* (New York: Scribner, 1922), 97.

6. PRAGMATISM AND MEANING

Epigraph: William James, "The Will to Believe," in *The Will to Believe and Other Essays in Popular Philosophy* (1897; New York: Dover Publications, 1956), 39.

1. William James, *Writings, 1902–1910* (New York: Library Classics of the United States, 1987), 487. All quotations of James are from this source unless otherwise noted.

2. Ibid., 149–50. This passage from *Varieties of Religious Experience* is conventionally understood to be autobiographical.

3. Ibid., 116.

4. Ibid., 463.

5. William James, *The Meaning of Truth* (1911; reprint, Amherst, N.Y.: Prometheus Books, 1997), 62.

6. Ibid., 597.

7. Ibid., 93–94. James makes a similar argument, with additional examples, in *Writings*, 596.

8. James, *Meaning of Truth*, 80.

9. Ibid., 185–86.

10. James, *Will to Believe*, 59.

11. Ibid., 24.

12. Ibid., 25.

13. James, *Writings*, 103.

14. James, *Will to Believe*, 61.

15. James, *Writings*, 618.

16. James, *Meaning of Truth*, 196.

17. James, *Writings*, 506.

18. James, *Will to Believe*, 16.

19. James, *Writings*, 575.

20. James, *Meaning of Truth*, 58–60.

21. James, *Writings*, 606.

22. Ibid., 618.

23. Ibid., 570.

24. Ibid., 762.

25. Ibid., 574–75.

26. Ibid., 453.

27. James, *Meaning of Truth*, 495.

28. James, *Writings*, 522.

29. James, *Meaning of Truth*, 80–81.

30. James, *Writings*, 755.

31. Ibid., 725.

32. Ibid., 745.

33. Ibid., 749.

34. Ibid., 746.

35. Ibid., 105–6.

36. Ibid., 762–63.

37. However, James is not entirely silent on the subject. He writes that just as "these passions put into the world is our gift to the world,

just so the passions themselves are *gifts*—gifts to us, from sources sometimes low and sometimes high, but always non-logical and beyond our control" (ibid., 141). These comments may fruitfully be examined in light of James Hillman's characterization of archetypes, discussed in chapter 7.

7. ARCHETYPAL PSYCHOLOGY AND MEANING

1. James Hillman, *The Force of Character and the Lasting Life* (New York: Ballantine Books, 1999), 73.

2. Ibid., 201.

3. James Hillman, *Re-Visioning Psychology* (1975; New York: HarperPerennial, 1975), xix.

4. Ibid., 128.

5. Ibid., 209.

6. James Hillman, "Peaks and Vales," in *Working with Images: The Theoretical Base of Archetypal Psychology*, ed. Benjamin Sells (Woodstock, Conn.: Spring Publications, 2000), 117.

7. Mircea Eliade, *Myth and Reality* (New York: Harper & Row, 1963), 92.

8. David L. Miller, *The New Polytheism: Rebirth of the Gods and Goddesses* (New York: Harper & Row, 1974), 55.

9. Hillman, *Re-Visioning Psychology*, 99.

10. Ibid., 128.

11. For an intriguing example of non-Western archetypes, see Taigen Daniel Leighton, *Bodhisattva Archetypes* (New York: Penguin Books, 1998).

12. Joseph Campbell, *The Inner Reaches of Outer Space* (New York: Harper & Row, 1986), 99.

13. George Lakoff and Mark Johnson, *Philosophy in the Flesh: The Embodied Mind and Its Challenge to Western Thought* (New York: Basic Books, 1999), 4.

14. George Lakoff and Mark Johnson, *Metaphors We Live By* (Chicago: University of Chicago Press, 1980), 3.

15. Hillman, *Re-Visioning Psychology*, xix.

16. Hillman, *Force of Character*, 6.

17. Hillman, "Peaks and Vales," 126.

18. Miller, *New Polytheism*, 59.

19. James Hillman, *ANIMA: An Anatomy of a Personified Notion* (Dallas: Spring Publications, 1993), 83.

20. Miller, *New Polytheism*, 18.

21. Hillman, *Force of Character*, 127.

22. Thomas Moore, *The Care of the Soul: A Guide for Cultivating Depth and Sacredness in Everyday Life* (New York: HarperPerennial, 1994), 137ff.

8. METAPHYSICS AND MEANING

Epigraph: E. F. Schumacher, *A Guide for the Perplexed* (New York: Harper Colophon Books, 1978), 38.

1. Walter Mead, quoted in Gayle White, "Europe's Loss of Faith," *Atlanta Journal Constitution*, May 28, 2005, B4.

2. E. M. W. Tillyard, *The Elizabethan World Picture* (1943; reprint, New York: Vintage Books, n.d. [196–?]), 54.

3. On this point, see Huston Smith's *Essays on World Religions*, ed. M. Darrol Bryant (New York: Paragon House, 1992), 206.

4. Huston Smith, *The Soul of Christianity: Restoring the Great Tradition* (San Francisco: HarperSanFrancisco, 2005), xvi.

5. Huston Smith, *Beyond the Post-modern Mind* (1982; 2d ed., Wheaton, Ill.: Theosophical Pub. House, 2003), 91.

6. Aquinas quoted in Schumacher, *Guide for the Perplexed*, 3.

7. In the following discussion, I rely entirely on Schumacher's work in *Guide for the Perplexed*.

8. Ibid., 16.

9. Ibid., 17.

10. Ibid., 25.

11. Ibid., 39. Section epigraph from Huston Smith, *Forgotten Truth: The Primordial Tradition* (New York: Harper Colophon Books, 1976), 60.

12. Ibid., 43.

13. Huston Smith, *The Way Things Are: Conversations with Huston Smith on the Spiritual Life*, ed. Phil Cousineau (Berkeley: University of California Press, 2003), 50.

14. On this point, see Smith, *Beyond the Post-modern Mind*, 67.

15. This discussion of Hinduism relies entirely on Huston Smith's *The World's Religions* (San Francisco: HarperSanFrancisco, 1991). The specific quotation is found on p. 17.

16. Schumacher, *Guide for the Perplexed*, 38.

17. Smith, *Forgotten Truth*, 52.

18. Ibid., 53.

19. Schumacher, *Guide for the Perplexed*, 71. On the intellectual connection between Smith and Schumacher, Smith on one occasion approvingly reported that his book *Forgotten Truth* was being packaged and sold as a set in some bookstores with Schumacher's *Guide for the Perplexed*.

20. Rabi'a quoted in Karen Armstrong, *A History of God: The 4000-year Quest of Judaism, Christianity, and Islam* (1993; reprint, New York: Ballantine Books, 1994), 226.

21. Smith, *Forgotten Truth*, 18.

22. Smith, *World's Religions*, 8.

23. Schumacher, *Guide for the Perplexed*, 35.

9. NATURALISM AND MEANING

Epigraph: George A. Sheehan, *Running and Being: The Total Experience* (New York: Simon and Schuster, 1978), 39.

1. Ursula Goodenough, *The Sacred Depths of Nature* (New York: Oxford University Press, 1998), 11.

2. Robert C. Solomon, *Spirituality for the Skeptic* (New York: Oxford University Press, 2002), 23.

3. Section epigraph from Chet Raymo, *Honey from Stone: A Naturalist's Search for God* (New York: Dodd, Mead, 1987), 150, quoting Edward Abbey.

4. That the human spirit is an evolutionary accomplishment, fully within a naturalistic scheme, is advanced by proponents of neurotheology such as the surgeon and bioethicist Sherwin Nuland.

5. Edward Abbey quoted in Raymo, *Honey from Stone*, 153.

6. Henry Samuel Levinson, *Santayana, Pragmatism, and the Spiritual Life* (Chapel Hill: University of North Carolina Press, 1992), 259. My reliance on Levinson's work is obvious. The book is not only a wonderful study of Santayana but a contribution in its own right to a naturalistic spirituality. Section epigraph from George Santayana, "War Shrines," in *Soliloquies in England and Later Soliloquies* (New York: Scribner, 1922), 97.

7. George Santayana, *Realms of Being* (New York: Scribner, 1942), 833.

8. Levinson, *Santayana*, 133.

9. William James quoted ibid., 166.

10. Josef Pieper, *Leisure: The Basis of Culture*, trans. Gerald Malsbary (1948; South Bend, Ind.: St. Augustine's Press, 1998), 11. My debt to this classic work is obvious.

11. Ibid., 79.

12. M. H. Abrams, *Natural Supernaturalism: Tradition and Revolution in Romantic Literature* (New York: Norton, 1973), 381.

13. Samuel Taylor Coleridge, *Biographia Literaria*, quoted in Abrams, *Natural Supernaturalism*, 378.

14. Ibid., 47.

15. Solomon, *Spirituality for the Skeptic*, xv.

16. D. H. Lawrence, *Apocalypse* (New York: Viking, 1932), 190, quoted in Abrams, *Natural Supernaturalism*, 324.

17. Goodenough, *Sacred Depths of Nature*, 47.

18. Robert C. Solomon, *The Passions: Emotions and the Meaning of Life* (Indianapolis: Hackett, 1993), 7.

19. Ibid., 29.

20. Henry David Thoreau, *Walden: or, Life in the Woods: and, On the Duty of Civil Disobedience* (New York: New American Library, 1960), 66.

10. CONCLUSION

Epigraph: Søren Kierkegaard, *Philosophical Fragments*, ed. and trans. Howard V. Hong and Edna H. Hong (Princeton: Princeton University Press, 1985), 37.

1. A conclusion is an exercise in seeing unity behind apparent diversity. As such, it is a task for the philosophic mind. In contrast, a postmodern or pragmatic perspective is pluralistic and accepting of a diverse collection of approaches according to circumstances and motive. Another way to look at the issue of unity versus diversity is to see each of the approaches we've studied as an archetype whose meaning chooses us. Recall that we do not deliberately and self-consciously choose archetypes; they choose us, and in choosing us they seem all the more compelling. Each archetype is a compelling force. If this is the case, the question becomes: are we monotheists or polytheists? Must we have one god/archetype/meaning above all the rest, or do we practice a form of polytheism? I invite others to arrive at their own conclusions.

2. One aspect of the relationship between knowing, commitment, and meaning is to acknowledge the essential role of communities. Paradigms and languages are legitimated and sustained by communities of users. Although knowing, and, in turn, meaning, seems like an individual achievement or failure, what we know is acquired through our participation and socialization in these communities, as the postmodernists most directly remind us. Though meaning is acquired individually, we need to correct any impression we may have left that meaning is the purview of isolated individuals making choices about what to believe. Meaning is in large measure defined and resolved within communities of fellow pilgrims.

APPENDIX: HOW MEANING AFFECTS OUR SENSE OF RIGHT AND WRONG

1. James Davison Hunter, *Culture Wars: The Struggle to Define America* (New York: Basic Books, 1991), 42.

2. The dichotomy between progressive and orthodox is not absolute, as I hope this study shows. A good example is the nineteenth-century Bible criticism that attempted to combine scientific method with belief in biblical myths. For more on this, see Van Austin Harvey, *The Historian and the Believer: The Morality of Historical Knowledge and Christian Belief* (New York: Macmillan, 1969).

3. Hunter, *Culture Wars*, 131.

BIBLIOGRAPHY

Abrams, M. H. *Natural Supernaturalism: Tradition and Revolution in Romantic Literature*. New York: Norton, 1971.

Anderson, Walt. *Reality Isn't What It Used to Be: Theatrical Politics, Ready-to-Wear Religion, Global Myths, Primitive Chic, and Other Wonders of the Postmodern World*. New York: HarperCollins, 1990.

Appleyard, Bryan. *Understanding the Present: Science and the Soul of Modern Man*. 1993. New York: Anchor, 1994.

Armstrong, Karen. *A History of God: The 4000-year Quest of Judaism, Christianity, and Islam*. New York: Knopf, 1993.

Barber, Benjamin R. *Jihad vs. McWorld*. New York: Ballantine, 1995.

Barbour, Ian G. *Myths, Models, and Paradigms: A Comparative Study in Science and Religion*. New York: Harper & Row, 1974.

Barfield, Owen. *Saving the Appearances: A Study in Idolatry*. New York: Harcourt, Brace & World, 1957. 2d ed. Middletown, Conn.: Wesleyan University Press, 1988.

Barrett, William. *The Illusion of Technique: A Search for Meaning in a Technological Civilization*. Garden City, N.Y.: Anchor Books, 1978.

Baumer, Franklin L. *Religion and the Rise of Skepticism*. New York: Harcourt, Brace & World, 1960.

Becker, Carl L. *The Heavenly City of the Eighteenth-Century Philosophers.* 1932. 2d ed. New Haven: Yale University Press, 2003.

Becker, Ernest. *The Denial of Death.* New York: Free Press, 1973.

Berger, Peter L. *The Heretical Imperative.* Garden City, N.Y.: Anchor Books, 1980.

Berger, Peter L., and Thomas Luckmann. *The Social Construction of Reality: A Treatise in the Sociology of Knowledge.* 1966. Garden City, N.Y.: Doubleday, 1967.

Berman, Marshall. *All That Is Solid Melts into Air: The Experience of Modernity.* New York: Viking Penguin, 1988.

Bettelheim, Bruno. *The Uses of Enchantment: The Meaning and Importance of Fairy Tales.* New York: Knopf, 1976.

Boldt, Laurence G. *Zen and the Art of Making a Living.* New York: Penguin Books, 1999.

Borg, Marcus J. *Reading the Bible Again for the First Time: Taking the Bible Seriously but Not Literally.* 2001. San Francisco: HarperSanFrancisco, 2002.

Burtt, E. A. *The Metaphysical Foundations of Modern Science.* Mineola, N.Y.: Dover Publications, 2003. Originally published as *The Metaphysical Foundations of Modern Physical Science* (1932; rev. ed., Atlantic Highlands, N.J.: Humanities Press, 1980).

Caldwell, Roger. "Hot to Get Real." *Philosophy Now,* www.philosophynow.org/issue42/42caldwell1.htm (accessed October 2, 2006).

Campbell, Joseph. *The Inner Reaches of Outer Space.* New York: Harper & Row, 1986.

———. *Myths to Live By.* 1972. New York: Bantam Books, 1978.

Campbell, Joseph, with Bill Moyers. *The Power of Myth.* Edited by Betty Sue Flowers. New York: Doubleday, 1988.

Clark, Thomas W. "Spirituality without Faith." Center for Naturalism, July 2001, www.naturalism.org/spiritua1.htm (accessed October 2, 2006).

———. "Towards a Naturalistic Spirituality." Center for Naturalism, www.naturalism.org/naturali.htm (accessed October 2, 2006).

Cornford, F. M. *From Religion to Philosophy: A Study in the Origins of Western Speculation.* 1912. Princeton: Princeton University Press, 1991.

De Botton, Alain. *The Consolations of Philosophy.* New York: Pantheon Books, 2000.

———. *How Proust Can Change Your Life: Not a Novel.* New York: Pantheon Books, 1997.

Derksen, Mario. "Causality and the Metaphysics of Change in Aristotle and St. Thomas Aquinas." Catholic Apologetics, www.catholicapologetics.info/catholicteaching/philosophy/cause.htm (accessed October 2, 2006).

Douglas, Susan J. *Where the Girls Are: Growing Up Female with the Mass Media.* New York: Times Books, 1995.

Edwards, James C. *The Plain Sense of Things: The Fate of Religion in an Age of Normal Nihilism.* University Park: Pennsylvania State University Press, 1997.

Eliade, Mircea. *Myth and Reality.* Translated by Willard R. Trask. New York: Harper & Row, 1963.

———. *The Sacred and the Profane.* New York: Harcourt, Brace & World, 1959.

Finley, John H., Jr. *Four Stages of Greek Thought.* Stanford: Stanford University Press, 1966.

Frankl, Viktor E. *Man's Search for Ultimate Meaning.* Cambridge, Mass.: Perseus, 2000.

Friedman, Maurice. *To Deny Our Nothingness: Contemporary Images of Man.* New York: Dell, 1967.

Fromm, Erich. *Escape from Freedom.* 1941. New York: Avon Books, 1965.

———. *Man for Himself: An Inquiry into the Psychology of Ethics.* 1947. Greenwich, Conn.: Fawcett, 1965.

———. *The Sane Society.* Greenwich, Conn.: Fawcett, 1955.

Frye, Northrop. *The Great Code.* New York: Harcourt Brace Jovanovich, 1982.

Goodenough, Ursula. *The Sacred Depths of Nature.* New York: Oxford University Press, 1998.

Gould, Stephen J. " Faith, Science, and the Soul." Center for Naturalism, www.naturalism.org/faithsci.htm#faith (accessed October 2, 2006).

Greene, Brian. *The Elegant Universe: Superstrings, Hidden Dimensions, and the Quest for the Ultimate Theory.* 1999. New York: Vintage Books, 2000.

Harvey, Van Austin. *The Historian and the Believer: The Morality of Historical Knowledge and Christian Belief.* 1966. New York: Macmillan, 1969.

Hauerwas, Stanley. *The Peaceable Kingdom: A Primer in Christian Ethics.* Notre Dame, Ind.: University of Notre Dame Press, 1983.

Havelock, Eric A. *Preface to Plato.* 1963. Cambridge, Mass.: Belknap Press, Harvard University Press, 1982.

Hawking, Stephen. *The Universe in a Nutshell.* New York: Bantam Books, 2001.

Herman, A. L. *The Ways of Philosophy.* Atlanta: Scholars Press, 1990.

Hibbs, Thomas S. *Shows about Nothing: Nihilism in Popular Culture from the Exorcist to Seinfeld.* Dallas: Spence Publishing, 1999.

Hillman, James. *ANIMA: An Anatomy of a Personified Notion.* Dallas: Spring Publications, 1993.

———. *The Dream and the Underworld.* New York: Harper & Row, 1979.

———. *The Force of Character and the Lasting Life.* 1999. New York: Ballantine Books, 2000.

———. *Re-Visioning Psychology.* 1975. New York: HarperPerennial, 1992.

———. "Peaks and Vales." In *Working with Images: The Theoretical Base of Archetypal Psychology,* ed. Benjamin Sells. Woodstock, Conn.: Spring Publications, 2000.

Hunter, James Davison. *Culture Wars: The Struggle to Define America.* New York: Basic Books, 1991.

James, William. *The Meaning of Truth.* 1911. Reprint. Amherst, N.Y.: Prometheus Books, 1997.

———. *A Pluralistic Universe: Hibbert Lectures to Manchester College on the Present Situation in Philosophy.* New York: Longmans, Green, 1909.

———. *The Varieties of Religious Experience.* New York: Longmans, Green, 1903.

———. *The Will to Believe and Other Essays in Popular Philosophy.* 1897. Reprint. New York: Dover Publications, 1956.

———. *Writings, 1902–1910.* New York: Library Classics of the United States, 1987.

Jenkins, Mark. "The Hard Way." *Outside Magazine* 28, no. 11 (November 2003): 55.

Johnson, Mark. *The Body in the Mind.* Chicago: University of Chicago Press, 1987.

Kierkegaard, Søren. *Philosophical Fragments.* Edited and translated by Howard V. Hong and Edna H. Hong. Princeton: Princeton University Press, 1985.

Kuhn, Thomas S. *The Structure of Scientific Revolutions.* 1962. 3d ed. Chicago: University of Chicago Press, 1996.

Lakoff, George. *Moral Politics: How Liberals and Conservatives Think.* Chicago: University of Chicago Press, 1996, 2002.

———. *Women, Fire, and Dangerous Things: What Categories Reveal about the Mind.* Chicago: University of Chicago Press, 1987. Paperback edition, 1990.

Lakoff, George, and Mark Johnson. *Metaphors We Live By.* Chicago: University of Chicago Press, 1980. Paperback edition, 1981.

———. *Philosophy in the Flesh: The Embodied Mind and Its Challenge to Western Thought.* New York: Basic Books, 1999.

Lasch, Christopher. *The True and Only Heaven: Progress and Its Critics.* New York: Norton, 1991.

Lauritzen, Paul. *Religious Belief and Emotional Transformation: A Light in the Heart.* Lewisburg, Pa.: Bucknell University Press, 1992.

Leighton, Taigen Daniel. *Bodhisattva Archetypes: Classic Buddhist Guides to Awakening and Their Modern Expression.* New York: Penguin Books, 1998.

Levinson, Henry Samuel. *Santayana, Pragmatism, and the Spiritual Life.* Chapel Hill: University of North Carolina Press, 1992.

MacIntyre, Alasdair. *After Virtue.* South Bend, Ind.: University of Notre Dame Press, 1981.

Marinoff, Lou, *The Big Questions: How Philosophy Can Change Your Life.* New York: Bloomsbury, 2003.

Matson, Floyd W. *The Broken Image: Man, Science and Society.* New York: George Braziller, 1964.

Menand, Louis, ed. *Pragmatism.* New York: Vintage Books, 1997.

Miller, David L. *The New Polytheism: Rebirth of the Gods and Goddesses.* New York: Harper & Row, 1974.

Moore, Thomas. *The Care of the Soul: A Guide for Cultivating Depth and Sacredness in Everyday Life.* New York: HarperPerennial, 1994.

———. *The Re-Enchantment of Everyday Life.* New York: HarperCollins, 1996.

Murdoch, Iris. *Metaphysics as a Guide to Morals.* New York: Penguin Books, 1993.

Niebuhr, Reinhold. *The Nature and Destiny of Man: A Christian Interpretation.* 2 vols. New York: Scribner, 1941.

Nielsen, Kai. *Naturalism and Religion.* Amherst, N.Y.: Prometheus Books, 2001.

Nisbet, Robert. *History of the Idea of Progress.* 1980. New ed. New Brunswick, N.J.: Transaction Publishers, 1994.

Novak, Michael. *The Experience of Nothingness.* 1970. New York: Harper & Row, Colophon Books, 1970.

Nussbaum, Martha C. *Upheavals of Thought: The Intelligence of Emotions.* Cambridge: Cambridge University Press, 2001. Paperback edition, 2003.

Palmer, Parker J. *The Active Life: A Spirituality of Work, Creativity, and Caring.* 1990. Reprint. San Francisco: Jossey-Bass, 1999.

Phillips, Christopher. *Socrates Café: A Fresh Taste of Philosophy.* New York: Norton, 2001.

Pieper, Josef. *Leisure: The Basis of Culture.* Translated by Gerald Malsbary. South Bend, Ind,: St. Augustine's Press, 1998. Originally published as *Musse und Kult* (Munich: Kösel, 1948).

Plato. *The Dialogues.* New York: Bantam Books, 1986.

———. *The Republic.* Translated and edited by F. M. Cornford. Oxford: Oxford University Press, 1945.

Polkinghorne, John. *Science and Theology.* Minneapolis: Fortress Press, 1998.

Postman, Neil. *Technopoly: The Surrender of Culture to Technology.* 1992. Reprint. New York: Vintage Books, 1993.

Raymo, Chet. *Honey from Stone: A Naturalist's Search for God.* New York: Dodd, Mead, 1987.

Rébuffat, Gaston. *On Snow and Rock.* Translated by Eleanor Brockett, with technical assistance from J. E. B. Wright. 1963. New York: Oxford University Press, 1968.

Rieff, Philip. *The Triumph of the Therapeutic: Uses of Faith after Freud.* 1966. Chicago: University of Chicago Press, 1987.

Rosenau, Pauline Marie. *Post-Modernism and the Social Sciences: Insights, Inroads, and Intrusions.* Princeton: Princeton University Press, 1992.

Santayana, George. *Realms of Being.* New York: Scribner, 1942.

———. *Skepticism and Animal Faith: Introduction to a System of Philosophy.* New York: Dover Publications, 1955.

———. *Soliloquies in England and Later Soliloquies.* New York: Scribner, 1922.

Schumacher, E. F. *A Guide for the Perplexed.* New York: Harper Colophon Books, 1978.

———. *Small Is Beautiful: Economics as if People Mattered.* New York: Perennial Library, 1975.

———. *This I Believe and Other Essays.* Foxhole, Devon, UK: Green Books, 1997. Repr. with corrections, 1998.

Sells, Benjamin, ed. *Working with Images: The Theoretical Base of Archetypal Psychology.* Woodstock, Conn.: Spring Publications, 2000.

Sheehan, George A. *Running and Being: The Total Experience.* New York: Simon & Schuster, 1978.

Smith, Huston. *Beyond the Post-modern Mind: The Place of Meaning in a Global Civilization.* 1982. 3d ed. Wheaton, Ill.: Theosophical Pub. House, 2003.

———. *Essays on World Religions.* Edited by M. Darroll Bryant. New York: Paragon House, 1992.

———. *Forgotten Truth: The Primordial Tradition.* New York: Harper Colophon Books, 1976.

———. *The Soul of Christianity: Restoring the Great Tradition.* San Francisco: HarperSanFrancisco, 2005.

———. *The Way Things Are: Conversations with Huston Smith on the Spiritual Life.* Edited by Phil Cousineau. Berkeley: University of California Press, 2003.

———. *Why Religion Matters: The Fate of the Human Spirit in an Age of Disbelief.* San Francisco: HarperSanFrancisco, 2001.

———. *The World's Religions.* San Francisco: HarperSanFrancisco, 1991.

Smith, Wilfred Cantwell. *Faith and Belief: The Difference Between Them.* Boston: Oneworld Publications, 1998.

Solomon, Andrew. *The Noonday Demon: An Atlas of Depression.* New York: Scribner, 2001. Paperback reprint, 2003.

Solomon, Robert C. *The Passions: Emotions and the Meaning of Life.* 1976. Indianapolis: Hackett, 1993.

———. *Spirituality for the Skeptic.* New York: Oxford University Press, 2002.

Tarnas, Richard. *The Passion of the Western Mind: Understanding the Ideas That Have Shaped Our World View.* 1991. Reprint. New York: Ballantine Books, 1993.

Thoreau, Henry David. *Walden: or, Life in the Woods: and, On the Duty of Civil Disobedience.* New York: New American Library, 1960.

Tillich, Paul. *The Courage to Be.* New Haven: Yale University Press, 1952.

Tillyard, E. M. W. *The Elizabethan World Picture.* 1943. Reprint. New York: Vintage Books, n.d. [196–?].

Tolstoy, Leo. *Confession.* Translated by David Patterson. 1983. New York: Norton, 1983, 1996.

Wallis, Jim. *God's Politics: Why the Right Gets It Wrong and the Left Doesn't Get It.* San Francisco: HarperSanFrancisco, 2005.

White, Hayden. *Figural Realism: Studies in the Mimesis Effect.* Baltimore: Johns Hopkins University Press, 1999.

———. *Tropics of Discourse: Essays In Cultural Criticism.* Baltimore: Johns Hopkins University Press, 1985.

Wilson, Colin. *The Outsider.* Boston: Houghton Mifflin, 1956.

Wong, Paul T. P., and Prem S. Fry, eds. *The Human Quest for Meaning: A Handbook of Psychological Research and Clinical Applications.* Mahwah, N.J.: Lawrence Erlbaum Associates, 1998.

Zavarzadeh, Mas'ud. *The Mythopoeic Reality: The Postwar American Nonfiction Novel.* Urbana: University of Illinois Press, 1976.

INDEX

Text:	10/15 Janson
Display:	Janson
Compositor:	International Typesetting and Composition
Printer and binder:	Maple-Vail Book Manufacturing Group